LETTERS FROM PRISON

Publication Number 1095
AMERICAN SERIES
IN
BEHAVIORAL SCIENCE AND LAW

Edited by
RALPH SLOVENKO, B.E., LL.B., M.A., Ph. D.
Professor of Law and Psychiatry
Wayne State University
Law School
Detroit, Michigan

LETTERS FROM PRISON
A Cry for Justice

By

GEORGE B. PALERMO, M.D.

Clinical Professor of Psychiatry and Neurology
Director of Criminological Psychiatry
Department of Psychiatry
Medical College of Wisconsin

Adjunct Professor of Criminology and Law Studies
Department of Cultural and Social Sciences
Marquette University

Lecturer, Department of Psychiatry and Bioethics
Loyola University, Stritch School of Medicine

and

MAXINE ALDRIDGE WHITE, J.D.

CHARLES C THOMAS • PUBLISHER, LTD.
Springfield • Illinois • U.S.A.

Published and Distributed Throughout the World by

CHARLES C THOMAS • PUBLISHER, LTD.
2600 South First Street
Springfield, Illinois 62794-9265

ISBN 0-398-06851-8 (cloth)
ISBN 0-398-06852-6 (paper)

Library of Congress Catalog Card Number: 97-51866

With THOMAS BOOKS *careful attention is given to all details of manufacturing
and design. It is the Publisher's desire to present books that are satisfactory as to their
physical qualities and artistic possibilities and appropriate for their particular use.*
THOMAS BOOKS *will be true to those laws of quality that assure a good name
and good will.*

Printed in the United States of America
SM-R-3

Library of Congress Cataloging in Publication Data
Palermo, George B.
    Letters from prison : a cry for justice / by George B. Palermo and
Maxine Aldridge White.
       p.   cm. -- (American series in behavioral science and law)
    "Publication number 1095."
    Includes bibliographical references and index.
    ISBN 0-398-06851-8. -- ISBN 0-398-06852-6 (pbk.)
    1. Imprisonment--United States. 2. Prison sentences--United States. 3.
Prisoners--United States. 4. Prisoners--United States--Correspondence. 5.
Punishment--United States. 6. Criminal justice, Administration of--United
States. I.. White, Maxine Aldridge. II. Title. III. Series.
HV9471.P25   1998
365'.6'0973--dc21
                                          97-51866
                                              CIP

To the memory of our parents who taught us fairness and responsibility. To the children, and to our hope that we can learn enough to help make their future brighter.

INTRODUCTION

A truly staggering total number of 1.6 million persons are behind federal, state, and local penal bars in the United States. Who are these people? Why are they there? What are the personal and societal factors that cause so many to be imprisoned? What is being done in the prisons to punish them? To rehabilitate them? Why do we as a democratic and free society have numbers in penal custody which rival those of despotic nations?

Dr. George Palermo, a psychiatrist, and Judge Maxine White, a criminal court jurist, provide with this very readable book informed and concise answers to these and other critical questions which ought to trouble every thinking person aware of the problems of crime and expanding imprisonment in the United States. While both authors are persons of erudition, their responses are intelligible and articulated in understandable terms rather than in the psycho-babble found in so many psychiatric studies or the mumbo jumbo so prevalent in legal treatises. The patent purpose of the writers is to inform a concerned public of the magnitude of imprisonment in the United States, and of the personal and social seminal dynamics leading to so much incarceration, and to invite considered reflection on what ought be done to reform imprisonment as it is today.

To adequately assess and fully appreciate the soundness and wisdom of their insights, some knowledge of the backgrounds and experience of the authors is helpful. Palermo was born in Tarquinia, Italy, and educated at Rome University Medical School and Bologna University Medical School where he received his medical degree. He completed graduate studies in psychiatry in the United States. He has practiced widely as a psychiatrist and as a forensic expert. He is a well-recognized authority in his field and holds faculty appointments both in the United States and abroad, teaching psychiatry, forensics and medical ethics. In his position as a consulting psychiatrist for the courts of Milwaukee County, Wisconsin, he has conducted thousands of offender mental assessments stretching from the minor miscreant to his service as the court-appointed psychiatrist in the trial of Milwaukee necrophilic serial slayer Jeffrey Dahmer.

Maxine White was born the daughter of an economically impoverished Mississippi sharecropper. Her advance from the rural cotton fields of her birthplace through college and law school is a bootstrap story worthy of a book itself. She received her BA in Sociology and English from Alcorn State University in Mississippi; a Master's Degree in Public Administration from the University of Southern California; and a Juris Doctorate from Marquette University in Milwaukee, Wisconsin. First as an assistant United States Attorney and now as a circuit court judge, she has been involved in the investigation, trial, and sentencing of thousands of offenders. As an African-American born woman of humble means in the rural South who has lived much of her life in the urban North, she is well aware of the critical roles race and poverty play in the lives of blacks who are disproportionately incarcerated in the United States. Both Dr. Palermo and Judge White subscribe to the concept that a person is responsible for his or her own actions, but they bring to that perception a compassion born of their own extensive experiences with troubled persons.

We have in this volume not the remote musings of academicians distant from the scene whose observations are born of studying statistics, but instead the keen insights of a doctor and a judge who toil daily and directly with the often unwashed and frequently semiliterate dysfunctional persons who crowd our jails and prisons. Palermo and White, while realists who relate the cacophony of problems which cause so many in the prison to return to crime upon release, also bring a message of hope that the criminal justice system can and ought to do better.

Readers will find a concise history of the use of imprisonment and of the development of the judicial system in the United States. Statistics reflecting current rates of incarceration are set forth. Scrutiny is provided of various subsets of prisoners: the substance abuser, the older offender, the mentally ill, and gang members.

Palermo and White present in a concise, lucid and interesting fashion the various socio-criminological theories bearing on antisocial human behavior prevalent in the last 100 years with an emphasis on the more current thought. Reams have been written on such theories and in this volume one finds a readable survey of the principal concepts of many professionals skilled in sociology, psychology and law who have wrestled with the problem of the causation of criminal behavior. The roles of character traits of impulsiveness and hostility, and the absence of self-esteem, and the milieu in which the prisoners live are all considered.

In the chapter entitled, "Prisonization," reflection is provided on the impact of imprisonment on the offender. Prison, itself, is the punishment. But pressures from the prisoners' own serious inadequacies, relations with guards, conflict with other prisoners, overcrowding, a sense of desolation, and other problems set upon the incarcerated affecting their experience and how they will emerge from prison. The chapter, "A View from the Bench," helps one feel the dilemmas, both moral and practical, that are encountered by a righteous and compassionate judge.

Palermo and White present letters from the prisoners themselves to judges and others to capture the thoughts of the incarcerated. While letters written to judges pleading for leniency will often be self-serving, the letters nevertheless capture remarkable insights into the thought processes, feelings, and life stories of the offenders. The promises of what the criminals will do if provided a "second chance" by the judge are mere velleities for some offenders but for others are surely an expression of genuine hope. That the love of family, a spouse and children, sustain some prisoners against the horror of imprisonment is beyond cavil. At the same time, letters relating backgrounds of economic deprivation and parental depravity and abandonment, often confirmed by court-ordered pre-sentence studies, provide the mournful backdrop of the lives of many offenders. While the authors clearly believe that dangerous persons belong behind bars, the letters inevitably will stir understanding hearts with the sense of immense tragedy for the untoward waste of human lives.

Those who search this volume for easy answers to the crime problem and its ensuing sequelae of imprisonment will be disappointed. Those who recognize that the problems of crime and punishment are varied, multifaceted, and not infrequently arcane, will find much in this volume to illuminate their knowledge of the issues. The authors, reflecting the fire of their own strong commitment to improvement of the criminal justice system, close by summoning society to a greater effort to rectify particular social problems connected with criminality and to make more rational use of imprisonment.

E. MICHAEL MCCANN
District Attorney
Milwaukee County
Wisconsin

FOREWORD

Prisons in early American history were used only to house the accused until trial and the convicted until corporal punishment or execution was carried out. With the declining use of flogging and stocks came the invention of the penitentiary–to encourage penitence while housing the convicted for longer terms of punishment, reflection and ideally, rehabilitation.

But are prisoners penitent as the term "penitentiary" would imply and as the Quakers who promoted the penitentiary in the place of corporal punishment suggested that they would be? In the early penitentiary, at the English Pentonville, prisoners upon admittance were immediately put in a solitary cell for a period, originally of 18 months, although as more and more prisoners went insane, that was reduced to nine months. The practice aroused the ire of the public and cries went out for prison reform. After two centuries of reform efforts, the same complaints are made: criminals come out of prison more hardened and vicious than they went in. They are called "overcrowded graduate schools in felony."

The number of people in prison in the United States has quadrupled during the past 20 years. The reasons include: deep concern about crime; the erosion of the rehabilitative ideal; increased emphasis upon punishment as an overriding goal of the criminal justice system; changes in sentencing practices, including the increasing use of mandatory minimum sentences; and the escalation of crime.

The prison plays an essential role in isolating dangerous offenders from the community, but that raises the question of identifying high-risk offenders who should be isolated from the community, and whether increased incarceration results in less overall crime. Are the benefits worth the financial costs of increased reliance on imprisonment? Of course, the only effective way to curb crime is for society to work to *prevent* the criminal act in the first place, but that is a utopian ideal.

The authors of this book–prominent forensic psychiatrist George Palermo and Judge Maxine Aldridge White–explore the prison system and they study the prisoners. They write not from the ivory tower but from the trenches, so to speak. They are in daily contact with the prison system and prisoners. They write:

> ...[M]ost of the offenders in the prisons are lonely people who for many reasons have been extruded from society, punished for minor infractions, often confined because of public fear, in prisons that should only imprison the violent and dangerous, those who are really a threat to the stability of the community. In addition, we also confirmed our idea, shared by many others, that sociological factors are highly contributory to their misbehavior. Though we wish to view people as autonomous and responsible agents for their actions, we recognize that the great majority of these offenders are educationally limited, socially handicapped, and at times figuratively chained by their poor economic conditions and by alienating prejudice. They may not be able to exercise, therefore, good common sense because of the anger, frustration and disappointment in a society that makes them the object of ambivalent messages. We do not condone the many shades of their behaviors, but we question the co-responsibility of society at large. The present way of dealing with the problems of antisocial offenders seems to be a bandage type of approach, possibly good for the economy of the nation, to the business of correctional institutions, as some people claim, certainly too expensive for the taxpayers,and supportive of a vicious circle of resentment, misbehavior and incarceration. Often, as part of transitional social periods such as the present technological one, one encounters confusion about roles, about personal responsibility, about just or unjust laws.

It is a fundamental principle in psychiatry that "all symptoms are overdetermined." That is to say, they have more than one cause. In his recent book *In Search of Stones*, Dr. M. Scott Peck makes the point over and over again, "For any single thing of importance, there are multiple reasons." But because we assume there is a reason for everything, we go looking for *it* when we should be looking for *them*.

The decline in family values may be one reason for crime, but it is only one of a whole complex of reasons. The criminal law, however, can do no more than focus on the individual. It cannot condemn society as a whole though it may be said: society loads the gun and the individual pulls the trigger. It is thus easy for one who commits crime to deny responsibility or to cast the blame on others or on circumstances. Also, to feel a sense of guilt is painful, so it is denied.

The authors expand their personal experiences with offenders by looking at the correspondence that they sent to judges, district attorneys, public defenders, prison chaplains and mental health professionals. Following their discussion of the prison system, the authors focus on these letters. Of course, as is well known, the writing skills of criminals are often limited to graffiti, and they are renowned as con artists. These letters can be expected more or less to be self-serving, but they are nonetheless revealing about the writers' upbringing and social maladroitness.

Will the time come when the costs of imprisoning so many people cause taxpayers to demand alternatives? In 1996 a total of 5.5 million people or 2.8 percent of the population in the United States were in state and federal prisons or on parole. Of this number well over one million were in jail or prison. Expressed differently, of every 100,000 people in the U.S., 260 were incarcerated, at an annual cost of $16 billion. The U.S. has the world's highest imprisonment: incarceration rates in Europe generally range from 35 to 120 per 100,000 residents and in Asian countries from 21 to 140 per 100,000. The high rate of incarceration has not made the U.S. a safer nation. Would it be a less safe place with a different policy?

It was 1888 when Cesare Lombroso published his book, *Palimpsests from Prison,* in which he collected stories, messages, writings and graffiti of prison inmates of Turin, Italy. Now, more than a century later, Dr. Palermo and Judge White in this book look at the communications of prisoners to provide a picture of the offender in today's world. It is a major contribution to the study of criminal behavior.

RALPH SLOVENKO
Editor, *American Series in Behavioral Science and Law*

PREFACE

They silently move through incarceration as if they are going to a familiar place. They are young people, strong and apparently healthy, handcuffed or chained to one another. They are Blacks, Whites, Hispanics and Asians, but they are mostly Blacks. They remind us of a scene from old movies, or of what one reads in books, of the interminable lines of black slaves getting off the boats that had transported them to a new land that will later be known as the land of freedom. They do not seem sad, their facial expressions do not express anguish or puzzlement. They look into the distance, seeming resigned, almost as if what they are going through was expected, part of a routine in a dreadful life. When looking at the deputies who accompany them one may catch the same facial expressions of routine performance. One senses, however, the silent atmosphere which is typical of a funeral wake.

The scene changes: two small groups of people are just outside the visiting section of the jail. The women are young adults, three of them—two Blacks and one White—surrounded by a group of ten children, ranging in age from three to eight. One woman holds an infant in her arms. The baby smiles, the children run around, playing with one another, calling out to each other, while the mothers chat among themselves. They talk about their men who are jailed, those whom they have come to visit. There is no sadness or anguish on their faces, and one has the feeling that they are paying a normal social visit to a neighbor's home. The entire atmosphere is divested of anxiety or embarrassment. Certainly, there is no shame. The young ladies' laughter and their teasing of one another supports the perception of their apparently implicit acceptance of the men's imprisonment as an ordinary fact of life. The crying of the infant and the sounds of the innocent children resounding through the adjacent corridor gives the appearance of a normal, run-of-the mill situation.

In a court setting, the offender stands before the judge, his attorney next to him. The offender is given the opportunity to say whatever he wants in his own defense. The young defendant, one of many, speaks up and states: "I'm sorry, your Honor, for the hurt I caused to other people, but I would like to tell you about myself, my life, who I am." The judge stops him and asks him to limit his statements to the offense he has been charged with. The man, apparently frustrated and sad, does not continue his speech, and, after thanking the judge, sits down and says no more.

The three scenes described above are an everyday occurrence. These are some of the facts that motivated us to inquire about the incarcerated offenders: this silent, multitude of people who go through the justice system, who are confined in the correctional institutions, who seem to be resigned and accepting of whatever Lady Justice dispenses to them. One senses that they are going through a rite of passage, through a revolving door of incarceration and non-productive freedom. Who are these prisoners, we asked ourselves, who apparently assume such a compliant attitude towards imprisonment? We asked how we could get to know more about them. We thought that our personal experiences with them, either during examinations or their court appearances, could be amplified by reading their correspondence which they directed to judges, district attorneys, public defenders, prison chaplains, and mental health professionals. We, therefore, reviewed a large number of these letters, typical examples of which are reported in the chapter, "Letters from Prison." We believe we have acquired from the letters a better appreciation of who they are, the silent people who day in and day out go through the carceral system, and whose number increases yearly. While looking into their characteristics and in order to better understand them, we studied and give a brief report on the evolution of the prison throughout the world and of the American judicial system. We also dealt with theories and types of punishment.

We ended this long journey with the realization that most of the offenders in the prisons are lonely people who for many reasons have been extruded from society, punished for minor infractions, often confined because of public fear, in prisons that should only imprison the violent and the dangerous, those who are really a threat to the stability of the community. In addition, we also confirmed our idea, shared by many others, that sociological factors are highly contributory to their misbehavior. Though we wish to view people as autonomous and responsible agents for their actions, we recognize that the great majority of these offenders are educationally limited, socially handicapped, and at times figuratively chained by their poor economic conditions and by alienating prejudice. They may not be able to exercise, therefore, good common sense because of the anger, frustration and disappointment in a society that makes them the object of ambivalent messages. We do not condone the many shades of their offensive behaviors, but we question the co-responsibility of society at large. The present way of dealing with the problems of antisocial offenders seems to be a Band-Aid type of approach, possibly good for the economy of the nation and to the business of correctional institutions, as some people claim, but certainly too expensive for the taxpayers, and supportive of a vicious circle of resentment, misbehavior and incarceration. Often, as part of transitional social periods such as the present technological one, one encounters confusion about roles, about personal responsibility, about just or unjust laws. It is well known that eventually a readjustment to a more objective and equilibrated *modus vivendi* takes place, and it is then that possibly and hopefully social injustices will be rectified, aiding in the diminishment of crime and bringing about a more fair dispensation of justice.

In searching for the causes of the prisoners' proneness to antisocial behavior, we asked ourselves what if anything can be done in order to reduce it. These people are frequently jobless and lose their own self-esteem and respect. They are not part of the mainstream society and many of them continue to live, with society's help, a vegetative type of existence. Most of the offenders we come across share the above social conditions. They are imprisoned, as above stated, by socioeconomic chains, and we wonder how their present state is different from the slavery of the past? Sociological issues are, indeed, present, and in our limited way we have reflected on them and attempted to give some answers throughout our book. It is our contention that it behooves all members of society, including the prisoners themselves, to rectify the social, moral conditions of the criminogenic communities. This attempt should not only take place during periods of incarceration, or after release from the carceral system, but primarily before incarceration becomes necessary.

We should view the prisoners as human beings and ask ourselves whether we interpret correctly the meaning of their antisociality. Indeed, the word antisocial speaks for itself. Is their rebellious, antisocial behavior against a society that in many ways rejects them and deprives them of their right to be responsible, productive human beings?

G.B.P.
M.A.W.

ACKNOWLEDGMENTS

Before thanking those who have been of encouragement to us in this endeavor, we should thank that multitude of offenders/prisoners whose behaviors have, unknowingly to them, stimulated us to look more attentively at the causes of their plight.

We wish to thank the Hon. Louis J. Ceci, Justice, Supreme Court of Wisconsin, (ret.), and the following Circuit Court Judges for reading various chapters of the manuscript: Dominic Amato, Timothy Dugan, David Hansher, Jeffrey Kremers, Elsa Lamelas, Stanley Miller, Diane Sykes, Jeffrey Wagner. We appreciate their comments and their suggestions. We are also grateful to Edward Gumz, Ph.D., Associate Professor of Social work and Chair, Undergraduate Social Work Program, School of Social Work, Loyola University, Chicago; to Prof. Edward M. Scott, Professor Emeritus of Psychiatry, Oregon Health Sciences University; and to Phoebe Weaver Williams, Associate Professor of Law, Marquette University, for reading and commenting on the manuscript. Our thanks are also extended to attorneys Deon Green, Leonard E. Martin, and Lew Wasserman.

We thank Joyce Evans, journalist for the *Milwaukee Journal Sentinel*, Chaplain David Sorensen of the Milwaukee County House of Correction, and Brother Jerry Smith, St. Benedict the Moor Church, Chaplain of the Milwaukee County Jail, for letting us read and use some of the letters addressed to them, and all the Milwaukee County Circuit Court Judges who allowed us to use excerpts from letters they received. We also wish to thank the Milwaukee County District Attorney, E. Michael McCann, J.D., Mark S. Williams, J.D., Assistant District Attorney and Head of the Homicide Division of the Milwaukee County District Attorney's Office; and William Hanrahan, J.D., Assistant District Attorney and Head of the Domestic Violence Unit, Milwaukee County District Attorney's Office, for their suggestions after reviewing the manuscript.

Special thanks are owed to Anna Green, the librarian of the Milwaukee County Mental Health Complex, for her prompt assistance in furnishing us with pertinent literature, and to a cohort of students from the Criminology Department of Marquette University who aided in the collection of some data. Our special gratitude goes to the indefatigable Adriana Palermo for her work in the preparation and pre-editing of the manuscript.

CONTENTS

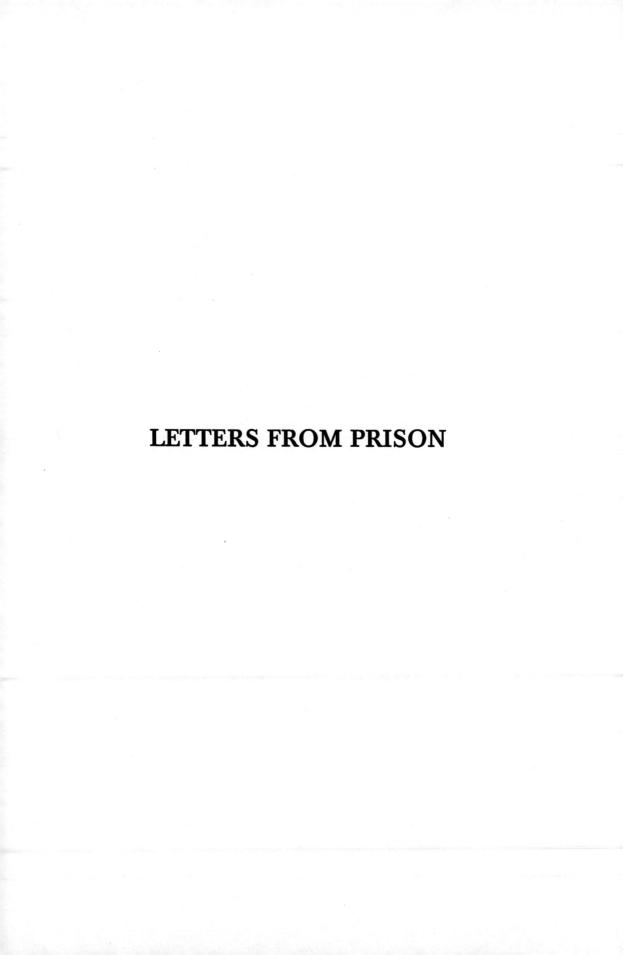

LETTERS FROM PRISON

Chapter 1

THE CRIMINAL COURT IN AMERICA: ITS HISTORY

At present, in very many cases, if we want to know why a rule of law has taken its particular shape, and more or less if we want to know why it exists at all, we go to tradition.... The rational study of law is to a large extent the study of history.

Mr. Justice Oliver Wendell Holmes

INTRODUCTION

Fox Butterfield, in his recent book titled *All God's Children, The Bosket Family and the American Tradition of Violence*, described a jury trial in which the defendant, Butch Bosket, was being tried for first-degree murder of two victims who Bosket had stabbed to death at a local hotel, and faced life imprisonment. The trial began on February 26, 1963, before Judge Herbert J. Steffes, an experienced jurist in the Milwaukee criminal court who had handed down over 100,000 hours' worth of sentences.

The defendant pled insanity and was examined by three psychiatrists and found to be competent to stand trial. Bosket was represented by a public defender who was faced with representing a "confessed murderer" and arguing for a lesser degree of homicide based on the defendant's claim that he lacked the intent to kill. Defendant Bosket contended that one of the victims pushed and argued with him which resulted in him stabbing each of the victims six times in "the heat of passion." On March 1, 1963, a jury consisting of ten men and two women deliberated from 3:40 to 10:00 p.m. that evening, with a break for dinner. The jury found Bosket guilty of murder in the first degree. After Judge Steffes excused the jury, the judge asked the defendant, "Have you anything to say as to why sentence should not be pronounced upon you?" The defendant "stood up, looking the judge in the eye and said:

> Your honor, murder is a hard pillow to sleep on, but the verdict that was brought back, I think, was an unjust one. For I never had the intention of hurting anyone. It is going to cost me years in prison and maybe the loss of my wife and children. But I am not going to let myself become embittered. That would just prove what the District Attorney tried so wholeheartedly to prove, that I am an animal. I can sincerely say that I am no animal, and I will spend every day educating myself to prove otherwise. I will become the best educated prisoner you have ever had. (Butterfield, 1995, p. 131.)

The judge was not moved, because he considered the defendant's statement "just another self-serving plea." The judge, reading from a prepared statement, pronounced sentence: "There is only one sentence the court can pronounce and that is life imprisonment. The defendant displayed, in my view, a homicidal temper, which demonstrated a lethal quality, a lethal history, which this community cannot tolerate." The judge paused and continued: "I do hope that in the passage of time the parole board will remember very clearly that this was not just one cold-blooded murder, but two cold-blooded murders." The judge closed by indicating that "the sentence commences at noon today; the sheriff will transport you to prison, I presume, with alacrity" (Butterfield, 1995, pp. 130-132). Although 34 years have passed since the Bosket trial, the criminal trial process and many of the factors present in the Bosket trial, right down to the defendant's response to the conviction and his "lethal background" are still evident in the cases before the criminal court.

The state criminal trial courts in America have always been at the heart of what is now known as the criminal justice system. In general, the state criminal court is the preeminent institution involved in the legal process, often creating, primarily applying, the laws in our society. Criminal courts are recognized as a small, yet powerful component in a criminal justice system which is actually a complex web of institutions. These institutions are designed to deal with those who violate the law.

The criminal court is a symbol of law and order and the embodiment of the law's involvement in the lives of its citizens. For crime victims, the criminal court is a critical institution in that it presents a nonviolent avenue for retribution. In fact, the criminal justice system, contemporary law, and the Constitution are the only legal mechanisms that crime victims can use to recover justice for themselves and punishment for the offender. Since its inception, the objectives of the criminal justice system have grown to include more than punishing offenders. A few of the "newer" goals include the deterrence of unlawful or injurious conduct and monetary compensation for crime victims.

The historical development of the criminal trial court involves not only the establishment of court structures but also adjudication of guilt or innocence and imposition of discipline. Accordingly, the history of the criminal court must encompass more than a mechanistic review of criminal laws and procedures. In order to understand the role of the criminal court at any given time in our history, it is essential that the courts' operations be viewed within the context of the social, economic, cultural, and political events of the time period in question. Through its operation, the criminal court ties the relationship of law to the needs and values of the community. An analysis of the history of the criminal court gives immense insight into the role of law in a community and how the laws of the land affect the social lives of its citizens. Defining criminal conduct, procedures for apprehending alleged offenders, victim and defendant rights, procedures and rules of the court, and the role of the judiciary in the criminal process are merely a few examples of the many quandaries which affect the business of the criminal court on a daily basis.

Local jails, state penile institutions, and federal prisons are filled with offenders whose misdeeds range from petty misconduct to violent crimes. These violations involve a substantial number of lesser offenses such as theft, operating a vehicle without a license, and disorderly conduct on the low end of the spectrum. Fewer offenders commit extremely violent crimes which mandate lengthy periods of incarceration for violent conduct such as sexual assault, armed robbery, and murder. Unfortunately, a trend is emerging where more and more of the inmates housed in both state and federal prisons have been convicted of drug possession and drug trafficking offenses. The fate of all of these miscreants, at some time, in some manner, was or will be affected by some sort of criminal court proceeding.

The purpose of this chapter is to provide a brief discussion of the evolution of the state criminal trial court, with various references made to federal court developments when applicable. This chapter is not about the philosophical, jurisprudential, or legal underpinnings of the court but a description of the development of the justice administration which originated from the chaotic, authoritarian-dominated procedures of yesteryear, to the professionally regulated modern-day criminal justice system we use in America today.

AN INTRODUCTION TO THE CRIMINAL COURT

The history of the American criminal court, like that of legal institutions in general, is a history of methods used to mold criminal laws and procedures with the practices of the criminal courts in an effort to meet changing societal conditions and public expectations. The federal government and each of the fifty states has adopted a criminal code (Friedman, 1993). With the exception of certain variations in strategy, procedure, and substantive law designs, there are certain general characteristics shared by criminal courts across the United States, especially in urban areas. Although they may be worded a bit differently, charges such as "thou shalt not kill" and "thou shalt not steal" are found in every jurisdiction (Friedman, 1993). The responsibility of the criminal court, in its most basic sense, is to refine, interpret, and transform legal concepts of criminality as defined by society at particular times. State criminal courts have evolved, through sheer necessity, into venues which are forced to grapple with devastating societal problems such as drugs, family violence, child abuse, and violent juveniles. These are all situations which other institutions have undoubtedly failed to unravel; yet, criminal courts are expected to crochet quilts from these scattered pieces of yarn.

The perplexing accumulations of criminal laws, policies, procedures, and judicial decisions found in every jurisdiction serve as guidelines in a system whose theoretical goals include community safety, crime prevention, offender punishment, and maintaining order. It is these laws which the criminal courts have used to develop the myriad rules and processes that all expanses of the criminal justice system utilize in the apprehension and discipline of lawbreakers.

Lawrence Friedman (1993) has written the most comprehensive and convincing research about the history of the modern-day criminal court system, and his research is used extensively throughout this overview of the evolution of the criminal court in America. Friedman's books reference a compilation of material gathered from court systems across the country and around the world. Significant portions of our knowledge about the history of the American legal system is based upon records from jurisdictions such as Massachusetts in the colonial period and Wisconsin during the nineteenth century. However, the court system which currently governs modern-day America can trace its beginnings as far back as biblical times. Through centuries of religious domination, theoretical evolution, and cultural conquests the criminal justice system has matured into our current system. Through this tedious maturation, criminal courts have evolved from meager beginnings to become comprehensive processing centers for ever-growing quantities of offenders (Friedman, 1993).

IN THE BEGINNING

Evidence of codes and customs having the effect of law can be traced as far back as the origins of mankind. Approximately eight centuries after Hammurabi promulgated his famous code for Babylonia, Moses reviewed the code governing the Israelites in the land of Canaan. Moses appealed to the people to "[a]ppoint judges and other officials in every town.... These men [were] to judge the people impartially" (Deuteronomy 16:18). The judges "[were] not to be unjust or to show partiality in their judgments; and they [were] not to accept bribes, for gifts blind the eyes even of wise and honest men, and cause them to give wrong decisions" (Deuteronomy 16:19). The judges were admonished to "[a]lways be fair and just..." (Deuteronomy 16:20). (See also Exodus Chapter 23 verses 1 through 9.) In biblical times, the local judges were given the authority to decide disputes on everything from property rights to murder, and in difficult cases, the judge could seek the assistance of priests. In these early periods, the accused had to "accept [the] verdict [of the judge and the priest] and follow their instructions in every detail" (Deuteronomy 17:8-13). Those who failed to conform to the law were severely punished. The rationale behind such punishment was to show members of the community the harsh consequences one would suffer in failing to adhere to the laws of the land. Biblical laws such as the Ten Commandments, along with various other well-quoted directives, formed the basis for the laws developed in preceding time periods and continue to act as the foundation for legal systems worldwide.

Religious influence can be found in Anglo-Saxon edicts, English law, and most any other legal system in the world. Consequently, the imprint of religion was clearly stamped on the customs and procedures of the colonial courts and in the history of America's judicial institutions. In fact, the influence of religion continues to be almost as prevalent in the legal systems of today as it was in the epoch of Moses.

ANGLO-SAXON INFLUENCE

The American colonial settlers originating from England were descendants of Germanic tribes. The members of these tribes later became known as "Anglo-Saxons." These clans operated a crude legal system and delivered a primitive sort of justice much less sophisticated than the courts which were later established in England. The tribal communities were connected by blood, kith, and religion. The tribes organized a primitive system of justice around tribal subdivisions which were presided over by an elected magistrate. Thereafter, power was distributed according to noble birth and wealth (Walsh, 1923).

The magistrate was assisted in his duties by a hundred elected "companions." These companions defended the magistrate in all endeavors and were rewarded with shelter and additional subsistence in return for their loyalty. To some extent, the magistrate operated as a military leader or feudal lord administering justice with the help of aides who were compensated through gains derived from inter-tribal conquests.

In the middle of the first millennium, the Anglo-Saxons migrated from North Germany, bringing with them an archaic system of laws primarily based upon primitive rituals and customs (Walsh, 1923). During their early migration period, the Germanic tribes kept very few written records concerning their legal processes. However, misdeeds which the Germanic tribe rulers considered to be crimes of violence, such as theft, disloyalty, treason, homicide, wounding assault, and rape, were listed among the "dooms" of the Anglo-Saxon kings. "Dooms" were registers which set forth penalties for crimes of violence. These registers have served as a written remnant of Anglo-Saxon laws in a time period which left very few other written records (Walsh, 1923).

Through warfare and conquest, magistrates and their forces combined the various Germanic tribes into larger kingdoms and settled in the area currently known as England. The Anglo-Saxons assimilated their laws, religion, and tribal customs into the lives of the populace they conquered. These laws were further developed by the Anglo-Saxons upon settlement into the area which later became England (Walsh 1923).

Upon migration and settlement in primal England, the Anglo-Saxon tribunal system changed. A king was elected from "royalty" and became the central power. This represented a radical change from the archaic tribal system which had consisted of a magistrate elected from a "national assembly" and assisted by a group of one hundred subordinates. During his tenure, the king granted jurisdiction to certain courts. One court, known as the "hundred court," was presided over by a individual known as a "reeve." The reeve was given province over all crimes and private disputes which arose within a district. The party which had been defeated in the hundred court could appeal to the king or a higher court known as the "shire court." However, such an appeal could only be undertaken if the defeated party had been denied their requested recovery three times by the hundred court. Another court, known as the shire court, was presided over by the sheriff, and its purpose was to represent the king to the locals and enforce judgments rendered by the hundred court. Each court—the hundred court and shire court—had twelve "thegns," also known as household officers, through whom most judicial business was conducted. Thegns, who had been warriors at one time, were given a non-transferrable tract of land in exchange for their service to the king (Walsh, 1923).

Anglo-Saxon courts were ineffectual, as evidenced by the myriad problems the courts encountered, such as the inadequate enforcement of judgments and the courts' inability to apprehend charged persons and bring them before the court. There were no skilled lawyers or judges in Anglo-Saxon courts. In fact, it appears that the system was primarily run by illiterate men. These decision makers answered questions of "law" based on their knowledge of local customs which had been handed down by word of mouth. Due to the ineptness of the newly formed Anglo-Saxon court system, vengeance and retaliation continued to be widely used as acceptable forms of retribution. It appears that the courts themselves perpetuated such actions. For those disputes which were eventually adjudicated before the court, there were several forms of discipline available. These options included compensatory allotments, requests for corporal punishment, and allowing the victim, or the victim's family, to privately retaliate against the offender (Walsh, 1923).

During the latter portion of the Anglo-Saxon period, the laws were aimed at granting victims and their families compensation in an effort to dissuade bloodshed. Anglo-Saxon kings worked diligently to compel the acceptance of a uniform legal system. The kings were equally tenacious in their efforts to coerce community members to accept compensation for injuries as opposed to private vengeance and self-help. During this somewhat lawless period, the church was an additional force in compelling the implementation of legislation directed towards obliging compensation for maltreatment as opposed to retaliation (Walsh, 1923).

Under Anglo-Saxon law, there were no prisons as we have come to think of prisons today. Accused persons were often placed in mines or dungeons merely to await sentencing. Accordingly, imprisonment was not an option. Outlawry was an offense that resulted from the persistent failure of an accused to appear in court. The lack of a system of incarceration was offset by the fact that when a person was declared an outlaw, the fugitive could "justifiably" suffer the loss of his property, or his life, without one shred of accountability on behalf of the thief or assassin. More plainly stated, failure to comply with the law essentially placed the fugitive outside the protection of the law. The Anglo-Saxon philosophy appeared to be that one must submit to the law or lose protection under the law.

During this time period theft was the most common crime, particularly of cattle and horses. Elements of civil property law and criminal law were not separated in cases from this period. In cases of robbery and burglary the primary objective was to capture the thief. Consequently, recovery of the property was routinely disregarded or neglected. Punishment of bandits was often swift and harsh. For example, if the thief did not make restitution to the victims, he or his family could be enslaved.

By the end of the Anglo-Saxon period, the judicial system had evolved enormously. Laws continued to be passed on predominantly by word of mouth; nonetheless, the customs and legislation developed during the Anglo-Saxon period lasted for five centuries.

THE NORMAN CONQUEST

Anglo-Saxon reign continued until the German conquerors were themselves conquered by the Normans. In 1066, William the Conqueror, a descendant of the Scandinavian conquerors of western France, entered England as a legitimate occupant of the throne. Prior to William's reign, the Normans had not followed a formal legal structure. After conquering the Anglo-Saxons, King William assimilated the Anglo-Saxon legal system into the Norman culture and further enhanced the Anglo-Saxon judicial processes with the aid of the extensive administrative skills which the Normans possessed (Walsh, 1923).

The Normans created the Great Council, or Magna Curia, which was composed of the king, the king's primary lords (to whom he had assigned large tracts of land), other English lords (who voluntarily joined the king's association), and the great religious leaders. This system later came to be known as the "House of Lords," to which was added the "House of Commons." American colonists would later establish their own bicameral legislatures, the House and Senate, modeled in part on the two houses of British government.

The Great Council was concerned with the overall operation of government and answered only to the king. The council performed numerous duties, including resolving land disputes, mediating agreements between the king and the church, and developing and enacting laws. The body of the council included the king's "justices." It was the duty of these individuals to watch over the king's interests, collect taxes from the sheriffs, supervise the shires, and oversee punishment of the guilty.

Over time, a court was established that would handle ecclesiastical matters separate from that of the county. For the most part, the hundred court was reduced to handling civil cases which did not involve land interests. On a semiannual basis, the presiding reeve of the hundred court would deliver criminal suspects before the county sheriff, who received "Pleas of the Crown." Some of these offenders were fined on the spot, while others, accused of more serious crimes, were held for trial before the shire court.

Norman kings appointed county sheriffs to preside over the shire court. The shire, or county, courts were then given a larger territory and jurisdiction over trials involving more grievous offenses. Court findings in both the hundred court and the shire court were binding unless the accused could prove prejudice or improper procedure. Appeals had to be requested from the king and his council.

The jurisdiction of the shire court was eventually altered when the sheriff became the king's primary aide. In the thirteenth century, the province of the shire court was transformed to that of a small claims court, a court which primarily handled lesser crimes and minor disputes. The removal of large land altercations, money disputes, and important criminal cases from these courts shifted the decision making to groups known as Royal Councils. The Norman kings also used personal confidants for judicial business. These officials were known as "lesser councils" who, along with the Great Council and Royal Councils, became an integral part of the "King's Court," known as the Curia Regis (Walsh, 1923).

The court structure that evolved under the Normans was demonstrative of the philosophy that the relationship between a vassal and his lord was primary. The Norman system was more like continental feudalism—landholding based on a personal relationship. A military type system was developed whereby the land tenant perpetually served the overlord, even to the extent of providing military service when needed.

Seignorial courts, locales where lords held court for their underlings, were also in existence during the Norman conquest era. There were as many levels in the seignorial courts as there were tenants in the service of the land-granting ruler. Each tenant could have their dispute decided in the seignorial court (Walsh, 1923).

There were also manorial courts or courts contained within the territory of the manor. The judiciary which supervised these courts were known as Villeins. These manorial courts had the authority to try most civil and criminal cases. For example, a thief caught stealing from the manor could be tried in the manorial court which governed that manor and sentenced to die by the same court (Walsh, 1923).

Moving forward in history, a series of events which occurred during the reign of Henry II culminated in the establishment of a system of royal courts. In the twelfth century, the king entered a decree which allowed him to seize jurisdiction over all important interests in land. The people could no longer deal with land interests in the lord's court unless the king granted jurisdiction by writ of right. This system was directed toward bringing these disputes before the king, as land was one of the most precious commodities during this time period. The writ system grew to include various powers which allowed the king to order a person, or a group, to perform, or not perform, a particular function (Walsh, 1923).

It was during the reign of Henry II that criminal defendants were regularly allowed to have an assistant accompany them in English courts to execute a technical pleading. These assistants evolved into the professionals we currently refer to as lawyers. By the thirteenth century, lawyers were recognized as professionals. By the time Henry III began his governance in England, judges were gaining respect as professionals and had begun to establish legislation and adjudicatory procedures in English courts (Walsh, 1923).

The king governed with the assistance of his "court," at least in theory as his power was rarely questioned. The king's court was the most exalted of the English courts and the ultimate court of appeal. Although the king's court was comprised of citizens from every elite group in English society, including priests, earls, knights, and barons, few of the court members ever actually participated in decision making, as the king himself usually chose to make all of the judicial decisions (Walsh, 1923).

In 1195, the king appointed lay people to aid in the apprehension and detention of citizens accused of misconduct. In 1344, the king granted these laymen, and additional citizens, the power to try those accused of misconduct and breaches of the peace. By 1368, these lay persons became known as justices of the peace and were endowed with the power to try prisoners.

During the Anglo-Saxon period and on into the period following the Norman Conquest, the criminal justice system separated criminal conduct into "emendable" and "unemendable" crimes. Emendable crimes were crimes that could not be satisfied through mere monetary reparations. An example of an emendable crime would be rape or murder. Unemendable crimes could be satisfied by money payments (examples include thefts, arson, housebreaking, breach of the peace with the king or church when accompanied by homicide, and a form of aggravated homicide committed secretly, such as by poisoning). For example, a convicted criminal could pay restitution for wilful homicide with the monies going to the victim's kin, the lord of the victim, and the king. Nonpayment would result in the offender being outlawed or sold as a slave. This system of payment continued until the twelfth century and was replaced by the common law of crimes (Walsh, 1923).

The new system of criminal law had three categories. Felonies, more serious crimes punishable by death or mutilation, lesser crimes for which the offender was fined, and the use of outlawry as a tool to procure the presence of the accused before the court. These early courts took a very narrow and direct reading of the laws. It was not until the fourteenth and fifteenth centuries that criminal intent was acknowledged as a legitimate basis for distinguishing felonious behavior from civil liability.

The Star Chamber Court, named after the room in which it was held, was first conferred jurisdiction under Henry VII, the first Tudor. This court was charged with administering justice to persons who refused to follow the dictates of other courts and to try cases which threatened the security of the realm, such as criminal libel, conspiracy, forgery, fraud and the punishment of judges. The Star Chamber was originally a court of equity. It appears that the court eventually developed into a locale which used unfettered discretion and torture to gain evidence and, upon passing judgment against the accused, imposed inhumane penalties. The Star Chamber was abolished by Parliament in 1641. With the demise of Star Chamber, the judicial power of the then antiquated "King's Council" disappeared (Walsh, 1923).

POST-NORMAN CONQUEST

In the era which followed Norman dominance, the new settlers in ancient England began to use the inquest, a distant forerunner to the grand jury, as their primary form of adjudication. This type of early inquiry was initially restricted to the king's congregation of landowners which was utilized to establish a system of taxation and the collection of feudal dues. Under this ancient system, the inquest was more likened to a declaration, under circumstances in which the ruler could obtain information from citizens. Township residents would be called upon to indicate their understanding of the immemorial rights of the king. This "understanding" was then adopted by a central group (Kempin, 1963).

In criminal cases, the inquest was initially a voluntary procedure in which 16 men were summoned from various jurisdictions to accuse an alleged offender of a crime. By 1166, the inquest procedure had become mandatory and was referred to as "a presenting jury." Once apprehended, the accused was tried in accordance with the pagan practice of "ordeals." These ancient modes of trial were little more than a series of tests, purported to appeal to the supernatural, which were purported to have the power to assess the guilt or innocence of the accused (Kempin, 1963).

One of the "ordeals" used during this period consisted of binding a hot iron to the hand of the accused and requiring him to carry it a certain distance. If there was no evidence of unclean matter on the hand of the accused in a three-day period of time, he was proved innocent. Another example was the ordeal of cold water. During this ordeal, the accused was dunked into cold water at the end of a rope, if he sank he was judged innocent. These ordeals were generally arranged to allow the accused a prospect of deliverance, as divine intervention was expected to play a role in the outcome (Kempin, 1963).

Trial by oath helpers, another form of trial which surfaced during this time period, required the taking of a formal oath by the accused along with his "chosen oath helpers." Oath helpers were not real witnesses of the facts involved in the accusation, they were people who were familiar with the defendant's character for truthfulness. Trial by oath helpers were used in cases involving an unspecified debt between parties who had no proof except for the claim of the plaintiff and the denial of the defendant. Essentially, eleven other men who were familiar with the defendant's veracity were called upon to provide support for the defendant's position. If the accused escaped punishment, it was again believed that divine intervention played a part in the process. It was further believed that even if the guilty escaped, the truly guilty would suffer divine retribution as a result of their perjury. Trial by oath helper continued to be used as late as 1833 when it was abolished by law (Kempin, 1963).

Beginning in 1215, the high powers of the church, the Fourth Lateran Council, prohibited churchmen from participating in the trial by ordeal process. As these trials had been being administered amidst the rituals of the church, trials by ordeal were essentially rendered unworkable. Although judges had acquired respect as professionals, the idea of replacing "divine intervention," as was thought to have existed in trial by ordeal, with judges authorized to perform the fact-finding duties was unacceptable. In fact, such a contention was likened to having a judge replace "the voice of God" (Kempin, 1963, p. 27). However, as time passed, judges were accepted as leaders of the court and proper decision makers.

Judges began to rely on the presenting jury as early as 1166. A presenting jury was made up of a number of men, mostly knights and lawmen, from the various townships. The jury consisted of twelve members who presented to the sheriff persons who were suspected of crimes. The jury then passed judgment and entered a referral. The sheriff had the discretion to accept or ignore the jury's referral. The jury members would sit in judgment of the accused regardless of their relationship with the accused or their prior knowledge concerning the alleged offense. Jurors did not merely hear testimony or the presentation of evidence; medieval jurors would personally investigate the matter, discover facts, and decide the guilt or innocence of the accused (Kempin, 1963).

These trials by chance, or appeals to a higher power, were replaced during Henry II's reign with a method of trial by the neighborhood. The trial did not include fact finding through the examination of witnesses. The jury, chosen from the neighborhood where the controversy existed, both researched and judged the facts. Medieval juries were drawn from fully informed prominent men of great financial means. Unlike modern jurors who are chosen for their impartiality, medieval jurors were chosen for their awareness and partiality. In a trial during this time period, if the accused died before submitting to the process, he was deemed not guilty. Once absolved of guilt, the heirs of the alleged offender were allowed to retain their interests in his property or possessions, as opposed to those interests being forfeited to the king (Kempin, 1963).

Over time, the jury process gradually evolved from a witness-type function to the development of a jury which solely served as judges of the facts. Moreover, whereas modern juries deliberate in private and decide cases as it sees fit, early English jurors were significantly less independent, as it was the judge who truly governed the proceeding.

Initially, trials were only held for felonies. However, by the end of the thirteenth century the practice extended to all accused of a crime punishable by imprisonment. In 1327, a system, supported by statute, incorporated the use of justices of the peace to replace more of the self-help remedies and to assist the sheriff in preserving the peace. People accused of committing crimes were initially asked to voluntarily submit to a presenting jury (Walsh, 1923).

Many of the accused were reluctant to do so, as the presenting jury was essentially comprised of his accusers. This gave the appearance that a guilty verdict was certain no matter what facts were eventually uncovered. By the year 1250, if the alleged offender declined to submit to the presenting jury, he could be tortured until he either cooperated or died. In 1275, a law was enacted which essentially authorized rigorous imprisonment for an accused person who refused to consent to a jury trial. By 1351, the laws were relaxed allowing an accused to challenge any indictor from participating as a trial juror (Walsh, 1923).

It was not until approximately 1450 that jury verdicts were not "truly" based on the testimony of witnesses. Nonetheless, even during the medieval time period when juror decisions were based more on personal bias than case facts, if a judge concluded that a juror had knowingly come to a false verdict, the judge could appoint a jury of twenty-four, known as an "attaining jury," to try the allegedly biased members of the presenting jury for perjury. A guilty verdict rendered by the attaining jury resulted in imprisonment of the juror(s) and forfeiture of his property to the king. The imposition of fines against jurors who failed to follow judicial instructions was an additional process used during this period to induce jurors to render unbiased verdicts (Kempin, 1963).

In the seventeenth century, juries were used more frequently in England. By the eighteenth century, the English model more closely resembled the modern American format: Jurors were drawn from the community and the courts endorsed the idea of randomly selecting an "impartial" group of jury members. Early on, it was a common provision, even codified in the laws of some jurisdictions, that the jury was the judge both of law and fact in criminal cases. Because of the threat to judicial power, this maxim was later modified allowing the jury to solely determine the fact element in criminal cases (Friedman, 1985).

THE COLONIAL COURTS

The criminal justice system has traveled a considerable journey from the colonial period, a time in which the criminal justice system was controlled entirely by laymen, to the current system which is predominantly operated by professionals. These early colonial criminal courts, conceived from the experiences and beliefs of the settlers, have been modified through thousands of legislative enactments and judicial decisions (Friedman, 1985).

In colonial America, the courts did not separate civil cases from criminal cases or property disputes. The division of labor which is so entrenched in the contemporary criminal court system did not exist until much later, after populations and living conditions evolved. Nonetheless, the proceedings which transpired before contemporary state criminal trial courts which were developed bore a striking similarity to those which were held in what was commonly referred to as "county courts" in colonial America. The system then, as it does now, processed ordinary criminal cases in large volumes without much fanfare. Apparently, spending excessive time on the "mostly" guilty has always been viewed as a waste of resources, especially in routine cases such as theft and simple assaults (Friedman, 1985).

Before the English settlers came to America, the country belonged to the Indians. Other cultures also preceded the English, including the French, Spanish, Swedes, and Dutch. When Christopher Columbus "discovered" America in 1492, North America was already home for an estimated two to ten million people. Archaeologists have discovered many pre-Columbian Native American cultures, some of which date back centuries before the arrival of European man. Columbus mistakenly believed that he had found the Asian mainland and, therefore, called the indigenous inhabitants of America "Indians." These Native Americans had developed hundreds of distinct cultures and spoke over two hundred different languages. There were impressive Indian groups who governed myriad administrative organizations, formed distinct cultural and religious practices, and developed intricate legal processes of their own (Friedman, 1993).

Early colonial settlers from England were generally one of three types. Some settlers were religious dissidents, others were people seeking new opportunities for wealth in the new land, and a fair segment of the colonial settlers were criminals sent over to rid England of their presence (Kempin, 1963, p. 22). Instead of attempting to merge Indian law with English law, these outcast colonists chose to nullify, or at the very least discourage, use of the bureaucratic system which had been utilized by the Native Americans. The use of force to supplant the customs of other cultural groups was deeply rooted in the history of the Germanic tribes, Anglo-Saxons, Normans, and early English settlers. Accordingly, the colonists used force and subterfuge to supplant any and all legislative procedures which were unlike those found in England. The result was a set of laws which bore significant similarities to those found in England but were shaped by the crude living and bloody battles which were fought between the Native Americans and the English settlers (Kempin, 1963).

In analyzing early American courts, it appears that a few of the practices and procedures used in colonial courts stemmed from remnants of Anglo-Saxon times. The early thirteenth century was the beginning of the period in which the common law system began to develop in England. Common laws were a set of laws developed using biblical edicts, customs, and other rules amassed and codified in words commoners could understand. It was this evolution, further influenced by the laws of England, upon which the colonial system was based (Kempin, 1963).

When the colonists established the colonial courts, the native tribes and African slaves had no protection under the newly established laws. Indentured servants received limited protection, yet even those protections differed significantly from those enjoyed by the other English settlers. Landowners, those of noble birth, and ordinary freemen controlled the legal system in England. Following in the footsteps of their Germanic forefathers, whose customs included the classification of people into ordinary freemen and the unfree, or serfs, the colonists began their new settlements under the cloak of social rank, race, and status. Historical data make it quite clear that the primary philosophy of the colonists was that property rights were more important than personal rights, or at least more important than the personal rights of select groups of people (Friedman, 1985).

The roots of the American legal system are inextricably intertwined with the "common law" legal system of England. By the beginning of the eighteenth century, the larger colonies had established court systems which possessed many of the characteristics found in English courts and continue to be utilized in modern-day American courts. Originally, the colonies established a two-tier judicial system that was similar to that used in England during the post-Norman time period. It was only after the colonists had gained their independence from England that the American court was converted to a three-tier system (Friedman, 1993).

The colonies were subject to England's rule for over 175 years. During this period the criminal justice system was really not a system at all. Members of the public bore the burden of assisting in the apprehension of the accused, reporting of the incident, and investigation of the crime. The colonial system relied on lay persons, who were either appointed or simply stepped forward to offer assistance, in apprehending and punishing criminals (Friedman, 1985).

Although there were similarities from colony to colony, each colony had its own system of laws, courts, and governance. All of the colonies, comparatively speaking, were densely populated, small communities with harsh living conditions. The definition of crime and punishment which was used by the colonists had been shaped by religion, years of subordination to the English monarch, and marred by the circumstances under which the colonists had been flung to the shores of America (Friedman, 1993).

The colonial system incorporated what the settlers could remember of the codes, customs, and jargon from English law, however, differences in social conditions made much of the English legal system unworkable for use by the colonists. The English legal system had evolved over a long period of time and existed in a well-established, refined society. England had about a hundred different courts, including specialized courts and courts with distinct powers, governing specified provinces. The elaborate tangle of courts operated in England would not have been sustainable in the colonies where life was much more crude than that of the "gentry" in England (Friedman, 1985).

The goal of the amateur players in the colonial system was to quickly find the accused, determine the strength of the evidence, and administer swift, often brutal, punishment. Unlike England, the colonists preferred the written word to word of mouth and, accordingly, codified colonial laws so that the community would know what type of behavior would and would not be tolerated. Another purpose, which was served by the change to written laws, was that people were able to keep the power of judges and other community leaders in check, as the laws also delineated the proper etiquette which these high-ranking officials were charged to follow (Friedman, 1985).

Essentially, one of three different types of legal systems, in varying degrees, were developed in each of the colonies. The first system was based on English law as remembered through folk talk. Another system was based on the norms and practices which developed as the settlers were coping with the problems in the new land. A third system was based on various ideologies the settlers brought with them from England, such as religion and the Bible. The colonies also varied in the manner in which they were structured. Several of the colonies were established as "crown colonies," others were structured as "chartered colonies," and still others were organized as "proprietorships." Chartered colonies explicitly agreed to conform the law of the colony to that of England, thereby providing the king with some continuing authority. In crown colonies and proprietorships, landowners merely assumed that the law of England controlled their interests in some way (Friedman, 1993).

The English legal system was greatly influenced by the wealth and power of the landed gentry of England. Ergo, the laws and legal customs in the colonies were similarly influenced. Comparably, religion, and its leaders, had a powerful influence on what was considered good and just in the colonies. This influence was so powerful that judges in colonial America were chosen not only from among political leaders but also from religious leaders (Friedman, 1993).

In many of the various stages of the criminal law process, including police operations, apprehension, prosecution, and punishment, the American criminal justice system adhered to many of the procedures which had been utilized in English courts. Colonial courts also incorporated additional safeguards into the American criminal process, such as the right to counsel, although such protections had not been firmly established in English courts. When a particular criminal law procedure was deemed to be nothing more that an outmoded ceremony, the procedure was either discarded or adapted to meet the needs and desires of the colonists (Friedman, 1985).

Although there were variations from colony to colony, the criminal court in colonial America typically had a tiered system. In the lowest level court, a single magistrate, or justice of the peace, handled petty crimes in a particular locality. This court bears great similarities to present-day municipal courts. Mid-level courts, also known as "county courts," were the trial courts which served a dual purpose as an administrative body and an assembly which presided over criminal cases. The county court was considered the "workhorse" of colonial government (Friedman, 1985).

Many of the colonies maintained a court of appeals. There were also specialized courts in the urban areas. In addition, the original American justice system even contained provisions which enabled colonists to appeal the decision of a colonial court to a tribunal in England (Friedman, 1985).

Although colonial courts chose to adopt many of England's judicial processes, there were countless variations in American criminal procedures. Colonial criminal procedures were not as formal and sophisticated as those found in England. For example, in colonial Massachusetts, a grand jury process was not employed because the population was so sparse. However, the procedure was later incorporated once the population in Massachusetts increased. In addition, early American courts took on an inquisitorial view. This type of thinking deviated greatly from the view of English courts which held that the decisions of jurors were appropriate, whether or not those decisions were actually based upon the facts of the case (Friedman, 1985; Friedman, 1993).

Colonial criminal law was much less formal, more direct, and contained fewer capital crimes, such as murder, in its code than in England. Essentially, in the colonies, the enforcement of criminal laws were tempered in cases involving "insiders" and more severe in punishing the deviance of outsiders. For example, in England, death could be ordered for any theft. However, in Massachusetts, death was ordered only for repeat offenders. Alternatives to death, such as hard labor and restitution, could also be ordered. In ordering alternatives to death and compelling offenders to comply with these mandates, American courts promoted confirmation with communal laws and discouraged personal forms of retaliation (Friedman, 1985).

Prior to the notorious Salem executions, which began in 1692, few executions were ordered in the colonies against English settlers. Notwithstanding that fact, severe punitive measures, such as hanging and castration, were widely used against slaves. Slave trafficking in England involved enormous quantities of people. Religious practices and laws passed during the early 1800s discouraged and ultimately quashed slave sales in England. Notwithstanding that fact, American colonists continued this practice hundreds of years after their migration from England to the point of incorporating the right to enslave another human being into colonial codes. Moreover, the "slave codes" created by the colonists were absolutely heinous in comparison to the general criminal codes. It took more than 100 years for these brutal, separatist codes to be destroyed (Friedman, 1993).

Moral laws regulating drunkenness, idleness, and lying were common. However, more often than not, the upper echelon of the community typically managed to avoid prosecution under these laws. The laws governing moral and social conduct were administered against those at the lower rungs of the social order—slaves, servants, and the poor (Friedman, 1993).

The role of the magistrate in colonial courts included much more that the finding of facts and application of laws. The magistrate initiated the judicial process and enforced orders solely with the assistance of only a sheriff or marshall. It was the sheriff's duty to arrest suspects as ordered by the magistrate. The presiding magistrate acted as investigator, interrogator, and prosecutor in deciding the fate of an accused person (Friedman, 1993).

The magistrate, and others involved in the criminal justice system, were not professionals. Most participants were chosen from among the lay population to carry out various duties in the criminal process. During this early colonial period, no lawyers were present. Moreover, there were no police in the modern sense of the word. Even sheriffs, constables, and watchmen were chosen from lay people or drafted by the magistrate (Friedman, 1985; Friedman, 1993).

When a colonial defendant was charged with a crime, the alleged offender was usually allowed to roam free until trial. The concept of bail had not been developed and, obviously, was not required. The size of the community and the familiarity of defendant to the locality was sufficient to force appearance for trial. Colonial trials were little more than forms of public embarrassment and teaching tools. Most colonists carried the belief that the magistrate had concluded the fate of the accused prior to trial, however, trials were conducted nonetheless. In fact, the more serious the crime, the more important it was for the magistrate to conduct the trial as a teaching tool. Colonial trials were used to publicly affirm the wrongful act, allowing the "sinner" a chance to show remorse and repent, as well as a chance to warn others of the consequences of such "wickedness" through publicly displayed punishments (Friedman, 1985).

The history of the colonial court and its use of the criminal process for social drama and local governance is well documented. The fact that lawbreakers were treated as instructional diagrams by colonial courts underscores modern-day perceptions that courts are not only interpreters of the laws in any given community but also are "safety valves for society" (Friedman, 1993, p. 30).

In the middle of the eighteenth century, the criminal court in Richmond County, Virginia was described as follows:

> Criminal courts met at the county courthouse. In Richmond, this was a small square building at a crossroads two miles from the river. Administration of justice was a wholly public event. The courts' yards were open to crowded places, magnets for the commoner and the curious. Merchant, lawyer, and passerby mingled to do business, hear cases and perhaps serve on a jury. The ceremonial of the courthouse, coupled with the colonists' interest in criminal cases involving neighbors, filled courthouses to overflowing.... The seating arrangement and placement of the bench in the courtroom gave visual emphasis to the power of the justices. The whipping post, to which many of the guilty were removed immediately after the justices had ruled, stood next to the courthouse. The gaol, with its yard, could be seen nearby. Whipping, branding, and pillory were public displays of the fruits of crime designed to warn the immoral. In a face-to-face society, public rituals of this nature strengthened the legitimacy of the criminal proceedings. (Hoffer & Scott, 1984, p. xx.)

Criminal procedure and the rights of the accused were transfigured over time. Although most cases were resolved without trial, the institution of trial by jury, as early as the seventeenth century in the some colonies, is evidence of these changes. Under English law, certain factors could operate to defeat the requisite mental state of the offender, such as violence of passion, temptation, or an extreme need to extenuate the offender's criminal conduct (Blackstone, 1851, 4. I.). Moreover, those who claimed a "benefit of clergy" were exempt from extreme penalties.

Both the king and Parliament had the power to forgive a forfeiture or reverse an attainder. However, penalties were usually inflicted as ordered. Two exceptions to that rule were that the death sentence of a pregnant woman could be delayed until after the birth of her child and a prisoner suffering insanity after conviction could be granted a reprieve (Blackstone, 1851).

England had an elaborate system of criminal procedures which had been developed over many years. American courts utilized the legal language which had been brought with them from England, but deviated from formal procedures and instead chose to create simple guidelines for use in attempting to preserve law and order. For example, in the seventeenth century, in situations where the judge was also a religious leader, that judge ruled with both the power of the robe and the authority of the church.

In colonial America, the judge handled cases in an "inquisitorial" way. For example, an alleged offender was often arrested based solely on rumor. Once apprehended, the accused was routinely interrogated by the presiding judge while the marshall and other magistrates observed. Upon completion of this inquiry, the magistrate made the decision on whether to dismiss or prosecute the accused.

When it was determined that a trial would be conducted, the magistrate called and questioned all witnesses and made findings of guilt or innocence. The majority of cases which were brought to trial in colonial America resulted in convictions. Once deemed guilty by the magistrate, the offender was expected to show remorse and repentance. The court used these opportunities to reaffirm the importance that punishment had on effectively enforcing law and order for the moral benefit of the community (Friedman, 1993).

The magistrates and justices of the peace were not formally trained. It was believed that these officials were people with an astute sense of right and wrong, convictions which were derived from their beliefs in God. There are additional components of this common-law system which are still in existence today. For example, the concept of a district attorney's office is Dutch in origin. In addition, the use of a jury to determine guilt or innocence, reliance on oral testimony at trial, and the exaltation of the trial judge as a revered super umpire were all characteristics found in English law which modern-day American courts continue to employ on a daily basis (Friedman, 1993).

THE CONTEMPORARY CRIMINAL COURT

Most offenders who come before today's criminal courts are subjected to fast-paced proceedings and are "punished" through the imposition of fines, correctional supervision (probation), or imprisonment. In addition, the criminal justice system in modern-day America is highly professional. These professionals include police officers, detectives, prosecutors, public defenders, parole and probation officers, and experts in myriad areas such as forensic medicine and psychiatry. Ultimately, most cases are resolved through plea bargaining. As it was in colonial times, trial by jury is still a staple of the American justice system. Moreover, the grand jury continues to be used in federal and state courts.

Significant changes in the American criminal justice system have been most pronounced during certain periods: the colonial period in America when the English-speaking settlers established their own law-ways after revolting against the motherland; the post Civil War period when, at least in theory, the legal system was expanded to include blacks who had previously been excluded from the protection of the law; the Miranda period, beginning in 1966, which, again, mostly in theory, extended the law to protect those being held on charges from police brutality which had been previously used unscrupulously to coerce confessions; and the period involving search and seizure issues, in which courts first refused to consider evidence which had been obtained from the accused in violation of the Fourth Amendment to the Constitution.

The latter two periods immediately preceded or, quite possibly, lead up to the era of the civil rights movement. The civil rights movement brought with it numerous cases which had a significant effect on both the substantive and procedural aspects of the criminal justice system. During these two periods, courts were faced with issues which reached far beyond those of crime and punishment. The criminal justice system was required to redefine who the Constitution would protect and under what circumstances and, to an even greater extent, was forced to reexamine the rights of those who previously had been stripped of their God-given rights to freedom and humanity.

The popular election of judges was not sanctioned until the middle of the nineteenth century, and, once elected, these judges were rarely impeached. Nineteenth-century judges emphasized that it was their job to interpret and harmonize previously decided cases, the Constitution, and common law, not to invent law. Consequently, America's modern criminal courts have been inundated with meandering ledgers of criminal laws which they are expected to strictly adhere to as guidelines in interpreting crimes and calculating appropriate penalties (Friedman, 1993).

Throughout the history of the American criminal court system, the greatest emphasis has been placed on the sentencing phase of the criminal process. The phase of the case which determines the guilt or innocence of the accused has historically been performed without much fanfare for the vast majority of offenders.

In most criminal cases throughout American history the accused confessed guilt. This continues to be the case in modern American courts. Due to the tremendous number of criminal cases disposed of by plea bargaining, American courts are beginning to look more like an administrative body than a trial court engaged in deciding disputed issues of law and fact (Laurent, 1959).

The criminal justice system has emerged as a compilation of several systems which function simultaneously (Friedman & Percival, 1981). Criminal cases fit within three different categories and each of these categories are managed in distinct ways. In one category there are the "show" trials which have unique characteristics, generally fame, gore, or some other high profile media subject. It is these show trials which have served to create an impression of the criminal justice system even though these cases are not representative of the masses. These trials usually consist of extensive pretrial hearings and detailed trial proceedings.

Another category of criminal cases are classified as routine felonies. Routine felony cases rarely go to trial and are generally disposed of in a highly informal and methodical procedure. These trials are usually brief and involve a minimal number of participants. The third category of criminal offenses involve petty crimes such as misdemeanors, criminal traffic offenses, and similar local ordinance violations. The third category of cases are hastily processed en masse by municipal courts with scant attention being given to criminal procedures.

CONCLUSION

The American criminal court has evolved over eight hundred years. In the early years, laws in the form of codes and customs were available, yet remained unenforced because the courts were governed by a tripartite scheme consisting of the judge, king, and religious leaders, all of whom enjoyed some form of control. From 1800 to 1960, laws were primarily enforced by judges who were considered to be genuinely independent. Unfortunately, costly and cumbersome litigation discouraged many citizens from utilizing the system; this essentially rendered the judicial process and governing laws ineffective.

The focus of modern-day courts must be on ensuring that our legal system is capable of enforcing the decisions it renders and renders judgments while equitably protecting legal rights, such as providing counsel to indigent criminal defendants, excluding illegally obtained evidence from criminal trials, and providing a trial by jury or other court process fairly and impartially. When a system ceases to serve even those minuscule functions, that system ceases to serve its citizens and must be revamped or discarded. The American criminal law system contains frailties and imperfections the same as any other system, yet it is the flexibility of our Constitution and the dedication of the professionals who develop the legislation and enforce the laws which ensures that our criminal justice system transforms to meet the demands of society.

Chapter 2

THE EVOLUTION OF THE PRISON

I do not know whether laws be right, or whether laws be wrong. All that we know who lie in gaol, is that the wall is strong. And that each day is like a year. A year whose days are long.

Oscar Wilde

INTRODUCTION

The development of the prison is strictly connected with the development of the jail. Historical data going back to the past 3,000 to 4,000 years indicate that the birth of the jail preceded that of the prison and that both of them reflect social changes involving increasing population growth, the growth of towns and cities, the right of owning property, the agrarian society, the industrial revolution and the urbanization movement. Further, jails/prisons served a social/utilitarian purpose. Hand-in-hand with the development of these places of confinement, a legal system evolved.

The original function of jails/prisons was that of a place of confinement, primarily for brief periods in a jail and for longer periods in a prison. The etymology of the word jail is apparently the Latin *capeola*, the diminutive of the Latin *cavea*, meaning cage or cavity, and probably describes the hollow ambience where prisoners were kept at times when apprehended. In fact, many of the jails in antiquity were actually underground caves. Prison, on the other hand, derives from the Latin verb *prehendere*, meaning to seize, and from the noun *prehension*, the act of seizing.

It is acceptable to presume that early humans had no code of laws and at first lived their lives in an aggressive-defensive mode in order to assure survival. Eventually, primitive humans grouped together

29

under a leader who showed a capacity for organization and decisional power. There was minimal political organization exemplified by basic rules of communal living, but those rules did not give a clear idea of what crime was—either against the individual or against property. Without a judicial system, even though primitive, to which one could make recourse, people reacted to offenses on the basis of their emotions and emotional ties. Generally, these reactions were based on the "hurt" or victimization suffered from someone else. Retaliation and blood feuds were acceptable and at times even expected. It was the way to rectify wrongs received—murder, rape or kidnaping of kin. This type of retaliation was essentially a normal reaction, fueled by the emotions of a person confronted by the killing or maiming of a loved one. Today, we would call it a gut reaction. This reaction was spontaneous and natural, not codified as eventually will be done, following the dictum "an eye for an eye, a tooth for a tooth."

Later, as the group became more involved with the welfare of its people, the concept of what should be considered right and wrong made its appearance. As time progressed, crime, which was at first dealt with on an individual basis, became the affair of the entire community. It is logical to think that the community, well aware of the aggressive impulses of its members, began to lay down rules and codified accepted behavior and penalties for misconduct. At the same time, religion came to offer a value system and a way for humans to control their destructive instincts. Religious precepts attempted to contain the spread of the blood feud which could have undermined the cohesiveness of the group. As people became property owners and property came to be viewed as an extension of the self and the fruit of people's labor, crimes against property slowly became part of a developing system of punishment. Personal retaliation soon gave way to various types of penalties such as exile, banishment, forced labor, which were aimed not only at punishing but at shaming the offender, or, at times, to capital punishment (Peters, 1995).

As the population grew and urbanization became more pronounced, the dispensation of justice moved progressively from physical punishment or shaming of the offender to incarceration, more or less lengthy, for the offenses that the guilty party had committed. The anonymity of larger towns minimized the emotional and social effect on the guilty person achieved by the previous methods of punishment which were aimed at shaming him in front of the people whom he was acquainted with. He was no longer under the scrutinizing eyes of people who knew him. In a society with a progressively increasing population, incarceration–i.e., removing the offender from society–came to be seen as a better way of dealing with offenders.

The penalties for all types of crime, against persons or property, were at first indiscriminate. The system of punishment began to change during the Age of Reason, aided especially by the insight of Charles-Louis de Montesquieu, the French philosopher and political theorist, and the Italian criminologist and economist Cesare Beccaria. It slowly lost its spirit of vengeance, becoming an expression only of retribution. In retribution, punishment is assessed on the basis of the *just desserts* theory. It must fit the crime and the culpability of the offender while taking into consideration the rights and duties of the victim and the offender, him or herself.

Indeed, it was with Montesquieu ([1748] 1994) and Beccaria ([1775] 1993) that the idea that the penalty should be congruous with the offense was promoted and that penalties, therefore, should not be based on arbitrariness. It was believed that if the penalty was made determinate rather than indeterminate, the defendants would become more aware of its disadvantages and perhaps defuse their proclivity for and interest in committing criminal acts.

Beccaria ([1775] 1872) summarized his theory, stating that "a punishment may not be an act of violence, of one, or of many against a private member of society, it should be public, immediate and necessary; the least possible in the case given; proportioned to the crime, and determined by the laws" (p. 99). He also stated, "Crimes are more effectively prevented by the *certainty*, than the *severity* of punishment" (p. 62, emphasis in original).

HISTORICAL NOTES

During the Middle Kingdom of ancient Egypt (2,050–1,786 B.C.) the pharaohs used public beating and imprisonment as punishment for those offenses which upset their orderly society. Prisoners were regarded as slaves and were placed in workhouses and subjected to hard labor. Their confinement varied according to the type of offense, and an official scribe kept a record of the inmates.

In Babylonia, the Hammurabi Code (1792–1750 B.C.), one of the most ancient codes of law, reports the use of prison and at that time people were confined for minor crimes and sentenced to hard labor. This type of punishment was also used by the Assyrians between 746–539 B.C.

In Genesis (39:20-23) it is reported that Joseph was confined to a prison for several years. Samson, when captured by the Philistines, was placed in a prison. The Hebrews are reported to have placed offenders in temporary custody, especially prior to execution (Leviticus 24:120-23; Numbers 15:32-36). When they were thought to have violated the covenant with God, offenders were also sentenced to exile or death through lapidation, burning, decapitation and beating. It is reported that the prophet Micah was imprisoned for a period of time. Jeremiah, the prophet, was imprisoned in the upper gate of Benjamin (Jeremiah 20:1-2) because his behavior had irritated Pashur, the son of the high priest and King Zedekiah. The Acts of the Apostles 4:3 report that both Peter and John were detained by the Sanhedrin, even though briefly. Saul imprisoned the Christians (Acts 8:3; 9:2), and St. Paul, in his Letter to the Hebrews (10:34), mentions imprisonment in addition to confiscation of property as a form of punishment (Peters, 1995).

In ancient Greece, from the seventh century B.C. to the fifth century B.C., the *polis* was responsible for the punishment of criminals and for the laws which applied to both major or minor crimes. During the period of Draco (620 B.C.), strict laws were enacted and enforced in cases of homicide. The expression Draconian laws derived from that. These laws were later revised by Solon, the great Athenian jurist (594 B.C.). A commonly held opinion of Athenians was that the guilty persons had to be confined in a prison and that their lack of freedom and/or their punishment should serve as an example to other citizens. Greek offenders were held in confinement, at times chained, in the *desmoterios* (place of chains). Confinement was viewed not only as retribution but also as a deterrent to further crime and a method of redemption for offensive behavior (Peters, 1995).

While Plato believed that people who committed serious crimes must be subjected to severe punishment, viewed by him as deterrent and retributive, he was of the opinion that an uneducated offender who did not have the capacity to appreciate the nature of his wrongdoing needed primarily corrective sentencing, what today could be termed behavioral modification. In Athens, at times punishment consisted in "stoning to death, throwing the offender from a cliff, [or] binding [the offender] to a stake so that he suffered a slow death and public abuse while dying..." (Peters, 1995, p. 5). The recidivistic offender was hanged. At times the offenders were denied burial. In Athens, punishment was three-pronged: physical, moral, and patrimonial. Patrimonial punishment consisted in fines, the confiscation of property, or the destruction of the condemned person's home.

In the prison, Greek offenders were also subjected to torture, and at times their execution even took place there. However, the Greek *phylake* (prison) was also used as a place of temporary confinement prior to trial or prior to punishment or, often, for long-term confinement. This is remindful of the present-day function of jails.

The Romans had specific courts for particular offenses, with statutory penalties. In ancient Rome, persons found guilty of physical assault, theft, or destruction of private property were punished either with a pecuniary payment or, when that was not possible after a sixty-day period passed by the offender in prison, with a death sentence. Prior to trial for any offense, the individual was imprisoned and the types of confinement were various. There was confinement to the home, called *ergastolo*; the *carcer*, or prison, where the individual at times was chained; the quarry-prison, or *latumiae*, which was initially within the city walls on the Capitoline hill, one of the seven hills of Rome. The prison often had a pit, which one could consider as corresponding to the so-called "hole" of contemporary prisons, where people were confined and, at that time, were often killed. As the city developed in importance and population, the Romans built prisons outside of the city walls. Those prisons were often underground dungeons—dark, noisy and overcrowded. It is reported that the prisoners were chained, at times abused and tortured, poorly fed and without supervision. The supervision of the prisons was made mandatory under the code of Emperor Theodosius (fifth century) and judges were mandated to inspect the jails or prisons. When they became emperors of Rome, humanistic leaders like Hadrian and Constantine made the jail/prison a less harsh place for the prisoners and punishment was less severe.

After centuries of social, military and political splendor, Rome, founded in 476 B.C., and capital of the Roman Empire, went through its decadent period and disintegration around the end of the fifth century A.D. Roman law, with the Twelve Tables, dating back to 451

B.C., became the basis of the Justinian Code in 434 A.D. The Justinian Code consisted of a complex of judicial norms protecting private and public rights in the administration of justice in the Roman State. It was based on *jus civile* and *jus gentium*, meaning the common good of the individual and the nation (Dizionario Enciclopedico Italiano-Treccani, 1970). It survived beyond the fall of the empire and still continues to influence the jurisprudence of many European countries.

After the fall of Rome, the Christian church, already present for some centuries under the last Roman emperors, became more powerful and enforced its own law—the Canon Law—designed to maintain control over people's misconduct. In addition to the State prisons, ecclesiastical prisons began to appear. These ecclesiastical prisons were present in France until the seventeenth century. The church, which had already been an important agent of social control from the third century through the seventeenth century, was empowered over secular matters by Charlemagne. The bishop's tribunals date from that period and were not only for people guilty of heresy but also disposed of common criminal matters. People found guilty of serious crimes were confined in the bishop's prison, at times even for life. If the defendant was found to be incorrigible, he would be turned over to a higher sacral courts which usually meant capital punishment.

In England, between 600 A.D. and 1,000 A.D., during the so-called Anglo-Saxon period, punishment in towns or shires often consisted in the branding of the offender. This was the usual sentence for crimes of arson, robbery, murder, and false coinage—crimes that were considered as being against the king's peace. This was codified in the Constitution of Clarendon by Henry II in 1166 A.D. Later, there was increasing severity of punishment, including capital punishment for treason, heresy, swearing, adultery and witchcraft. In Anglo-Saxon England, people found guilty of theft and witchcraft were at times imprisoned but more often they were punished, as in other European countries, with "mutilation, death, exile or compensation" (Peters, 1995, p. 33).

In England, at the time of King William I, there were important prisons like the Tower of London, the so-called Fleet Prison, and the Bulk House at Winchester. During the reign of Henry II, each county of England had jails for offenders charged with felonies while awaiting trial. From the twelfth to the sixteenth centuries, punishment moved from harsh physical punishment to fines. Fines were often combined with imprisonment during the fourteenth and fifteenth centuries.

The use of prisons increased as time went on, and by the sixteenth century offenders guilty of crimes ranging from vagrancy to moral offenses could be sent to prison. Prisons were frequently franchised by the king, and the townships had the responsibility not only for building the prison but for its upkeep. Life in prison was obviously uncomfortable and the prisoners were subject to pay for their maintenance. There were communal rooms, single cells, and the so-called segregation rooms or "holes" when severe punishment was thought to be indicated at the jailers' discretion. At times prisoners sentenced to capital punishment were tortured before being executed. England had used capital punishment extensively for two hundred years and thousands of offenders were executed, even for misdemeanors. "Blackstone had listed one hundred and sixty capital crimes in English legislation in 1760, while by 1819 there were about two hundred thirty-three" (Foucault, 1979, p. 14).

The Milbank Penitentiary in England was built in 1816. Its design included the panopticon proposed by Bentham. A panopticon type of prison was also constructed in 1840 in Pentonville. "The theme of the Panopticon [was] at once surveillance and observation, security and knowledge, individualization and totalization, isolation and transparency..." (Foucault, 1979, p. 249). In 1842, five progressive stages of prison custody were actuated, including a diminished sentence for good behavior and/or the possibility for conditional discharge from the prison. The prison system was essentially reserved for callous and incorrigible offenders. The Pentonville and Milbank Prisons eventually housed first offenders who, after a period of observation, were utilized for public works and later at times profited from conditional discharge.

In thirteenth century France the prison was used for offenders charged with debt, perjury, conspiracy, robbery, blasphemy and kidnaping, when they were not exiled. There were prisons for the lower classes and for the nobility, those of the nobility being better supervised. Hardened criminals were to be separated from offenders who were not thought to be dangerous. There was some food available, at least bread and water, but if the prisoners desired they were allowed to purchase other food through the jailers or their relatives were allowed to bring it to them. There was also the possibility for prisoners to obtain very short furloughs.

While the Châtelet in Paris housed both upper and lower class prisoners, the Bastille, initially a royal prison, by the time of the French Revolution housed mostly members of the lower class. It contained dungeons and eight towers with cells for confinement; it was poorly kept and its conditions were unhealthy. It was used as a prison until the French Revolution in 1789 when it was destroyed by the revolutionaries. During the eighteenth century workhouses were instituted.

In Spain during the eleventh and the twelfth century, people were imprisoned for failure to appear in court or to post bond, but basically the prisons housed offenders of a type similar to those found in other European countries. Mutilation, blinding and execution were common forms of punishment. In 1265 A.D., Alfonse X of Castile issued the legislative work *Las Siete Partidas* which, among other things, forbade the branding or mutilation of prisoners, and upheld prison hygiene.

In Italy, Castel Sant'Angelo in Rome, which at times served as a walled and protected residence for aristocrats and popes, also served as a place of confinement for common criminals and for persons accused of political crimes. Pope Boniface VIII approved the *poena carceris* in 1298 A.D., becoming "the first sovereign authority in the Western tradition to determine that imprisonment as punishment was a legitimate instrument of a universal legal system" (Peters, 1995, pp. 29-30). Later, prisons were used by the church inquisitors for people accused of heterodoxy.

In Florence, during the thirteenth century, Le Stinche prison became an alternative to the death penalty. In Le Stinche prisoners were separated by age, gender, seriousness of the offense, and by their mental status. Later, Siena, Pistoia and Venice adopted the same approach and by 1559 Venice had constructed large prisons.

Prisons were used under Germanic law during the domination of Europe by the Franks. In Germany and the northern countries temporary confinement was used and alternated with forced labor until the sixteenth century. At times people were kept in underground prisons for years, or were chained in the towers of castles or kept in monasteries. However, mutilation and capital punishment were the primary form of punishment. Prisons were usually used in lieu of more serious punishment. Before the fifteenth century, the time of imprisonment was usually short.

Eventually, "[t]he prison became the representative institution of industrial society, the perfect realization of the modern state" (Morris & Rothman, 1995, p. viii). In the 1600s, while existing prisons were highly functional places, a social interest in the construction of workhouses appeared. In these workhouses, like St. Bridget's Well, also known as Bridewell, in London, minor offenders and beggars were detained. Similar workhouses were also used in the Netherlands and in America during the colonial period. The workhouses in Amsterdam date to 1596 and housed beggars, young malefactors and people who obtained a reduction of penalty for good behavior. There, work was mandatory and was performed as part of a group. In these workhouses the prisoners slept two or three to a bed and each cell contained between four and twelve people. They received wages for their work as well as religious indoctrination. This type of workhouse can be thought to be a forerunner of the reformed prison of the eighteenth century.

Exile was a frequent form of punishment in many European countries. Until 1750, criminals from Russia were exiled to Siberia; those from Spain and Portugal were sent to Africa; France sent its prisoners to South America. Since 1650 England had sent many criminals to the North American colonies, except for those who were still housed in the so-called convicts' ships on the river Thames. Prisoners sent to the colonies were those convicted of murder or other serious crimes. They were usually white English citizens who reached the American territory in chains. By 1776 the number of these exiled prisoners was in the tens of thousands. With the American Revolution the convicts were no longer sent to the New World, but England continued the practice of exile, substituting Australia as a penal colony.

In the United States the first prison was constructed in New Haven, Connecticut in 1773. By 1790 prisons had been built in several states and some of them were underground. The conditions in those prisons were very harsh. Some were located near taverns, men and women were housed together, food was scarce, the sanitary conditions were very bad and there was no discipline. In 1787, an organization called The Society for Alleviating the Misery of the Public Prisons, headed by Benjamin Rush, had been created in an attempt to implement necessary reforms.

In the eighteenth century, prisoners in the Maison de Force in Ghent, Belgium were obliged to do work for which they were remunerated. Their supervision was strict and their discipline was based on a system of moral pedagogy. Idleness was thought to be the cause of most crimes. The time length of a sentence was a bone of contention since a too-short sentence (less than six months) was thought not long enough to properly address the offender's bad habits, while it was believed that a life sentence would create despair in them, leading to a desire to rebel and escape.

THE BEGINNING OF REFORM

In Ireland, Lord Crofton, who became Chief of the Penitentiary Administration in 1854, instituted outdoor work for the inmates whom he subdivided into five different classes which progressed towards a final conditional release or total freedom for good behavior, good work or good educational achievement. The inmates were paid for their work and they received differential treatment on the basis of their behavior. Professional training was available while in jail leading to various occupational possibilities for the inmate upon discharge from prison. This Crofton system lasted for only a period of thirty years, during which time some of the Irish prisons were shut down because criminality had lessened. By 1880, however, the number of offenders had reached high levels and it was again necessary to reopen the prisons.

The previously mentioned prison in Ghent, Belgium was almost a precursor of the Walnut Street Prison model in Philadelphia which opened in 1790 and which was operated by the Quakers. The Walnut Street Prison became one of the first in the world to implement radical reforms. In the prison, the prisoners were isolated but worked while in isolation, going through a basic apprenticeship. It was believed that in so doing they would avoid the bad influences of other inmates and, through personal introspection, would rediscover the morals they had lost or had never had. The prison was essentially viewed as a place of confinement, the purpose of which was to transform the propensity of the prisoners for antisocial acting out into good habits. The men and women were separated; drinking of alcohol was not allowed; there were cells for solitary confinement where inmates were to meditate while avoiding, as above mentioned, moral contamination from other prisoners. Inmates received religious instruction, did Bible reading, and worked while in their cells.

"In 1786, the Quakers in Pennsylvania instituted incarceration as a humane alternative to hanging and torture. In an effort to have prisoners do penitence for their sins, the Quakers locked convicts in solitary cells until they died or were released. So many died or went insane that in 1825 New York State's Auburn Prison introduced the practice of hard labor performed in silence" (Stang, 1972, p. 25).

Already in 1815, the state of New York had established the Auburn Prison, a prison that came to be seen by many states as being more economical than the Walnut Street Prison, and therefore thought to be more successful. The inmates were exposed to harsh discipline with strong security measures. They were allowed to work together during the day even though they had to maintain silence; at night they were confined in individual cells. A certain competition developed between the two prison systems–the Walnut Street Prison and Auburn Prison: which would achieve better rehabilitation of the convicts? At the time that the above changes were taking place in Philadelphia and New York, the Puritans were active in prison reform in Boston. Doubtless, however, the above systems were more humane than the criminal court of England which enforced harsh penalties and showed "no concern at all about the reformability of the criminal..." (Dumm, 1987, p. 73).

Prior to the turn of the nineteenth century offenders were punished with pillories or galleys and/or executed. Their death was considered an honorable means of making amends for the wrongs that they had committed. The pillory was abolished in France in 1789 and in England in 1837. By 1810, detention had become the essential form of punishment in France except for those crimes requiring the death penalty. Cities and counties began to construct their own prisons, together with houses of correction where offenders were kept for sentences up to one year. Main prisons were generally used for prisoners whose penalty was longer than one year (Foucault, 1979).

Prisoners began to be assigned to public works as, for example, in Pennsylvania where prisoners cleaned the public streets and worked on highways. They were easily recognized by their shaven heads and convicts' attire. They wore iron collars and were chained together "to impede any reaction to the verbal and physical assaults of the onlookers" (Foucault, 1979, p. 9). Chain gangs which had also been present in Europe were abolished by the beginning of the nineteenth century. However, in 1995, "chain gangs" were reinstated in the state of Alabama, although the offenders cannot be chained together because of a recent ruling regarding their civil liberties. As of this writing, their implementation in the form of electronic bracelets is in use in the state of Wisconsin. Already in 1764, Beccaria had spoken against the above practice of exhibiting chained prisoners in public. He expressed the idea that the punishment frequently exceeded the crime itself.

The guillotine was used for the first time in March 1792, replacing the gallows, first used in England in 1760. The French doctor Joseph Guillotin proposed that the decapitation of a person condemned to death would bring about a more rapid death. Public execution preceded by torture had almost entirely disappeared by 1840. Even though still in use in 1972, execution by guillotine had slowly moved from the city square to the interior of the prison, becoming inaccessible to the public. Rush, who in 1787 had founded the aforementioned Society for Alleviating the Miseries of the Public Prisons, opposed public execution as a barbarous expression of punishment. He believed that it was the product of "the feeble influence of reason and religion over the human mind" (Foucault, 1979, p. 10). By 1835, a New York law ordered that executions (hangings) to be "inflicted within the walls of the prison...or within a yard or enclosure adjoining," (Friedman, 1993, p. 76) in the county where the prisoner had been tried.

The prison experiments in America by the Quakers and Puritans in Philadelphia, New York and Boston were based on a philosophy of moral and social rehabilitation of the offender. At the same time, the offenders were thought to be deserving of confinement for their own benefit and that of society. In support of the prison system, Desjardin stated, " 'Prisons were intended by the law not to punish, but to secure the persons of the offenders..." (Foucault, 1979, p. 119).

As previously mentioned, the philanthropic approach in dealing with criminals regarded solitary confinement as important because it was believed that it would bring about changes in the moral character of the offenders leading to modifications in their conduct. This was the approach of the Quakers in Philadelphia. "Central to the Quaker mission was a radical modification of the system of criminal punishment...to establish institutions which would redeem rather than torture" (Dumm, 1987, p. 65).

The Quakers believed that merely putting the offenders to work would not change their habits because, they asserted, the habit of a righteous life could only be achieved through inner moral changes and a return to God. They viewed crime as a sin and saw faith and the fear of God as the only means to happiness and rehabilitation.

In the Quaker approach friendly persuasion took the place of physical coercion and became another form of control imposed on offenders. The Quaker ideas were part of the historical reality of that moment in American society, but their application was, by necessity, limited to a small carceral community and could only be actuated when the larger community was cohesive in sharing humane goals.

The eighteenth century began to see crime in a secular, rational way, and people, more aware of the environmental influences on human behavior expressed by Locke, began to endorse the sociogenic factors in crime and to consider more fully its social consequences. The new carceral philosophy stressed crime prevention as the basic rationale of any just law. Retribution or severe punishment were thought to be insufficient for its control.

By the beginning of the nineteenth century long strides had been made towards a more humane approach in dealing with criminals throughout the world, but especially in the United States. The ideological basis for that approach had originated in Europe with Jean-Jacque Rousseau, Montesquieu, and Beccaria, but the Europeans derived organizational ideas also from the new and more humane prison system of the New World.

As the urban population grew, so, too, did the number of offenders who were sent to poorly planned city jails/prisons which actually functioned as a holding tank, keeping in custody those individuals considered to be the rabble of society. They began to house not only criminals but also vagrants, the destitute and the mentally ill. By the end of the nineteenth century most cities and counties had established jails/prisons that served the purpose of "the control of problem population in the community" (Stojkovic & Lovell, 1992, p. 73).

In 1885, an international prison congress was held in Rome, Italy. Sixty countries participated and some exhibited the type of cell used in the prisons of their country. Germany, Switzerland, Sweden, Norway, Italy, England, France, Denmark, Belgium, Hungary, Russia, Austria, Spain and the United States were some of the most important nations participating in the congress. The exhibition of the United

States included models of the Philadelphia prison and the House of Correction in Concord. The topics of discussion were centered around the sentencing of offenders and the possibility of their being assigned to public works. Luigi Daga (cited in Ferracuti, 1989) reported the radical changes that had occurred after 1885 when the penitentiary system altered its philosophy, embracing an efficient scientific approach to the correction and rehabilitation of offenders. Incarceration was mandated primarily in serious cases while probation and pecuniary sanctions were more frequently employed.

In 1901 at the International Law Congress of Amsterdam, and in 1925 at a similar congress in London, the attention shifted from the prison to the person imprisoned and to the importance of the offender's psychopathology. That again led to better understanding and better treatment of the inmates. At the time, the reduction of penalty for good behavior, already present in the Italian, French and German prison systems, had also become a part of the English correctional/judicial system. During the first part of the twentieth century, however, the German penal system advocated the new principle of *volksgewissen*, the conscience of the people, which gave the judges the power to annul any kind of sentence, even retroactively, if it were contrary to the interests of the German people (Ferracuti, 1989).

Following World War II, alternative measures of detention, such as probation and parole, were adopted throughout the world, and the judicial and the penitentiary systems became more interested in the social reintegration of the inmates than in their punishment or moral changes. The liberalization of the law and the penal system, with stress on rehabilitation and social reintegration of the offender, together with the application of various forms of diversion, was meant to reduce the rate of criminality.

Until 1960 most prisoners were held in antiquated prisons. The security prisons, like Sing-Sing and Alcatraz, offered primarily custody and at times harsh punishment but few rehabilitative programs. A comparison can be made between the prisons of 1860 and those of 1960. In 1860, petty criminals were treated more harshly. They were required to do hard labor on things such as a treadmill or a crank; they were given a small diet and forced to sleep on boards. They were allowed no visits or letters, and the only reading material they were supplied with was the Bible. However, they were able to wear their own clothes and they were able to order food from the outside. They could even hire someone to clean their jail cells. Every one of these prisoners was kept in solitude. In 1960, petty criminals were forced to do boring but easy labor. They were supplied with a good diet and had easy access to a variety of reading materials. They also had their choice of several forms of recreation, and they had the possibility to buy things in the prison system. However, they had to serve longer sentences than those in the 1860s. The felons in the 1960s were under constant surveillance and assigned tasks to do. However, if they worked themselves up in status they were allowed part- or full-time education. They were given supportive counseling and even the possibility of home leave. There was more possibility for them to have visitors and to receive correspondence.

LATE TWENTIETH-CENTURY VIEWS

As the twentieth century progressed, crime was increasingly thought to be the product of a criminogenic society. A new breed of professional criminologists began educational and therapeutic programs for prison inmates and attempted to make the prison routine more acceptable and the conditions more liveable, with less harsh discipline and more opportunity for recreation and rehabilitation for the inmates. However, with the rapidly increasing population in the penal institutions during the past decades, these rehabilitative measures soon became less available because more time was spent by the custodial officers in supervision and control of the often unruly behavior of the inmates. Indeed, the past decades have witnessed an increase in crime and in the prison population, and in order to contain the avalanche of felonious criminality the prison system is again moving towards a more rigid treatment of the inmates. Maximum security prisons have been built throughout the country, and, because of the increase in the number of inmates, the continuous construction of prisons is foreseen for the twenty-first century. Primarily because of the overcrowding, "discipline became much more difficult to impose, with the result that gangs began to flourish as never before, drugs to be more available, and brutality between prisoners to be an increasing threat" (Morris, 1995, p. 237).

The sixties had already witnessed a high level of violence within the maximum security institutions, violence perpetrated by inmates on other inmates. "The violence now may not be administered by prison officials as in the past, but the violence promulgated by inmates against each other is no less harmful, nor is it anything else but a deviant form of punishment for non-compliance to coercive rules, even if those rules are part of the inmate culture," stated Stojkovic and Lovell (1992, p. 58).

From 1961, the request for release from prisoners incarcerated in federal prisons permitted by the United Sates Supreme Court following the *Monroe v. Pape* (1961) decision became very frequent, and "Habeas Corpus suits themselves were to become so popular that by 1995 some 10,000 petitions were being filed each year in Federal courts" (Ball, 1997, p. 57). The two *Gram v. Bordenkircher* rulings (1981 and 1986), an action initiated by a group of inmates at the Moundsville [Virginia] Penitentiary, became a milestone in defining what should be an adequate correctional institution. The totality of the institution under scrutiny included building structures, heating, ventilation systems, lighting, food, recreational facilities, and strict hygienic conditions. Spatial density, social density and mobility within a given cell were also considered. Visitation, exercise, recreation activities, and access to education and rehabilitation "and even the adequacy of the institution law library were addressed by the rulings of the court (in *Rhodes v. Chapman,* 1982). Generally speaking, prisoners are assumed to require a certain amount of exercise and recreation to remain in proper physical and mental condition. Deprivation of these necessities may be regarded as cruel and unusual" (Ball, 1997, p. 63).

During the 1980s, disgust with prison conditions in the United States led to a veritable revolution of judicial intervention. "In most popular and scholarly accounts, this development is attributed to the efforts of civil liberties groups, prisoners' rights lobbies, enhanced media scrutiny, and other societal pressures that ended the autocratic reign of iron-fisted wardens" (DiIulio, 1990, p. 8). One of the major developments in judicial intervention regarding the reform of prison conditions was the closing of the above-mentioned state penitentiary in Moundsville on July 1, 1992. Until then, "prisons were almost entirely in the hands of prison administrators, and the courts had maintained the traditional hands off attitude" (Ball, 1997, p. 56) and the prisoners were considered to be slaves of the state (*Ruffin v. Commonwealth,* 1871), having lost their rights after being sentenced.

However, in the sentencing at time of appeal in *Coffin v. Reichard* (Coffin v. Reichard, 143F.2nd 443, 1994) the court ruled that any prisoner is entitled to better confinement conditions and that undue deprivation of liberties while already in prison could be beyond what the law would allow and therefore was unconstitutional.

At present, rehabilitation appears to be less important in the treatment of offenders, and ambivalent judicial and carceral policies together with a social climate which supports stricter sentencing and less diversion are the expression of a cyclical return of the past. Even though many attempts have been made to reform the jails and prisons by humanistic advocates and by legislators interested in the humane treatment of offenders, the results have been minor, temporary and intermittent. The unchanging, monotonous routine of the prison deadens the spirit of those prisoners who could be rehabilitated, and the often unpredictable behavior of other inmates is a source of continuous fear for many of them.

PRISON OVERCROWDING

Overcrowding, which is one of the major problems encountered in jails and prisons at present, has brought about difficult management of the prisons. As stated by Morris (1995): "The most common prisons are the overcrowded prisons proximate to the big cities of America; they have become places of deadening routine, punctuated by bursts of fear and violence. Nor is there a clear trend in either direction: additional massive prisons and modern small prisons both proliferate" (p. 227).

Prison conditions of overcrowding are ubiquitous. Italy, for example, has 300 penal institutions; by spring 1995, the Italian prison system had 54,000 inmates while the capacity is for 36,000 (Sofri, 1995, p. 138). The San Vittore Prison, positioned almost in the center of Milan, built in 1879 with a panopticon design, houses 2,400 prisoners instead of the 1,000 for whom it was built. One thousand are prisoners who have entered Italy illegally from other countries. These offenders are usually charged with crimes of violence, robbery, drug use and abuse, and 60 percent of drug trafficking. Approximately fifty new prisoners enter the prison daily while about forty are discharged daily. In Italy, too, the prisons have become the repository for the indigent, minorities, and misdemeanants. The prison has lost its reeducative and rehabilitative programs and has become just a place of confinement. The overcrowding is so high that a cell of nine square meters may house six inmates at night and for most of the day (Deaglio, 1995, pp. 14-16). In Milwaukee, Wisconsin, a recently built jail often houses two offenders in cells built for one.

In France, prisons are overcrowded as well, usually because of a large misdemeanant population. In 1990, 20 percent of the French prisoners were reported to require psychiatric care and 15 percent were considered psychotics or seriously mentally disturbed (Lamothe & Gravier, 1990). In England, the prison population "rose sharply in the wake of strong media and political pressure for harsher policies towards offenders, including a greater use of imprisonment [during 1993 and 1994].... Overcrowding is felt most sharply in the Victorian-built city center local prisons, which always bear the brunt of rising numbers. On 30 November 1994, 18,383 prisoners were held in local prisons, which had a total of 15,594 places. Overall, therefore, local prisons were 18 percent overcrowded" (http://www.penlex. org.uk/pacoverc.html, [1997, June 24]). However, some prisons were 30, 40 and 50 percent overcrowded as of the same date. The prisoners are reported to be usually cramped and live in unpleasant conditions.

In St. Petersburg, Russia, up to twelve inmates are packed into each one of the cells of the famous Kresty Prison which, built in 1882 for 3,300 inmates, presently houses more than 10,000 inmates. "Last year a group of Council of Europe dignitaries revealed that up to 14 prisoners were packed into most of the 1,100 cells. Their damning report also criticized harsh treatment meted out to prisoners at the hands of guards" (http://www.spb.su/sppress/100/ugent/html, [1997, June 24]).

In Canada, "the Federal inmate population grew by 22 percent between 1990 and 1995." Incarceration rates are also very high— 130/100,000. The rates are exceeded by those in "Russia (558), the United States (529) and South Africa (368)." The incarceration rate, however, is "far above countries such as the United Kingdom (92), France (86) and Germany (81)" (The above statistics are from: http://www.sgc.gc.cw/news/factsheets/eovercd.htp [1997, June 24].) The situation is no different in South Africa where "on January 31, 1995, [the] overall occupational rate in South African jails [was] 122.3

percent. The prisons had on this day available space for 95,754 inmates whilst there were 117,153 held–an overpopulation in excess of 21,000 people.... South Africa has 380 inmates per 100,000 as compared to Zambia with 102 and Tanzania with 86" (Nesser & Takoulas, 1997, p. 1). And finally, it is interesting to note that in the Netherlands, a nation which has always attempted to avoid putting people in prison, "an additional 1,600 cells were added to the [prison] system in April [1997], bringing the number of cells to 12,000 and there is a proposal to build an additional 3,000 cells by the turn of the century.... Recidivism [is] at about 70 percent.... Funds [were also asked] to expand prison rehabilitation and crime prevention programs" (http://www.acsp.ui...BS/CJE/060306b.htm [1997, June 24]).

PRISON STRUCTURE AND ORGANIZATION

The structure of prisons is changing. The prisons, larger and technologically avant-garde, are generally of a more functional direct/podular supervisory type. This type of jail/prison allows not only more interaction among prisoners but also better supervision of them by the custodial personnel. This recent evolution of the jail/prison structure reflects a change in correctional philosophy towards a management-oriented approach to incarceration and stresses the personal responsibility of the inmate. "Prison has changed in some ways since I was here the first time....Today's prison system is geared more towards custody than treatment," wrote an inmate (van Court, 1994, p. 51). However, as Friedman (1993) correctly states: "The picture is, and remains, extremely mixed" (p. 463).

Organizationally, the correctional system may have multiple components, including "the prison," community-based facilities, halfway houses, home confinement, bracelets and monitoring. People in city jails come and go, and the jails are overpopulated not only with many recidivistic misdemeanant inmates but also with felons in transition to prison. In addition, a large cohort of mentally ill are now incarcerated and, in our experience, the paranoids are highly represented among them. These are inmates who need psychologic/psychiatric treatment which, unfortunately, the system cannot usually offer. Also, during the latter part of the twentieth century the jail has become increasingly the repository of persons who have been arrested for minor offenses. Indeed, most of the incarcerated offenders are charged with non-violent crimes. Many offenders are often over-charged for their criminal offenses. Further, their jail stay is frequently longer than it should be because of due-process delays and delays in sentencing due to an overcrowded court calendar. At times they spend their sentences in houses of correction, or their jail stay may be brief, since they are returned to the community on probation. However, many of them do not go through that period of reflection and integration of their carceral experience that might lead to new wholesome behavior, and they frequently become recidivist.

The great number of prisoners, their frequent recidivism, and the unsuccessful rehabilitative approach of the past decades, are leading to a robotization of the prison system. We do not believe that the courts overstep their boundaries when they try to address the conditions in correctional institutions. The institutions should be administered without infringing upon the constitutional rights of the prisoners, and the judges, as those who sentence people to prison, should have a voice in how the jails/prisons are run. Again, we would like to state that prisons are meant to confine offenders and deprive them of their freedom—not to further punish them by exposing them to unhealthy surroundings which would take us back 200 years to the pre-reform period of correctional institutions.

CONCLUSION

Prisons, serving a basic function in the penal system, are here to stay. The theories that advocate the abolition of the prison, such as those espoused by Lee Griffith (1993), are irrational and utopistic. The prison should be used with utmost discretion, for particular cases, and certainly not in the cases of those offenders who could benefit from the assistance of social agencies whose basic purpose is to reeducate offenders. Mediation, already present throughout the world with satisfactory results, should be enhanced, especially in cases of misdemeanor or even in some minor felonious offenses. "With the guidance of a mediator [the victim and the offender] share their feelings, discuss the facts and develop agreements about restitution" (Haley, 1994b, p. 24). Mediation should be viewed as a cathartic method which allays fears and anger and gives the offender the possibility to express guilt and remorse directly to his victim.

Even though we do not fully agree with Griffith's (1993) application of biblical perspectives to the problem of prisons, we certainly agree with him when he states: "Rather than leaving people isolated behind locked doors and barred windows, community movements for change help to empower neighborhoods.... Such efforts seek to make peace in the neighborhood. They represent movements away from habitual reliance on police, courts, and prisons" (p. 224).

Chapter 3

WHO ARE THE PRISONERS?–I

The more laws and order are made prominent, the more thieves and robbers there will be.

Lao-Tzu

SOCIO-CRIMINOLOGICAL VIEWS

The personality traits most prominent among the offenders we come in contact with in our professional lives led us to consider their patterns of behavior and the main characteristics of their personality in action, from which it is possible to derive an identikit which may be supported by the type of their crime. While the characteristics of the offenders give a clue to their personality type, since they do not live in a vacuum but in a social setting the suggestion that crime should be looked upon as behavior may be more helpful in assessing who these offenders are. We reviewed some of the major studies on the behavioral tendencies of offenders.

It was the belief of Emile Durkheim (1972) that crime is a normal occurrence "because a society exempt from it is utterly impossible," and that "crime...consists of one act that offends certain very strong collective sentiments" (p. 5). Crime is seen, then, as necessary, bound up with the "fundamental conditions of all social life and by that very fact it is useful because these conditions of which it is a part are themselves indispensable to the normal evolution of morality and law" (p. 7). Durkheim expressed the belief that the collective conscience will designate the offenders as criminals, and wrote that, "What confers this character upon them is not the intrinsic quality of a given act, but that definition which the collective conscience lends them" (p. 7). Further, he believed that "contrary to current ideas, the criminal no longer seems a totally unsociable being, a sort of parasitic element, a

50

strange and unassimilable body, introduced in the midst of society. On the contrary, he plays a definite role in social life. Crime, for its part, must no longer be conceived as an evil that cannot be too much suppressed" (p. 8). Durkheim defined as criminal that type of behavior which is prohibited by the criminal code, and wrote that "the criminal norms, i.e., the conduct norms embodied in the criminal law, change as the values of the dominant groups are modified or as the vicissitudes of social growth cause a reconstitution of these groups themselves and shifts in the focus of power" (p. 13).

In looking at the personal background of prisoners, wrote Guttmacher (1972a), "almost without exception one finds...not only economic want, but cruelties and miseries of every kind" (p. 99). Most of them have characteristics typical of the antisocial personality, such as frustration, reckless disregard for human life, a complete lack of family cohesiveness, and social maladjustment. He believed that, "[i]n all probability, the genesis of such defective personality structure has resulted from the defective ethical standards which flourish in the milieu in which they were spawned, rather than from hidden neurotic complexes" (p. 105). For them, people are just objects on whom to prey.

Looking at the inmates not just as offenders–persons who have committed a punishable act–but also as delinquents whose biographical life, personality and predisposition to crime may enlighten us regarding the motives for and the circumstances surrounding the crime they have committed–raises the question of the typology of the offender/delinquent. Indeed, as Michele Foucault (1979) aptly stated, "The delinquent is...to be distinguished from the offender in that [the offender] is not only the author of his acts...but is linked to his offense by a whole bundle of complex threads (instincts, drives, tendencies, character)" (pp. 252-253).

Sellin believed that people are born into a culture, and intrinsic to that culture are "customs, beliefs, artifacts," as well as people's relationship to their fellow humans and to social institutions. These ideas become "cultural elements...fixed into integrated systems of meaning" (p. 15). Together with the biological makeup of the individual they will influence and help to form the personality itself. The above views are useful in the rehabilitation of offenders since the examination of their life will aid in their classification regarding the many degrees of dangerousness and possible recidivism and attend to their rehabilitation in the best, most adequate and specific manner.

There has been in the past a tendency to an ethnography of crime which viewed criminals as part of "quasi-natural classes, each endowed with its own characteristics and requiring a specific treatment" (Marquet-Wasselot [1841], cited in Foucault, 1979, p. 253). The ethnography of crime was certainly the forerunner of criminal typology. Foucault reports Ferrus' [1850] classification of prisoners into three types of convict. The first group consisted of those of above average intelligence, perverted by "the tendencies of their organization...a native predisposition...pernicious logic...iniquitous morality [or]...a dangerous attitude to social duties" (p. 253). Ferrus believed that these persons were in need of "isolation day and night, solitary exercise," and some bizarre precautions if they ever came in contact with other inmates, such as a "light mask made of metal netting" (p. 253). The second group was described as "vicious, stupid or passive...led into evil by indifference to either shame or honour,... cowardice...laziness" (p. 254). For these, he proposed a regime of education, work in common during the day, allowing only conversation or reading in a dayroom with indoctrination and isolation at night. This is what the carceral system consisted of at the Auburn Prison in New York. The third group of convicts classified by Ferrus comprised those "incapable...of any occupation requiring considered effort and consistent will...incapable of competing in work...having neither enough education to know their social duties nor enough intelligence to understand this fact or to struggle against their personal instincts" (p. 254). He suggested for these convicts life in common, in small groups "stimulated by collective operations and subjected to rigid surveillance" (p. 254).

The Sutherland Differential Association Theory holds that criminality is learned in interaction with others in a process of communication. "A person becomes delinquent because of an excess of definitions favorable to violation of law over definitions unfavourable to violation of law. This is the principle of differential association" (Sutherland, 1955, p. 78). The offenders define and interpret the situation, codes and mores differently from non-criminals.

Robert Merton (1972) theorized the doctrine of "socially derived sin...[in which] the social order is solely a device for impulse management and the social processing of tension...[and in which] certain phases of social structure generate the circumstances in which infringement of social codes constitutes a normal response" (p. 379). Two elements, culture goals and institutional norms, are instrumental in the integration and stability of social groups. He believed, therefore, that "[a]berrant conduct...may be viewed as a symptom of dissociation between culturally defined aspirations and socially structured means" (p. 382). Various forms of adaptation derive from the above interplay: conformity, innovation, ritualism, retreatism, and rebellion. Merton further believed that people whose conduct is maladjusted are, strictly speaking, in the society but not of it. "Sociologically they constitute the true 'aliens,'" he wrote (p. 386). He also believed that the social sources of antisocial behavior centered around the cultural emphasis upon pecuniary success. Any lack of equilibrium between "culturally designated means and ends" may promote antisocial behavior and anomie, especially when conventional and legitimate access to means for attaining success are not present (p. 389).

Walter Bromberg's (1965) proposal to regard the individual offender as a "behaver" rather than a wrongdoer "offers a freer view of the actual interaction between the criminal psyche and his society" (p. 90). He thought of crime as deliberate, highly personalized behavior, the outcome of an "inner struggle between instinctual desire and the residue of moral and ethical ideals seated uneasily in the conscience" (p. 91). However, at times there is no struggle within the individual, and his instinctual desires have free rein, without the presence of any vestiges of moral conscience. It is the lack of inner control, stated Colin Wilson (1984), that allows what he termed the inner tension to become aggression.

LONGITUDINAL TRAITS STUDIES

Even though the inmates behind the bars of a jail or prison are usually viewed as an amorphus group, generally differentiated only on the basis of the type of crime they have been charged with or found guilty of, one cannot dismiss *tout-court* the fact that behind each crime and even behind the same category of crime there is an individual with his own character and attitudes, unique in his own right.

Longitudinal trait studies of delinquents have greatly contributed to the understanding of the continuity of misconduct. Sheldon Glueck and Eleanor Glueck's seminal study in 1930 took into consideration two groups of 500 fourteen-and-one-half-year-old adolescents (delinquent and non-delinquent) matched by age, ethnic background, neighborhood, family income, IQ and the corresponding delinquency rate. Specific differences, such as the delinquent boys' lower educational background, the fact that their homes were more crowded, less clean and with poor hygienic facilities, and the generally lower average income and low occupational level of their parents, were taken into consideration. The study revealed that the delinquents were more self-assertive, defiant, hostile, suspicious, narcissistic, impulsive, resentful, and ambivalent towards authority, while the non-delinquents were more anxious, compulsive, more conventional in their behavior, fearful of failure, and more dependent on others. The study revealed that by age thirty-one, the delinquent group had committed a much higher number of criminal offenses, "15 homicides, hundreds of burglaries, hundreds of larcenies, hundreds of arrest for drunkenness, over 150 robberies, dozens of sex offenses, and so on" (Glueck & Glueck, cited in Wilson & Herrnstein, 1985, p. 178). Instead, only sixty-two of the 442 non-delinquents, by age thirty-one, had committed minor crimes—drunkenness, offenses within the family, and a few armed robberies, one assault with a dangerous weapon, and an abuse of a child.

John Conger and Wilbur Miller's (1956) longitudinal study of 368 cases of tenth graders in the Denver Colorado Public Schools, comprising 184 delinquent and 184 non-delinquent boys, showed that the delinquents were emotionally unstable, impulsive, suspicious, hostile, egocentric and generally more dissatisfied than the non-delinquents. Their third-grade teacher's evaluation had already pointed out these traits: "More poorly adapted than their classmates," the teacher's notes read (cited in Wilson & Herrnstein, 1984, p. 179). In addition, while in school they did not accept responsibility, had a negative attitude toward authority, and had difficulty in getting along with peers.

A prospective longitudinal study of 3,415 school boys was done by Terence Taylor and David Watt (1977) in England. They appraised the children's behavior retrospectively to assess correlates for delinquency. One child in ten had three deviant symptoms. A symptom was classified as deviant if it appeared in less that 10 percent of cases. Within a seven-year period 300 of the boys were referred to criminal court or clinic at a ratio of 3.1 to 1. Among the symptoms that were precursors of delinquency they cited restlessness, stealing, emotional instability, moodiness, school phobia, temper tantrums, and crying in court. They also had reading difficulties. It is interesting to note that seven years earlier the teachers had described the court-bound boys as assertive and disruptive, while those boys who were referred to a clinic were described as uncooperative and uninterested in school activities. The study of Glueck and Glueck, that of Conger and Miller, and the study by Taylor and Walt, above reported, reveal that the most disruptive youngsters came from poorer backgrounds and larger families, with an absence, or inconsistent presence, of parents.

Lee Robins, in a thirty-five-year follow-up of 526 white children in a guidance clinic in St. Louis, Missouri, initiated in the 1920s, reported that approximately one-third of adult sociopaths–an antisocial child having reached adulthood–had been described as impulsive, reckless and lacking guilt during their childhood. They were also reported to have been careless of their hygiene and appearance. Donald West and Donald Farrington's prospective study of 411 fourth graders in six neighborhood schools in London in 1961 analyzed a "self-report questionnaire, school and family records, and self reports and official records of offenses" (cited in Wilson & Herrnstein, 1984, p. 183). The study revealed that 30 percent had a record of delinquency already by age twenty-one, and of the 20 percent of sample boys rated by teachers and peers prior to age eleven about 60 percent were recidivist by age eighteen. Their study, also, showed that the boys were restless and impulsive and belonged to a rowdy or non-conventional groups.

Pothrow-Stith (1991) stated that "boys without fathers at home have a more difficult time managing their aggression than boys who do," and, referring particularly to black minorities, she added, "Young black males in the impoverished underclass setting usually grow to manhood in an environment where very few feel good about their manliness," (p. 79) and robbed of their pride and self-esteem, she believes that they are at risk for violence because of their narcissism. Narcissism, she wrote, even though "a normal and necessary part of adolescent sexual development,... impairs judgment, preventing young people, especially young men, from perceiving and fleeing from dangerous circumstances" (p. 55).

Donna Towberman (1994), in reporting the results of her study on the psychosocial antecedents of chronic delinquency, emphasized that "family functioning, defined as the degree of affectionate bonding between youth and parents, contributes significantly to all dimensions of chronic delinquency." She added as important contributory factors to delinquency the "numbers of out-of-home placements in institutions and foster homes, abuse in foster homes and institutional placements, commission of delinquent acts with peers and siblings, drug use during offense commission, poor school attendance, and early age at first adjudication" (p. 151). Families at high risk for delinquency, she stated, are "those whose children have been placed in foster homes or institutions" (p. 163). We frequently see in offenders before the bench or whom we examine for the courts or within correctional institutions the following triad during their adolescent period: absence of father, poor school attendance, and alcohol/drug use.

The above sample of prospective and retrospective studies supports the contention that social misconduct and antisocial traits, inherent to the personality, are already present in the delinquent's adolescent period and continue to be present and worsen during the course of the offender's life. One of the personality traits which stands out clearly among others is impulsiveness and is part of the psychopathology found in criminal offenders, especially evident in those jailed or imprisoned.

VIEWS ON CRIMINOLOGICAL TRAITS

Ernst Kretschmer believed that a person's character is the result of constitution, temperament and environmental interaction. Further, he thought that it may be difficult to mold the biopsychogenetic tendencies of the individual. Kretschmer was one of the most important scholars of the early 1900 German school of psychiatry and can be considered as a forerunner of Cesare Lombroso and the positivistic school of criminology. He distinguished two main behavioral reactions—the primitive and the organized. He stated that the primitive reaction of the individual does not process the stimulus that impinges upon him, but *impulsively* and *immediately* reacts to it as if he were a child. He explained the above as a consequence of an exaggerated stimulus (that which today is termed stressful) that "paralyzes the cognitive/noetic/moral part of the personality, either due to congenital or acquired anomalies of the self (such as traumatic infections, toxic noxae, intra- and extrauterine), or psychological deficiencies." He added that, because of physical and psychological deficiencies, at times even minor stimuli might provoke these primitive impulsive reactions (DiTullio, 1960, p. 23). This is quite characteristic of the psychopathic personality.

Lombroso described prisoners as people who "talked like savages, and showed violent passions, lack of foresight and frequency of tattooing...blunting of their moral and ethical selves, a superficiality of interpersonal contact such as lacking ambition, unable to show affection and real love...prone to lying and swindling and with a chaotic sexuality" (Palermo, 1994a, pp. 105–106). Arthur Noyes and Lawrence Kolb (1958) described the offenders of the antisocial type as having characteristics of emotional immaturity, impulsivity, absence of rational behavior, lack of conscience, affectionless. They had narcissistic feelings, lack of remorse, and did not show foresight. Hare and McPherson (1984) described the psychopath as impulsive and aggressive, needing and craving exciting and thrill-seeking behavior, prone to boredom, and as having a low-frustration tolerance, easy irritability and belligerent behavior. "All of the above studies and observations from Lombroso to Hare and McPherson basically agree that the offender, and in particular the psychopath, is endowed with a distinct personality...defiant of rules, laws and mores, usually pursuing a self-incriminating, impulsive, reckless and often nonsensical type of behavior" (Palermo, 1994a, pp. 108-109).

CHARACTER AND TEMPERAMENT

The ideas of W. Boven (cited in DiTullio, 1960) are interesting for the understanding of human behavior. Boven's belief was that man tends to overcome his biological self throughout his lifetime. He viewed character as the result of a struggle among the lower instinctive, vegetative and attitudinal stratum; the egocentric forces of the central stratum; and the higher stratum which comprises the intelligence and the willpower. Benigno DiTullio, himself, stated that an individual tends to develop his character on the basis of his natural instinctive and affective propensities, aided in his maturation by the environment and education, leading to habit patterns that become an intrinsic part of his daily activity.

Character is the composite of distinctive qualities formed by mental and ethical traits which, stimulated by an individual's emotional sensitivity and habitual mode of reaction, give to each one's personality its dynamism. Character is the personality in action and is due to the temperamental propensity of the individual. It is the outcome of life experiences, of togetherness, of give-and-take, of a conscious or unconscious adaptation of id and ego tendencies to the social dictates or appropriate modes of practical, moral and ethical behavior when confronted with choices. Absence of character is usually found behind much senseless crime, and the knowledge of the personality traits shared by many non-psychotic criminals is fundamental for the understanding of the criminal behavior that relegates any person to a jail or prison.

Recently, numerous studies have been done to assess the continuity of temperament over time. Stella Chess and Alexander Thomas (1991) rated temperament in nine categories. "These categories are activity level, regularity of biological functions, approach or withdrawal tendencies to new situations, adaptability to change, sensory threshold, quality of mood (whether predominantly positive or negative), intensity of mood expression (whether positive or negative), distractibility, and a combined category of persistence and attention span" (p. 205). They divided temperament into three types: difficult, easy, and slow-to-warm-up, comprising different numbers of the above categories. The purpose of their study was to determine whether some of the undesirable traits of each temperamental group showed continuity during the first five years of a person's life and whether the undesirable expression of one or another temperamental trait or pattern could be minimized. They even calculated "correlations between temperament in years 1 through 5 and early adult temperament" (p. 206). They found no significant correlation between single temperament traits and early adult adjustment, but did find that if temperament were looked upon in its globality, continuity in temperament continues into adult life. Traits may change during a lifetime due to individual reaction, to the environment, and to a person's developmental maturation. Continuity and change are thought to be not exclusive. "A temperamental characteristic pattern may be continuous throughout one time period and then change, and the opposite may also occur" (p. 210). In their goodness to fit theory, they theorize that "demands, stresses and conflicts, when consonant with the child's developmental potentials and capacities for mastery, will be constructive in their consequences" (p. 211). However, they further stated that disturbed behavior is due to excessive stress due to "poorness of fit and dissonance" (p. 211) between expectations and demands and the child's capacity to master the situation. They suggested that "short and long term correlations of continuity in temperament may reach the 50 percent level" (p. 210).

The above study is not only pertinent to children in their developmental life course but it applies, too, to adults, who also go through developmental stages. If they do not possess the ego resiliency and the intellectual/emotional capacity to properly assess and react to whatever situation confronts them, they may not master the situation. They will fail. We raise the above issue, extending the intentions of Chess and Thomas' study into adult development, because many young adult criminals show recidivistic behavior, frequent behavioral failures, and an incapacity to adapt to societal demands. That may also be the consequence of poorness of fit. It is probably due to poor assessment of their capacities and resiliency rather than to their enjoying the criminal offenses they perpetrate. We have all come across the young offender whose life history, gathered by us or by a social agency, well points out the frequent continuity of their temperament. Actually, one can easily observe in some of them the progression of antisociality from the oppositional defiance of a child to a conduct disorder and to the eventual antisocial personality disorder.

W. H. Sheldon (1942), well-known for his biotypology (endo-, meso- or ectomorphic body types), thought by him to be fixed elements of a personality, stressed the importance of human temperament, which adds a dynamic component to the personality itself. M. Verdun (cited in DiTullio, 1960) stressed the interaction between environment, constitution, and temperament. His emphasis on the importance of the neurovegetative system and its excitability at the basis of human behavior and human emotions anticipated the present-day neurotransmitter hypothesis in normal and disorderly conduct. He wrote of orthosympatic adrenalinergic, parasympatic cholinergic, and telesympatic histaminergic reactions. Verdun belonged to that school of thought that viewed human behavior as the outward manifestation of an individual neurovegetative predisposition to react to excessive or irritating stimuli—endogenous or exogenous, biological or psychological, acute or chronic—idiosyncratic to the individual. Such theories lead one to consider the possible predisposition of many offenders to criminal behavior and to the theory that, during the past fifty years, has attributed that behavior mostly to negative environmental factors, since many offenders seem to be recalcitrant to change, even though attempts have been made to change their environmental conditions. The pendulum of nature versus nurture at the basis of human conduct seems to be more on the side of nature.

Fr. Agostino Gemelli and Giorgio Zunini (1949) recognized the importance of personality traits and attitudinal disposition in the formation of character. They believed in the plasticity and variability of character and subscribed to the idea that character is the outcome of an interplay of traits, attitudes and stimuli in a given moment for a given individual. They believed that education, and not only a person's hereditary or organic personality traits, were basic to the manifestation of human conduct, and that an individual without education and lacking a notion of morality cannot be considered a mature being because without the above his basic self has not evolved to a level of acceptable adaptation to society. This is frequently observed among the criminals presently in the carceral system: a poor educational and moral level. Indeed, the vast majority of the thousands of offenders we have examined through the years had not finished high school, frequently dropping out of school around the tenth or twelfth grade, often displayed a third grade level of knowledge, and lacked a moral sense.

Because of a lifelong maladjustment in a world of anomie with characteristics of both amiability and hostility, hedonistic purposes, and immediate expediency, the psychopath has been defined as a rebel without a cause. Hervey Cleckley, in 1955, made a distinction between the ordinary criminal and the psychopath that still holds true. He believed that the first possessed purposive behavior and his aims are well understood by the average person, even though not accepted and shared with him. "The criminal, in short, is usually trying to get something we all want, though he uses methods we shun" he wrote (p. 292). The ordinary criminal is consistent and persistent in conniving in order to reach his own ends and is aware of the possible legal consequences of his actions. He is shrewd in his planning and in his attempt to avoid being apprehended.

As throughout past centuries, today the common criminal lacks a mature personality and his behavior is primarily driven by instinctual drives, drives that in the non-criminal are usually sublimated, channeled toward more acceptable behavior. Lack of education, and not of basic intellectual endowment, and the *lack of exposure to the socio-moral values* shared by the community at large have not allowed the psychological self of the future criminal to acquire that *socio-civic sense of responsibility* that allows one to live in the human consortium.

Crime can be looked upon as a psychobiologic social phenomenon. The offender gives a clue to his criminal character through the type of offense. This is the reason why crimes have been described as essentially aggressive (e.g., murder, robbery and rape) or passive aggressive in nature (e.g., burglary, forgery, arson, etc.), or as essentially related to psychophysiological stress (e.g., sexual crimes, pedophilia, indecencies in public, exhibitionism). Can one determine the personality of the offender from his or her crime? Don Gibbons (1965) devised a very complex typology mostly based on the type of crime that the individual offender had committed. Even though his description is more along the line of a so-called "criminal career," he included among the various categories the offender's self-assessment and his attitudinal predisposition. The above factors are helpful in forming an identikit of the offender.

Bromberg (1965), in his book *Crime and the Mind*, took into consideration the personality characteristics of the offenders from a psychiatric and psychological point of view. He listed various types of offenders: the aggressive (antisocial, released by alcohol, or a reaction to feelings of inferiority); the emotionally unstable; the unethical (criminal type); the maladjusted adolescent; and the immature adult type. Among the latter stand out the egocentric, inadequate, shiftless, suggestible, adynamic or dull types. Bromberg further proposed the interesting classification of the nomadic type, "unattached, schizoid to a degree," and the primitive type, whose behavior is "simple and instinctive" (p. 86). Among "adjusted" individuals he included those "adjusted to a low cultural level with its own ideologies and mores" and "those obviously maintaining a relationship to the so-called stable world" (p. 86). His first category of so-called adjusted individuals is quite interesting and is remindful of those groups described as belonging to the specific subculture of violence.

Subscribing to the idea that "we should be able to reconstruct the man from a sample of his violent acts" (1969, p. 133), Hans Toch formulated a typology of the violence-prone individual that includes nine categories: (1) those defending their reputation, such as a person whose role or status is given to him by others and makes him exercise violence/justice, like a Mafia godfather; (2) those enforcing norms, such as "a self-assigned mission involving the use of violence on behalf of norms that the violent person sees as universal rules of conduct" (p. 135); (3) those who are self-image compensating, including persons defending their self-image and those promoting their self-image. In the latter cases "the use of violence as a demonstration of worth by persons whose self-definition places emphasis on toughness and status" (p. 135); (4) persons who are self-defending with a tendency to perceive others as sources of physical danger requiring neutralization; (5) persons who are "pressure removing" and have a propensity to explode in situations due to an inability to deal with them; (6) bullying in which pleasure is derived by using violence against people who cannot defend themselves; (7) exploiting through the manipulation of others, taking advantage of their fears of violence; (8) self-indulging: making themselves the center of attention getting; expecting subservience and satisfaction of needs from others; and (9) cathartic: the tendency to act out their repressed aggression as part of rebuilding their internal homeostasis. The above characteristics, found in the offenders in jails/prisons, may also be present in people in the community at large, however.

It is interesting to note that the psychodynamics of the self-image promoter are described by Toch as "feelings of guilt, of being scared and of a lack of worthwhileness" (p. 139). We would like to generalize his statement, making it a common denominator for all the offender types that he described, and suggest that each of his offender types react to the same feelings in his own idiosyncratic way on the basis of a premorbid personality, family upbringing, and personal community experiences. The types he described aim at securing the insecure self, enhancing their weak self-esteem, gaining the approval of others and acquiring a pseudo-respectability, admiration and self-aggrandizement in the carceral community. These prisoners are unconsciously driven by feelings of insecurity, low self-esteem, fear of others, rejection, and the lack of attention and love experienced in their early years of life.

Manfred Guttmacher (1972b) subdivided criminals into groups: (1) The normal criminal, comprising 85 percent. They are dyssocial and identified with asocial elements of society [socially defective—morally defective parents]. (2) The accidental or occasional criminal which comprises a small group. This group is characterized by a healthy superego that is overwhelmed by a special set of circumstances. (3)

The organically or constitutionally predisposed criminal–a small part of the criminal group. To this group of offenders belong the mentally defective, the post-encephalitic, the epileptic, the senile deteriorative, and the post-traumatic disorders. (4) The psychopathic or sociopathic criminals make up approximately 10–15 percent of the offenders. They are not psychotic, but indulge "in irrational, antisocial behavior" and are in and of themselves the most "malignant and recidivistic offenders" (p. 295).

For David Abrahamsen (1952), there are several types of prisoners who present different characteristics which he grouped as follows: (1) the momentary offenders (alias situational, accidental or associational offenders); (2) the neurotic offenders (e.g., kleptomaniacs, fire-setters or pyromaniacs); (3) offenders suffering from unconscious guilt (have the unconscious desire to be punished); (4) offenders with a character disorder ("pathological liars, swindlers, marriage wreckers, nympho-maniacs, Don Juans, imposters, drug addicts and alcoholics, some types of homosexuals, rapists, and murderers, and some of those who commit pedophilia and incest") (p. 154).

An interesting typological classification is the 1979 study of 1,164 detainees in a federal prison done by Edwin Megargee and Martin Bohn. Using the Minnesota Multiphasic Personality Inventory (MMPI) they analyzed not only the frequency of the various types of personality in criminals but also their psychological structure. Among the ten follow-up groups classified as Item, Easy, Baker, Able, George, Delta, Jupiter, Foxtrot, Charlie, and How, it can be observed that 26 percent of the prison population was found to be either normal or with minimal pathological signs on the MMPI. These groups (Item and Easy) include persons classified as belonging to the middle class, who drank excessively or, in the most serious cases, had been found guilty of stealing, robbing, car theft or the abuse of illicit drugs. Violence was minimal in these offenders.

The Foxtrot group (8 percent of the population) included inmates whose characteristics were impulsivity, bossing attitudes, bullying, lon-ers, hostility, suspiciousness, and apathy. They appeared to be intro-verted and obviously antisocial, their crimes involving violence and auto theft. Similar to the Foxtrot group, the Able group included, however, mostly juveniles who, even though belonging to the middle class, came from a subculture of violence. Violence and drug abuse were part of their traits of amorality, opportunism, impulsive pleasure seeking, manipulativeness and recidivism.

The Delta group (10 percent of the examinees) was composed mostly of persons with psychopathic behavior, while the Charlie group (slightly less than 9 percent of the population) included primarily paranoiac psychopaths with acting-out behavior and who were poorly adjusted in youth and adulthood, abusing drugs and alcohol, lacking values and self-control, aggressive and impulsive. They were mostly African-Americans. The How group (13%) included mostly African-American, single offenders. The most frequent crime was theft. The intellectual/cultural level of the persons under consideration was below the norm. They dropped out of school more frequently than others and used LSD and barbiturates. (It must be noted that in 1979 crack cocaine was not yet the drug of choice among illicit drug users; it began in 1984-1985.) Those in the How group, frequently recidivistic, exhibited low stress tolerance. The Baker group showed behavior similar (4%) to that of the How group but they were more clearly neurotic, anxious, and passive-aggressive.

WHO ARE THE OFFENDERS?

Many of the offenders are very young. Nevertheless, their antisocial behavior is that of a superpredator. Their identikit shows "radically impulsive, brutally remorseless youngsters, [who]...do not fear the stigma of arrest, the pain of imprisonment, or the pangs of conscience...[and for whom] the words 'right' and 'wrong' have no fixed moral meaning" (Bennett et al., 1996, p. 27). These are offenders whose behavior is motivated by a profound disregard for societal rules, who try to manipulate others, both while in and out of jail or prison, and who generally display a macho attitude out of fear. They are frequently illiterate, but streetwise. They often abide by a group code of behavior, seemingly despising the social and moral codes shared by their communities. On further scrutiny, they are found to be repeat offenders and chronically irresponsible. Their character analysis reveals hatred toward a nonexistent father and benevolent appraisal of a frequently non-giving mother—an idealization of her—a previously frustrated longing for affection, and a misguided rebellion against authority in general. Mention must be made of their poor educational background, their lack of job training or very scarce employments records, their dysfunctionality, and their frequent search for escapism through the nirvana of drugs and alcohol, all of which are important contributory factors in their evolution as criminals.

The prison seems to be the right place for their unsolved emotional conflicts with their mother and father. It is in jail/prison that these young offenders unconsciously behave according to "a pathological, perceptual stance known as 'splitting'" (Hofer, 1988, p. 99). This is a defense mechanism, present in the antisocial personality, usually used by the child, however, in order to feel protected and nurtured despite real evidence to the contrary. As Paul Hofer well described, the splitting is between "the affection directed toward a fantasized, loving, perfect mother image and the aggression directed toward the fantasized abandoning, all-bad father image..." (Hofer, p. 99). The prison allows the inmates, especially the antisocial recidivist, to obtain, even though in a displaced fashion, a certain amount of the nurturing they crave for and the possibility to ventilate their resentment toward the paternal authority figure who let them down, displacing it on to the correctional institution guards.

Even though many jail/prison inmates belong to a low economic group and are without any basic training for a rewarding job in a competitive society, economic poverty cannot be subscribed to as the only determinant of their offensive behavior. We agree with Bennett and colleagues (1996) that "among all economic classes, including low income people and the poor, it is the irritable, impulsive, and poorly socialized males who are most likely to commit crimes" (p. 42). The question of moral poverty in these individuals should be raised. Is it at the basis of their offensive social behavior? And if so, does that apply to the criminal behavior flooding the streets, as well as to the subtle, widespread white-collar type of crime?

Just as the cognitive, intellectual self with its moral and ethical structure is important in decision making, so the affective state of an individual, with its variations, may influence human behavior. At times, fluctuations of a person's mood, not clearly pathological but limited to a feeling of sadness or joy, may bring about changes in conduct in relation to the people within his usual habitat. Occasionally, when this affective fluctuation becomes greatly exaggerated and is not controlled by the powers of objectivity, discrimination and the anticipation of future consequences, the individual may not be strong enough to hold back the negative instinctual, impulsive drives.

Indeed, as can be seen again and again, among the characteristic traits of individuals who commit crimes are impulsivity and an inability to exercise the effective willpower necessary to control their behavior when under the influence of strong, instinctual negative emotions, or alcohol and drugs.

IMPULSIVITY

For David Shapiro (1965), the subjective experience of impulse is not due to a by-pass of executive or "operative modes of functioning" (p. 140) by explosive behavior but part of a style of functioning. Whether the above dynamics are correct or not, it is a fact that the impulsive psychopath's actions are not fully deliberated and fully intended but the result of a whim–"I did it" is the resultant of "abrupt, transient, and partial experiences of wanting, choosing, or deciding" (p. 140) with impairment of reflection and deliberation. The impulsive offenders lack the capacity to organize their experienced reality and are unable to assess it properly through integrative and deliberating mental functions. The rapid way in which they execute whatever they do lacks reflection and planning. It is probably due to a type of mental short-circuiting which bypasses reflection and the assessment of the consequences of their actions, and moves them directly from thought to action.

The impulsive offender has shallow emotions, and in his interpersonal encounters he is more interested in his own satisfaction than in the person he is dealing with. He remains unattached, unempathic, self-limited, and frequently exploitative, and his actions are unmindful of consequences. Immediate gains and lack of long-range planning are at the basis of impulsive behavior. The impulsive persons lacks the active, searching, critical process we call judgment, which is used in any deliberative act by normal persons and abused by the obsessive-compulsive individual who is often unable to decide or to judge. It is possible that at times the impulsive behavior, the lack of empathy and remorse, vary in specific encounters, and that the impulsive character may show more psychological sensitivity under different circumstances. These people are often highly perceptive and good manipulators, but they do not direct their perceptive ability and their intellectual capacity toward the achievement of good, altruistic, or at least non-exploitative aims.

Many offenders give as a justification of their quasi anal impulsive actions their inability to resist temptation, being with the wrong crowd, being misled by other offenders, giving into outside pressure, a sense of weakness of personality. They certainly lack, as their strong, impulsive twin, the full capacity to process stimuli, social events and to deliberate according to moral responsible standards. They show short-circuiting of integrative processes and "defensive disavowal of responsibility, particularly in the form of so-called externalization of responsibility" (Shapiro, 1965, p. 169).

Hans Eysenck (1977) stated that among the characteristic traits of psychopaths and of many offenders, in addition to impulsivity, are shallow emotions and a dislike for norms. These are also part of the extroverted personality described by Eysenck. This widens the discussion on the traits present in offenders into two frequently encountered syndromes in many of their life histories: (1) attention deficit/hyperactivity disorder and (2) conduct disorder (CD). *The Diagnostic and Statistical Manual of Mental Disorders* (APA, 1994) gives the criteria for attention/deficit hyperactivity disorder as consisting of symptoms of inattention or of hyperactivity-impulsivity lasting at least six months. The symptoms of hyperactivity and impulsivity, six or more of which are considered necessary for diagnosis, are: the frequency of hyperactive fidgeting with hands or feet, or squirming in one's seat; of leaving the seat in a classroom or other places where it is expected that one remain seated; of inappropriate and/or excessive running about and climbing (may be limited in adults or adolescents to feelings of restlessness); of difficulty in engaging in quiet leisure or play activities; of excessive talking; and of being frequently "on the go" or acting as if "driven by a motor".

Impulsivity consists of frequently answering questions before their completion, difficulty in waiting one's turn, and interruption or intrusion on others. In addition, some of the above-listed symptoms are present before age seven; some of the impairment resulting from them is present in at least two settings (such as home and school), and clear evidence of "clinically significant impairment in social, academic, or occupational functioning" is necessary in order to make the diagnosis (APA, 1994, p. 84). "These symptoms do not occur exclusively during the course of a pervasive developmental disorder, schizophrenia, or other psychotic disorders and are not better accounted for by another mental disorder (e.g., mood disorder, anxiety disorder, dissociative disorder, or a personality disorder)" (APA, 1994, p. 85). In our experience, some of these children lack a nurturing and sustaining parent who helps them to grow up. Unfortunately, "The only important activity for [the child's] survival is securing the approval of the parent; they will nurture and sustain him, providing he pleases them" (Gaylin, 1991, p. 193).

Impulsiveness, together with planning ability and judgment, have been assessed by the Porteus Maze Test, a measure of nonverbal reasoning; its questionable results led to the Roberts and Riddle Q Score. "In tests of impulsiveness, defined as the inability to forgo a small, immediate reinforcer instead of waiting for a more valuable one to come later, more impulsive people earned higher Q scores than less impulsive ones" (Wilson & Herrnstein, 1985, p. 174). The Q score records the quality of performance by the testee who may allow the pencil either to move out of the maze channel, lifting it from the paper or cutting corners. The high score defines a poor performance. This test appears to be good in detecting delinquent characteristics. It is understandable on the basis of the frequent hyperactivity and nonconformity found in many impulsive criminals, that such a test would bring out their distractibility, their superficiality and their "I don't care" attitude.

RESTLESSNESS, HOSTILITY AND SELF-ESTEEM

A propensity to rage and destructive violence is also characteristic of many criminals, from domestic violence actors to murderers and rapists. Restlessness is a frequent anticipatory sign of rage and violence in many offenders. A sense of lost power or downright impotence also is often at the basis of an offensive reaction. Frequently, it is during a moment of rage that individuals may lose their objective, discriminatory powers and self-control. Many offenders feel powerless, overwhelmed by and unable to face up to their duties and social demands. They feel frustrated, and frustration brings about their acting out which is often destructive of things (property) and injurious to others. At times, hostility is also directed toward the self—a self that is hated because it is not responsive to what is demanded of it; a self that the offender believes must have no value because no one seems to accept him; a self that feels deeply rejected. In fact, other characteristic traits of people who act in a criminal fashion are feelings of rejection, frustration, hostility, tendency to self- and outer-destructive behavior, and, especially in the so-called psychopath, one finds the lack of a sense of duty and justice. Obviously, previous experiences in school and family played an important part in generating the above.

A modicum of stable self-esteem is essential in the development of a mature individual within a social context. Good self-esteem can be viewed as a psychological vaccination against the ups and downs of life. It is behind the capacity for resiliency to adversity. Criminals frequently exhibit fluctuations of self-esteem and, more frequently, low self-esteem. Many criminals have low self-esteem; not only do they feel inferior but their conscience talks to them in derogatory ways and they frequently pass negative judgments on themselves. At times, they experience sudden reactions—assertive reactions in self-defense—which assume the typical stance of antisocial behavior. Fluctuations of self-esteem, in an upward manner, may also bring about antisocial behavior in those individuals too proud of themselves, too sure of their capabilities, inconsiderate of others and of the social consequences of their actions.

THEORIES OF THE EVOLUTION OF ANTISOCIAL BEHAVIOR

The evolution of antisocial behavior seems to follow at times a sequential pattern from an oppositional type of behavior to a conduct disorder, which eventually becomes clearly antisocial in type. Age usually demarcates each of these periods as the actor moves from childhood to adolescence and then early adulthood. Hyperactivity seems to be frequently associated with all three stages, even though it may become a syndrome in and of itself. "The essential feature of Oppositional Defiant Disorder is a recurrent pattern of negativistic, defiant, disobedient, and hostile behavior toward authority figures" persisting at least six months (APA, 1994, p. 91). During that period, the individual has a frequent reoccurrence of at least four of the following behaviors:

> losing temper.., arguing with adults.., actively defying or refusing to comply with the requests or rules of adults.., deliberately doing things that will annoy other people.., blaming others for his or her own mistakes or misbehavior.., being touchy or easily annoyed by others.., being angry and resent-

ful.., or being spiteful or vindictive.... Negativistic and defiant behaviors are expressed by persistent stubbornness, resistance to directions, and unwillingness to compromise, give in, or negotiate with adults or peers. (APA, 1994, p. 91.)

The pattern of behavior is generally evident in more than one setting—home, school, or community. "Children or adolescents with this disorder often initiate aggressive behavior and react aggressively to others" (APA, 1994, p. 86). In some cases the onset is in childhood while in others during adolescence, and it may result in mild, moderate or severe conduct problems. The prevalence of conduct disorder, which appears to be higher in urban centers, seems to have escalated during the last decades. "Rates vary widely, depending on the nature of the population sampled and methods of ascertainment: for males under 18 eighteen years, rates range from 6% to 16%; for females, rates range from 2% to 9%.... [It] is one of the most frequently diagnosed conditions in...mental health facilities for children" (APA, 1994, p. 88). Studies have shown it to have both genetic and environmental components and it is increased in those children with a parent—either biological or adoptive—suffering from antisocial personality disorder or who have a sibling who suffers from conduct disorder (APA, 1994). This pattern of behavior is repetitive and persistent. It manifests itself by aggression against people and animals; the destruction of property, deceitfulness or theft; and a serious violation of rules. The disorder may begin in childhood (prior to age ten) or in adolescence (after age ten). These children often lack a sense of guilt or shame. "The absence of any constraining guilt or shame in [the child's] behavior implies a defective conscience mechanism. When a conscience-free individual emerges because of an inadequate or corrupting early environment, no amount of goodwill, understanding, compassion, or for that matter psychotherapy is likely to rectify the problem. Self-control in these individuals will reside in fear of retribution, not in remorse" (Gaylin, 1991, p. 62).

Longitudinal studies of children with hyperactivity-impulsivity-attention deficit problems (HIA) have shown that in adolescence and adult life they exhibit a relatively high incidence of delinquent, antisocial, criminal behavior. I. Nylander's (1979) study of 2,000 cases, ages nine to twenty-nine, in a child guidance clinic in Stockholm found that about one-third of the hyperactive boys were officially registered for criminal actions. A cross-sectional study of HIA children by D.

Offord and colleagues (1979) also pointed out the tendencies of these children to delinquent behavior. As one can easily anticipate, at times HIA groups also manifest conduct disorders (CD) as demonstrated in a study by H. Huessey and D. Howell (1985).

Further studies on the late manifestations of children diagnosed HIA or CD revealed a very interesting finding that can be easily supported on the basis of clinical experience. Children with HIA are more prone to lower academic achievement during their adolescence and some of them even during early adulthood. This is explained not on the basis of a lower level of intelligence (indeed, these youngsters are often quite intelligent) but as a result of their hyperactivity and very short attention span, with an incapacity to focus their attention long enough to do their schoolwork and, later, work tasks. In our experience, their delinquency is frequently not of a serious type, certainly not as serious as the future behavior of those children who suffer from conduct disorder. Nevertheless, the longitudinal study of R. Loeber in Oregon in 1988 (a five-year follow-up of 210 boys ages 10 to 16) and a previous one by D. Magnusson (1984), a follow-up study of children from age 10 to age 28, found that "HIA and aggression lead to an increase in the rate of offending" (cited in Farrington et al., 1990, p. 64). Even though more children with CD will eventually become delinquent, it is quite possible that the co-occurrence of HIA and CD (CP) correlates with more frequent antisocial behavior in adulthood.

Frequently, hyperactivity is concomitant with impulsivity and daring, as suggested by David Farrington and colleagues. Chronic offenders (recidivistic) were "independently predicted just as well by HIA or by CP, but HIA and CP (CD) interact significantly and "both assist in predicting the extent of a future criminal career at the time of the first conviction" (p. 74). An interesting finding of their study is the background of those children who suffer from HIA. They found that it was particularly related to criminal parents, low intelligence, large family size, poor housing and delinquent brothers. Conduct problems, on the other hand, were found to be "particularly related to poor parenting, poor supervision, low income, and separations from parents" (p. 74). We don't agree completely with this background of HIA children unless it applies to those children who continue to commit crimes. The background of HIA non-delinquent children, and those are the majority, is that of an average family, whose mother often is obsessive-compulsive and poses a great many demands on the child, apparently for what she believes to be the child's good. By and large, however, we agree with the statement made by Farrington and colleagues that CP (CD) was more predictive of "self-reported delinquency, adult convictions and recidivism" (p. 77).

A LOOK AT THE PSYCHOPATH

Egoism, selfishness, a wish to control, and evilness are frequently present in psychopathic personalities. They show a lack of remorse for their offense and an amoral behavior. Wilhelm Reich defined the psychopathic offenders as impulsive characters, Franz Alexander called them a neurotic character. Others described them just as psychopathic personalities (Abrahamsen, 1952). Psychopaths may also suffer from schizophrenia. Franz Alexander (1948) classified them as the primary psychopath and the symptomatic psychopath. The primary, a smaller group, is characterized by amoral behavior, lack of conscience, deficient superego, lack of anxiety, possibly violently aggressive, and often sadistic in their criminal behavior. Sellin (cited in Palermo, 1994a) cited studies showing that the criminal psychopath is more likely than the criminal non-psychopath to have committed serious violent assaults and property crimes. He reported that psychological studies showed that violent psychopaths exhibit more impulsive tendencies and more aggressivity than the symptomatic psychopath (cited in Palermo, 1994a).

Alexander also stated, as did Freud, that the psychopaths are a group of offenders "who engage in antisocial behavior in order to achieve punishment at the hands of the law...[because] they have intense guilt feelings over some deeply buried early life experiences" (Guttmacher, 1972b, p. 298). They are often tortured neurotics easily apprehended because of clumsy, stupid crimes. Psychopaths may suffer from paranoia and their ego may be overwhelmed by primitive, aggressive criminal drives. Silvano Arieti (1967) subdivided the psychopathic states into the pseudopsychopath and the idiopathic, attributing the psychopath's impulsivity and his desire for immediate gratification to his attempt to overcome unbearable inner tension due to short-circuited anxiety. He asserted that when the paranoiac psychopath is prevented from acting out, for instance by imprisonment or hospitalization, he becomes more paranoiac" (p. 248). Benjamin Karpman (cited in Wilson & Herrnstein, 1985, p. 206) reported that idiopathic psychopaths are less prone to fear, anxiety or guilt, while secondary psychopaths show symptomatic anxiety and their behavior is frequently accompanied or motivated by emotional disturbance.

The decisional capacity in psychopaths is also defective; even though they apparently seem to function normally they usually reach a decision too rapidly. Strong unsublimated impulses may be disruptive. Wilson and Herrnstein (1985) wrote: "Impulsiveness can be thought of as either the cause or the effect of the poor conditionability of the psychopath" (p. 204) and "[w]ithout the internal monologue, time horizons shrink; behavior becomes more tied to its immediate consequences" (p. 205). In fact, it is the quick decision making which is the expression of the lack of reflection before acting that is usually found in the psychopath. Self-control is essential for a person's achievements after he properly channels his impulses without giving vent to unbridled impulsivity. Impulses were viewed by Friedreich Nietzsche, for example, as important in a person's behavior. He wrote that "a man without impulses [interest?] could not do the good or create the beautiful any more than a castrated man could beget children" (Kaufmann, 1974, p. 244). Nevertheless, impulses need control, and Nietzsche viewed the man who is in control of his passions as powerful, able to organize the chaos, and able to give style to his character. He believed that "the passionate man [or woman] who is the master of his passions" will also be a good, intuitive and creative individual (Kaufmann, 1974 p. 280). He viewed the man who strives for power over others through bullying and criminal activity as a weak person, deeply frustrated. The man who imposes restraints on himself is not only "a 'rational' animal, but also a 'moral' animal" (Kaufmann, 1974 p. 213). The two are inseparable.

Henri Baruk (DiTullio) viewed the total lack of moral values, visible in the true psychopathic offender, as "one of the worst calamities that can affect a human being, because of its personal and social consequences" (p. 41). In assessing the offenders' characteristic traits we have observed that they often lack self-criticism in regard to their criminal acting out. Kaufmann (1974) stated that their offenses are not only irrational but intrinsically immoral because their impulsivity undermines their critical reflection.

Further, Nietzsche believed that true existence is not a passive accident but is a personal, progressive achievement toward bettering one-self, attempting to achieve those higher models of behavior one should aim for in order to become one's true self: "You shall become who you are (*Du sollst der werden, der du bist*)." He well-portrayed the criminal's restless, morally unhealthy personality when, in answer to his own question, he stated, "He's a heap of diseases, which through his spirit, reach out into the world: there they want to catch their prey...a ball of wild snakes, which rarely enjoy rest from each other: so they go forth singly and seek prey in the world" (Kaufmann, 1975, p. 39).

CONCLUSION

Edward Scott (1997) raised an interesting issue. Are prisoners' behavior or statements ever real, or responding to the real self? He theorizes that most prisoners, because of their state of subordination and forced compliance with the rules, cannot be totally sincere, either with the guards or with other inmates. "I am real in my cell, all the externals are off," he quotes one prisoner as saying, while another adds, "Hell, I am not real anywhere. I'm afraid of the other prisoners. I can't say what I want around the guards—and this is scary" (p. 99). It is clear that prisoners do not show their true selves while incarcerated. Even though Winnicott's (1965) thesis of the true and false self applies, we believe, to people in general, it is certainly more present for pragmatic reasons among the prisoners. It is a defensive mode of facing the reality of a correctional institution—by not being oneself, by being unreal. However, there are some prisoners who, once incarcerated, let down their defenses and show their real selves, because "Finally, I don't have to pretend any longer."

Loneliness is a feeling that all people experience, at least in particular situations in their life. "Moustakies...sees loneliness as an existential phenomenon in that it is so central to being human and it is at the core of every person's ordinary life experience" wrote Ami Rokach and Spomenka Koledin (1997, p. 168). Is loneliness present among prisoners? In the study of Rokach and Koledin on loneliness among incarcerated men, offenders scored high on the Growth and Discovery and the Interpersonal Isolation Factor. The dynamics of prisoners' loneliness centers around a lack of "closeness, attachment, warmth, and caring necessary for survival" so important to every human being

(p. 177). And it is natural for them, during a period of incarceration, to withdraw, and to reflect on their past life and behaviors, to make certain discoveries concerning the self. This type of behavior is at the basis of their high scores on Rokach and Koledin's questionnaire. Didn't the Quakers base their program of rehabilitation of inmates at the turn of the nineteenth century on the isolation of the prisoner which they believed promoted growth, self-discovery and changes in behavior?

Normal traits are important psychological structures that when exaggerated assume a pathological connotation. Their consistency in people's behavior is present regularly in "contexts of attitudes, interests, intellectual inclinations and endowments, and even vocational aptitudes and social affinities with which the given symptom or trait seems to have a certain consistency" (Shapiro, 1965, p. 3). Traits are part of the character of a person, and character may be regarded as "the configuration of an individual of...relatively stable forms of functioning..." (Shapiro, 1965, p. 5). Anomalies of character are frequent among prisoners.

Wilhelm Reich described the compulsive character as a living machine. His description encompasses quite well the doubting, the obsessive and rigid thinking, the dogmatism, the opinionatedness that borders in paranoia, with a frequent constriction of affectivity, interests and attention exhibited by some of the offenders. Often, paranoid modes of functioning, differing in degree and not overtly psychotic, are present behind a facade of suspiciousness and arrogant conduct. Since perception and judgment are part of the way any individual appraises events, in the case of the paranoid, perception may be correct but judgment faulty. The paranoid inmates show rigidity of thinking, hyperalertness, defensive antagonism towards other inmates, towards authority figures, often represented by the guards. Their sense of superiority is usually a sign of their underlying emotional insecurity (Palermo & Scott, 1997). The meticulous offender may become an organized type of criminal. He is programmed and only gets into difficulties when something happens that thwarts his planning, because he has limited flexibility and a slow capacity to change.

Even though we try to keep from boxing individuals into classifications, many of the traits we discussed as part of the offender's character are included in the antisocial personality disorder as well summarized in the DSM-IV (APA, 1994). Their antisocial conduct is only at times part of a schizophrenic illness or a manic episode. In our experience, there are shades of antisocial behavior, manifestations of a more basic personality. This is clearly observable in the many criminals we have seen. Indeed, one does not lose his individuality or uniqueness, even when committing a crime. The past behavior of the inmates in the jails/prisons and their relevant courtroom history testify to that.

A random group of professionals who come into frequent contact with prisoners was asked what, in their opinion and experience, were the most salient personality traits of the prisoners. Among the chaplains questioned, the views were that generally prisoners were not seen as citizens but as problems. They felt that some prisoners do look for answers to their behavior, and at times search for a biblical answer to justify their conduct. Further, they often search for a biblical solution to their practical problems, some even becoming very evangelistic in their thinking and conduct. They may become very dogmatic about religion, with a tinge of paranoia at times. Many prisoners are basically immature and look for guidance in the here and now. They would like immediate solutions to their problems and become demanding at times. They displace to the chaplains their long, frustrated dependency. They want support but are generally not interested in a growing experience. Sometimes they surrender to a higher power—an act of faith and a spiritual awakening. They come to believe in fellowship and, paradoxically, some of them, by using the Bible, manage to acquire control over themselves fairly well.

The prosecutors' answers to our questions were varied. They believe the prisoners to be irresponsible and that impulsivity is their major trait. They exercise poor judgment. They use denial and blame others for their conduct and their problems. A police detective stated, "They are demanding, argumentative, frequently belong to gangs. When they get a chance to exercise control they do it. They are sexually aggressive." Another police officer stated, "They are antisocial, impulsive, real psychopaths." Defense attorneys stated, "They show adolescent-like behavior and do not take into consideration the consequences of their actions. They want immediate gratification. They feel powerless and are dependent."

One prisoner stated, regarding his co-inmates: "They have an attitude like, 'I don't take that shit from nobody.' They are loud in the dorms or cells, talk as if the victims are the cause of their being in here.

What they say is unbelievable. For instance, they seem to be happy because they got to do only one year. They have a negative attitude about life. They are disparaging of women–their words are destroying their women."

A group of correctional officers said, "They are losers, they have been here three or four times. They will not stop their behavior. They don't have strong willpower." Several social workers added to the above: "They are like soldiers of some type. They don't care, they don't think of the consequences. They don't regret their actions." They added that they believe the prisoners, on average, to be smart.

Their acting out is viewed by most of the professionals as caused by psychological and social impotence. They believe that they have no stake in what is going on and feel powerless–a kind of invisible human being. All agreed that the majority assume a bossy, bullying attitude.

There is no doubt that as Havelock Ellis ([1870] 1973) wrote (citing Lacassagne): "The social environment is the cultivation medium of criminality; the criminal is the microbe, an element which only becomes important when it finds the medium which causes it to ferment, and every society has the criminals that it deserves" (p. 24). Indeed, while society breeds crime, the criminal is the one who executes them. The psychopathology of the offenders and their criminal actions are intrinsically connected with the milieu in which they live.

Chapter 4

WHO ARE THE PRISONERS?–II

We live in a morass of corroding lies and illusions, in which
terrible and monstrous things happen.

Gustav Janouch in Conversations with Kafka

POLYSUBSTANCE ABUSE OFFENDERS

Alcohol

Walking the city streets, especially in certain neighborhoods, is dangerous. One can be mugged, physically or sexually abused, even murdered–crimes often perpetrated by people intoxicated by alcohol and illicit drugs. Before addressing the topic of polysubstance abuse offenders, one should first have a clear idea of the extent of consumption of alcohol and drugs in society at large. Harold Kaplan and colleagues (1994), reporting epidemiological data for 1991 from the National Institute on Drug Abuse, stated that almost 85 percent of the United States civilian population, over age twelve and non-institutionalized (171.7 million people), had used alcohol one or more times in their lifetimes. They wrote, "The age group with the highest percentage of active alcohol users, which is also the age group that consumes the most alcohol, is the group in the ages from 20 to 35. That fact, however, risks overshadowing the fact that about 50 percent of adolescents aged 12 to 17 have tried alcohol-containing beverages at least once, and about 25 percent of that age group describe themselves as current users of alcohol" (p. 396). In 1996, Norman Miller reported that "The Epidemiological Catchment Area Study, a recent survey of mental health and addictive disorders in nearly 20,000 adult Americans, found a 13.5% lifetime prevalence of alcohol abuse or dependence, and 7% for drug addiction" (p. 1). Substance dependence is defined as a "maladaptive pattern of substance use leading to clinically significant impairment or distress" (APA, 1994:181). It is distinguished by an intense desire for the drug or alcohol, the large amount ingested, and its increasing compulsive use over time. It usually interferes with an individual's job or social/family life. There may be remissions and exacerbations

The widespread use and abuse of illicit drugs and alcohol is slowly becoming a social cancer in some sections of society but is certainly not limited to those persons who commit crimes. The use of alcoholic beverages is as old as humanity. Indeed, one finds comments in the Bible regarding both its positive and negative effects. It was used by various ancient cultures, including the Hebrews, the Egyptians, the Chinese and the Romans. In the nineteenth century, the recognition of its calming and soporific effects led to its increased use (Palermo, 1994). Presently, the moderate use of alcoholic beverages, particularly wine, is seen as possibly having some health benefits.

However, the excessive use of alcohol leading to alcoholism is a major cause of family dysfunction, domestic violence and child abuse. Miller (1996) reports that over 40 percent of adults are exposed to problem drinkers in their families. Alcoholism is a major contributor to poor job performance and productivity loss, as well as to incarceration because of offenses against persons. Fifty percent of all general psychiatric hospital admissions are associated with alcoholism; the elderly are not excluded. Miller stated that "[on] any given day, more than 800,000 clients are in active alcohol/drug treatment programs: 45% are in treatment for alcoholism, 29% for drug addiction, and 26% for both" (Miller, 1996, p. 2), even though studies have shown that approximately 18 million individuals require treatment for alcoholism, a far greater number than the above.

Kaplan and colleagues report that "about 51 percent of all United States adults are current users of alcohol.... Beer accounts for about half of all alcohol consumption, liquor for about a third, and wine for about a sixth" (1994, p. 396). Epidemiologically, alcohol-related disorders rank third as a health problem in the United States, preceded only by heart disease and cancer. Recent statistics state that "10 percent of women and 20 percent of men have met the diagnostic criteria for alcohol abuse during their lifetimes, and 3 to 5 percent of women and 10 percent of men" are classified as alcohol dependent during their lifetime (Kaplan et al., 1994, p. 396). During the past five years, alcohol has become the drug of choice for many juveniles, either alone or at times to come down from the "highs" of cocaine or crack cocaine. These juveniles are at present overrepresented in the correctional institutions.

The overindulgence in alcoholic beverages produces intoxication, and many prisoners we have seen appear to enjoy the knockout effect that alcohol causes. They are unaware that alcohol, by suppressing cortical inhibitory controls, unleashes emotions normally kept in check in the subconscious, emotions not of a positive nature but of an aggressive type. Because of these repressed feelings, conflictual or hostile, they frequently become loud, abusive, profane and aggressive. Under the influence of excessive amounts of alcohol, an intoxicated individual, especially the chronic abuser, may have illusions, delusions and hallucinations. Short of fleeting psychotic symptoms, unrestrained aggression is central to some intoxicated states because of the frequent misperception of reality on the part of the intoxicated person as in the following case:

> A middle-aged homeless, chronic alcoholic, frequently arrested for drunkenness and disorderly conduct, harbored persecutory delusions of a plot to take his money. He also believed that people wanted to steal his new [nonexistent] scientific discoveries and to kill him. One day, he violently attacked and manhandled another homeless man, believing him to be his persecutor. His chronic alcohol addiction was the cause of his delusional behavior. He was charged with disorderly conduct and eventually directed to a correctional institution having a mental health section.

The use of alcoholic beverages follows a pattern: from beer to whisky, to gin, to brandy or vodka, through a life span that goes from the early teens through the end of the third decade. Unless the individual has become addicted, alcohol consumption generally decreases after age forty. Those who abuse alcohol are frequently suffering from an antisocial personality disorder, or are depressed/manic or delusional persons, who at times use alcohol in an attempt to quiet their hallucinated voices. The offenders in these cases, in which alcohol addiction is superimposed on mental illness, are at times charged with serious offenses and are classified under the category of dual diagnosis, as in the case of the chronic paranoid schizophrenic who, not taking his medication and under the effects of alcohol, killed his mother, acting under the delusional belief that she was his persecutor.

Among the various addicting substances, it appears that only alcohol addiction has a family pattern and can be traced to genetic factors.

However, an analysis of drug dependence leads one to believe that the dependency is not on the drug itself but lies within an individual's predisposition and psychological need and his desire to escape from his own reality. "The drug addicts of our modern civilization, for a variety of reasons...are attempting to escape from what they consider an oppressive reality" (Fisher et al., 1987, p. 213).

Illicit Drugs

Cocaine has come a long way from the use of chewing coca leaves practiced in Central America and in South America. There, coca leaves are at times used as a source of physical energy. The current epidemic of cocaine use in the United States began around 1970 among rather affluent individuals. Slowly, during the following decades, this group expanded to include lower socioeconomic groups, especially in large metropolitan areas: "A community survey conducted in the United States in 1991 reported that 12 percent of the population had used cocaine one or more times in their lifetime; and 3 percent had used it in the last year; and less than 1 percent had used it in the last month" (APA, 1994, p. 228). A study by Dean Gerstein and Lawrence Lewin (1990) found that about 5.5 million people depended on or abused drugs. While many of those need treatment or counseling, they reported, in 1990, only 850,000 had received the necessary care. (These statistics are very close to those reported by Miller regarding persons receiving treatment for alcoholism.) This certainly may contribute to the fact that many inmates have used crack cocaine prior to, and at times during, the commission of their criminal offenses. They represent the acting-out group of cocaine users. Indeed, during periods of intoxication, some cocaine addicts become aggressive and violent. They do not stay within the confinement of their homes because they are fearful of imaginary persecutors. They may exhibit explosive behavior and at times may commit murder.

Presently, there has been an increase in the use of crack, a highly potent form of cocaine: "Crack use is most common in persons aged 18 to 25, who are particularly susceptible to the low street price of a single 50 to 100 mg. dose of crack..." (Kaplan et al., 1994, p. 423). At times, the use of cocaine has resulted in financial catastrophe or even indigent states. Many offenders seen for forensic psychiatric examination or appearing before the court, and who are receiving SSI, admit to spending most of their money on the drug.

In the sixties, drug and alcohol abuse increased to high levels among young people, and in the following decades even ten- and eleven-year-olds began to use marijuana and alcohol; at present, children this age even use cocaine. It seems that for many, "intoxication is...a rite of passage into adulthood and maturity" (Post, 1992, p. 36). Stephen Post wrote that substance abuse is often the outcome of the lack of self-esteem arising from a lack of love, as well as from many poverty-related environmental factors. It is, he stated, a form of unsuccessful "self-enhancement, making up for a lack of genuine self-esteem" (1992, p. 39). This becomes quite evident during the interviews with prisoners in the various correctional institutions.

In our experience drug use related offenses are quite common among African-Americans and are frequently associated with joblessness and SSI recipiency. In 1979, more than 4 percent (4.4%) of all prison inmates were in drug treatment; this figure climbed to 11.1 percent in 1987 (Winfree et al., 1994). Thomas Winfree and colleagues concluded in their study on drug history and prisonization that "inmates with histories of drug use, particularly major illicit drug groups such as cocaine and opiates, may be viewed as 'life's losers,' a condition that seems associated with deeper penetration into the prison subculture and higher levels of institutional maladjustment" (1994, p. 282). However, "...in a 1986 survey of state prison inmates, almost 50 percent of those who reported daily drug use had been employed full-time in the year prior to their offense...and 10 percent had been employed part-time (Benson & Rasmussen, 1996, p. 13). They claimed that their income also came from welfare, family, friends, and other criminal activities. Many of the offenders responsible for these crimes are not apprehended however.

Jails, prisons, and correctional institutions today house large groups of prison inmates who have been addicted to illicit drugs for years. They are usually arrested because of offenses against persons or property, generally in order to get money to support their drug and/or alcohol habit.

Today, these offenders are not considered psychopathic, as they once were, but are termed antisocial, an appellative that seems to minimize their personal responsibility for their actions and sees the actions not only as "against society" but as caused by society. They are frequently viewed as victims of a technological era, aggressive consumer-oriented advertising, and competitive job markets. "These young people have been raised in the glare of ceaseless media violence and incitement to every depravity of act and spirit. Movies may feature scores of killings in two hours time,...[and] show methods ever more horrific, many are quickly imitated on the street. Television commercials teach that a young man requires a new pair of $120 sneakers each week" (Walinsky, 1995, p. 53). These are the people who, as Dante stated in his *Divine Comedy*, have lost all hope once they entered hell.

The disruptive effects on the human mind of drugs like cocaine, together with their association with criminal behavior, is well known. Many offenders who are apprehended, frequently young, look for a quick solution to their tormenting inner conflicts, insecurity, and unsuccessful search for personhood, for acceptance. They may attempt to find a solution to their problems through the use of drugs—particularly cocaine and crack cocaine—and in the excessive use of alcohol. They use crack cocaine to get high and alcohol to come down to what they believe is normal behavior (less agitation and more integrated conduct). However, contrary to their expectations, they cannot stand the lows, and again as rapidly as possible, they search for the quick fix of cocaine, regardless of the way it is procured. The need for a quick fix in the cocaine users necessitates the availability of immediate financial means, often leading them to actions ranging from panhandling to the commission of theft, burglary or robbery, to carjacking, gang warfare and even murder (Palermo, 1996a). Their attempt to find a solution to their problems through the use of drugs brings, instead, only temporary oblivion. John DiIulio (citing Barbara Allen-Hagen and Melissa Sickmund) rightly stated:

> In essence, the inner city has become a criminogenic community, a place where the social forces that create predatory criminals are far more numerous and overwhelmingly stronger than the social forces that create virtuous citizens. At core, the problem is that most inner city children grow up surrounded by teenagers and adults who are themselves deviant, delinquent, or criminal. At best, these teenagers and adults misshape the characters and lives of the young in their midst. At worst, they abuse, neglect, or criminally prey upon the young. (1994:7.)

One of the unfortunate realizations is that even mentally ill persons, often abandoned by a system that has viewed mental illness as an inalienable right to be sick, and who frequently roam the streets, have been medicating themselves with illicit drugs and alcohol. They belong to the so-called dual diagnosis group, as above reported—schizophrenia, chronic depression, paranoid delusional disorders and poly-substance addiction—and frequently their offense is disorderly conduct, occasionally a felony. In a study conducted in 1992 (Palermo et al.), a group of 272 mentally ill jail inmates examined over a period of three years was analyzed. Of the 272 of offenders considered, a total of eighty-five had frequently used cocaine, marijuana and alcohol. The other offenders were also found to have occasionally used drugs and alcohol.

There are numerous drug users involved in misdemeanors or lesser types of felonies who form a group by themselves of dependent help-seekers, inmates who seem to give lip service to prison rules. They try to avoid the dominant gangs because of the fear of being jumped. They also seem to avoid the prisonization process, usually because of their short-time sentences. Could these classify under the legitimate subculture of dependent drug users? In a study on the correlation between substance abuse and arrests, B. K. Singh and G. W. Joe (1981) found that heroin, marijuana, alcohol, cocaine and amphetamine users were very high both in the number and percentage of arrests for criminal offenses. Many of these offenders are frequent users; "as much and as often as I can afford it" is a frequent answer given by persons addicted to drugs when questioned about frequency of use.

Another mind-altering substance frequently used by prisoners prior to incarceration is marijuana. Popularly called "weed," it is used because of its calming effects. Many adolescents start smoking marijuana around the age of twelve or thirteen, about the same time that they begin to use alcohol. After many years of decline, in 1996 the use of marijuana was reported to be increasing (Wren, 1996). Frequently, after several years of marijuana use, the users progress to cocaine and then to crack cocaine. A recent report states that drug users have begun to substitute heroin for crack cocaine, "dismissing crack as a ghetto drug and believing that heroin is easier to manage" (Wren, 1997, A12). The above seems to go hand in hand with the appearance of hyperactivity, conduct disorder, and the social aggressive personality. At times, marijuana users become psychotic or may suffer from a demotivation syndrome.

In 1993, Friedman stated that "sixty percent of the people who were asked felt that 'drugs' were the factor most responsible for crime in the United States [at that time]" (1993, p. 464). This holds true even today. The following case is typical:

> A middle-aged male, chronic alcohol and cocaine user, experienced delusions of a jealous paranoia type while under the effects of crack cocaine and alcohol. These delusions resulted in the stabbing death of his wife whom he believed to have been unfaithful to him.

The rather strong association existing between drug use and crime in different samples of adults coming into contact with the criminal justice system has been reported in various studies (Chaiken & Chaiken, 1982; Wish & Johnson, 1986; Wish, 1987; Palermo et al., 1992). This association is found not only in adults but also among juveniles. Among criminals, two distinct types of drug users exists: "First, a substantial portion of drug offenders apparently do not commit property or violent crimes. Second, many offenders arrested for violent and property crimes also use drugs...[but] many people arrested and convicted for drug offenses are not hardened criminals" (Benson & Rasmussen, 1996, p. 9). As previously stated, a high percentage of offenders in correctional institutions, both juveniles and adults, have used and abused substances like alcohol, marijuana, and cocaine, both before their crime and/or at the time of the commission of the crime. The use of this triad of abusive substances, alcohol, marijuana and crack cocaine, is a typical pedigree of many criminal offenders and contributes not only to their crimes, both minor and major, but also to their frequent abuse of family members. The young or relatively young addicts share demographic similarities. They often come from broken homes, with frequent absence of a father or other positive male role model. David Blankenhorn (1995) believes that "the most urgent domestic challenge facing the United States at the close of the twentieth century is the re-creation of fatherhood as a vital social role for men....To tolerate the trend of fatherlessness is to accept the inevitability of continued societal recession" (p. 222). The broken homes of these offenders are frequently just a meeting place, a place for breeding, and their poor upbringing often leads to truancy in school, association with gangs, and criminal activity.

Even though alcohol and illicit drugs, particularly cocaine, are the precipitants in many criminal actions, the factors at the basis of destructive violence are multiple. Drug users would certainly benefit from more socio-psychiatric attention and treatment than from stricter law-enforcement policies, even though at times their crimes are so heinous that incarceration may provide not only punishment but enforced treatment. For minor illicit drug users (and these are the majority), decriminalization may be more beneficial. Decriminalization of illicit drugs, wrote Benson and Rasmussen (1996), "should be considered as a method of decreasing drug use" (p. 47), theorizing that this would probably also lead to a decrease in crime. However, it is highly possible that the illicit drug industry would flood the streets or drug houses with new drugs, such as methamphetamine (ecstasy), and, more importantly, the government would be going into the illicit drug business. Barry McCaffrey (cited in Wren, 1997), the Clinton administration's director of national drug control policy, recently stated, "We believe there is a continuing increase in the use of drugs by young Americans and that there's a migration of new drugs into the population, especially heroin and club drugs" (A12).

Thomas Bonczar and Allen Beck (1997) report that among persons admitted for the first time to state or federal prison in the 12 months prior to 1991 the most frequent offense was drug trafficking (1997). Sol Wachtler reports that in 1996, 250,000 persons were incarcerated for drug offenses in the country and that 80 percent of new federal prisoners since 1987 have been drug offenders. He believes that "[w]e should recognize that some 75 percent of crime is related to drugs: using drugs, dealing drugs, committing crimes while high on drugs, and robbing to get money to buy drugs.... But locking up low-level drug dealers who are nonviolent will not stop the supply" (Wachtler, 1997, p. 265).

The question of how to deal with drug and alcohol addiction is difficult to answer because for some people drugs have become almost a way of life and are used to overcome both fleeting and long-lasting social distress. People must be helped to re-enter the reality of life. That reality (education, training for jobs and job availability, adequate housing, etc.) should be readily attainable. The creation of a drug court is an interesting idea, only useful if all the players in the system pursue the welfare of both the individual addict and society at large.

Except for some addicts and criminal offenders, the majority of these troubled and troublesome people who use and abuse drug/alcohol may still be sensitive to social disapproval. Social disapproval, indeed, is highly contributory to good behavior. It is advisable that, while showing compassion, professionals who come in contact with offenders strongly express disapproval of their conduct and minimize the commiseration often expressed for social misconduct. While we do not condone the criminal activities of polysubstance abuse offenders, we are compelled to ask ourselves, is the jail/prison setting the right place for these polysubstance abuse offenders or should they be diverted directly to appropriate rehabilitative institutions in those many cases in which the entity of the offense does not warrant incarceration in institutions whose aim is to imprison serious and dangerous offenders? We are of the opinion that doing so would decrease the overcrowding of courts and correctional facilities, so that these facilities would be utilized for their primary purpose: the confinement of dangerous offenders who pose a threat to society.

THE MENTALLY ILL OFFENDERS

Mental disorders are often thought to be linked to violent manifestations of behavior. This has been immortalized in biblical quotations, philosophical reflections, and often in dramatic, theatrical, cinematographic, and television representations. The presence of the mentally ill in jails/prisons has fluctuated during the past centuries, an expression of social-historical periods and prejudices, present at both a conscious and an unconscious level. At a conscious level is the necessity to guarantee the security of people from the impulsive, disorderly, and at times menacing behavior exhibited by the mentally ill, and the prejudice against mental illness itself. The latter is due primarily to ignorance about the origins and motives of the behavior of the mentally ill that is frequently bizarre and delusional, and secondarily to the unconscious fears that such strange behavior evokes in many people, a fear often connected with a deep sense of guilt—that guilt that possibly derived from humankind's repressed/suppressed past with its mythical archetypes, unacceptable thoughts and demoniacal tendencies. In the past, the insane raised the fear of death in people around them, and death is something that the average person wishes to deny. They were equated with the deterioration of the human race that had to be segregated from the larger society. At first they were imprisoned in unhealthy jails; then, prior to the humanitarian crusades of Pinel, Dix, and Chiarugi, in hospitals so inhuman and unhealthy, with antiquated structural and poorly functioning conditions, that they were not conducive to the improvement of any mental condition. Following the ensuing reforms, the mentally ill obtained better care but still far from really human.

Prior to the advent of psychopharmacology in the 1950s and 1960s, the asylums housing the mentally ill were, because of their appalling conditions, often referred to as "snake pits." Psychopharmacology liberated the mentally ill from the chains of their illness, but unfortunately, due to the inability of society to deal with them properly in the social setting to which they were discharged, and because of their at times disorderly behavior, they have often been relegated to the prisons, usually because of misdemeanors, again finding themselves in "chains." At present, jails and prisons are often the repository of the mentally ill, forgotten people, alienated from society, people in need of medical/psychiatric help.

Even though most jails have within their physical structures small departments for medical and psychiatric services and for the progressive rehabilitation of the inmates, they still remain huge facilities of human containment, their main purpose being the isolation of the prisoners from the outside world. Among these inmates, the mentally ill stand out as a hybrid category whose deviant behavior is due to their underlying mental illness. Indeed, they should be called pseudo-offenders, and their confused behavior is not like the silent delusional paranoid who, though withdrawn, remain law-abiding.

One finds mental illness of various types and severity at the basis of the conduct of a small number of the offenders charged with violent crimes; their violent conduct also varies in degree. Prisoners suffering from delusions or hallucinations are occasionally encountered among jail and prison inmates. At times, their emotional disorders, even though not psychotic in their manifestations, are nevertheless deeply ingrained in a mixed personality disorder which frequently goes unnoticed and untreated. Such mental disorders may motivate the worst types of crime. This is often seen in violent offenders of the serial killer type—the non-social-organized or the social-disorganized serial killer.

A question pertinent to the present topic is, Is there a strong link between mental disorders and antisocial violent behavior? Are there any manifestations of a disordered mind or behavior that one should look for as indicators of mental illness and possible dangerous behavior? In addition to the frankly delusional or hallucinating offender, the authors have had the opportunity to examine and/or review many offenders and their case histories. Violence is not always unpredictable, and a thorough assessment of the mentally ill offenders may give clues to their proneness to future explosive conduct. We have found that irritability is a frequent trait exhibited by offenders, often a precursor of offensive behavior. Because irritability often precedes acting-out behavior and can be a good predictor of it, both among the mentally ill–(especially the paranoid)–and the non-mentally ill offender, it should be monitored. Hostility, often masked as aloofness and non-communicative behavior, or at times verbally and openly expressed, may also be a precursor of acting out among paranoid offenders.

In a report by H. Brill and B. Malzberg (1962) of a review of 5,354 records of 10,247 discharged male patients from the New York State Hospital, the overall arrest rate for discharged patients was 122/10,000 while for the general population it was 491/10,000. However, the arrest rate for felons was found to be higher for ex-patients than for the general population (54.70/10,000 compared with 32.83/10,000, reported by Zitrin and colleagues in 1976). A previous report by Jonas Rappeport and George Lassen (1965) regarding discharged patients from the Maryland Institution for the Mentally Ill, a retrospective and projective analysis, revealed that schizophrenics accounted for more than 30 percent of the arrests before and after hospitalization in the 1947 group and 20 percent of the arrests for the 1957 group. The latter percentage appeared to confirm the fact that people suffering from schizophrenia exhibit a moderate degree of disorderly criminal conduct. This was supported by a study by J. M. Giovannoni and L. Gurel (1967) who reported that former mental patients had a higher arrest rate for felonies–95 percent were schizophrenics. H. Häfner and W. Böker (1973) reported that schizophrenics were frequently arrested for crimes of violence. J. Cocozza and colleagues, while stating that released mental patients committed higher rates of crimes, attributed the high percentage to the longitudinal tendency to criminal behavior in some of them. In 1980, J. F. James found that 10 percent of 246 inmates in Oklahoma prisons were acutely and seriously disturbed. John Monahan and Henry Steadman (1983) wrote that "among persons in jail and prison, serious mental disorders range from 1 to 7%, whereas rates of less severe mental disorder range from 15 to 20%" (cited in Palermo et al., 1992a, pp. 55-56). J. Johnson (1984) found that about 20 percent of those filing through the United States jails each year are mentally ill. Edward Guy (1985) and colleagues, on the other hand, found that among a group of ninety-six randomly chosen inmates in a Philadelphia prison schizophrenics and bipolar inmates numbered 14.6 percent. The percentage rate of the mentally ill in United States jails/prisons is variously reported as from 6.6 percent schizophrenics and bipolar illness, and 5.1 percent unipolar depressed in a Michigan study, to 8.4 percent for schizophrenia and bipolar illness, 10 percent unipolar depression, and 1.9 percent schizophreniform illness in a sample of 199 admissions to the Washington State prison system. Studying the relationship between mental illness and antisocial violent behavior, primarily depression, R. Bland and H. Orn (1986) reported a psychiatric diagnosis rate of 54.4 percent among the offenders they considered.

Steadman and colleagues (1987) found that 8 percent of a sample of 3,332 inmates in the general prison population had severe psychiatric disabilities that warranted mental health intervention, and 16 percent required periodic attention for mental disability. Anthony Swetz and colleagues (1989), in a study of 190 inmates age fifteen or older, found that 19.5 percent of them were suffering from a psychiatric disorder and in need of treatment. S. E. Strick (1989) examined the characteristics of eighty-one female offenders and found that 79 percent were psychotic on admission.

In a 1989 study from a Kansas City mental health clinic, 25 percent of violent psychiatric patients showed similar recidivistic behavior within one year from discharge. P. Lindqvist and P. Allebeck (1990), in a fifteen-year longitudinal study of 644 individuals with schizophrenia, reported a rate of violence four times higher than that in the general population. Linda Teplin (1990) reported that 6.4 percent of 728 offenders in the Chicago jail suffered from schizophrenia, mania or depression. E. Fuller Torrey (1996), in his recent book, *Out of the Shadows*, after reporting that "the most recent data available in 1995 indicated that there were 483,717 inmates in jails and 1,104,074 inmates in state and federal prisons in the United States, a total of 1,587,791 prisoners," estimates that "[i]f 10 percent of them are severely mentally ill, that would be approximately 159,000 people" (p. 31).

In order to assess the relationship between the typology of crime and mental illness, Salvatore Luberto and colleagues (1993) studied two groups of patients. The first group was composed of 1,855 outpatients from the Psychiatric Centers of the cities of Modena and Reggio-Emilia, Italy (total combined city population of 338,412). The second group consisted of 885 inpatients from the population of the

Psychiatric Inpatient Services of the same cities. The outpatient-mentally ill committed sixty-five crimes in 1990 (3.5%), while the inpatients had committed 104 crimes (11.7%): *the inpatient-psychiatrically ill had committed more crimes than the outpatients.* The total sample of the 169 patients (both inpatient and outpatients) who had committed crimes was further analyzed for gender, age, civil status, educational level, work record, type of work, birthplace and place of residence, family psychiatric pedigree, psychiatric diagnostics and mental status. In addition to the above, the authors scrutinized any previous contacts with the law for criminal charges and types of crime committed. Finally, they linked the type of crime committed by each patient to the patient's psychiatric illness, and this was followed by a list of major and minor crimes committed by the total group of 169 patients.

The results of the above analysis are quite interesting and differ somewhat from the average statistical analysis, showing that, at least in their study, the dangerousness of the mentally ill is rather low. First they listed 125 male and forty-four female patients. The age bracket with the most crimes was from twenty-six to forty-five years, with a total of 103 crimes (60.9%). The majority of the patients, 108 (63.9%), were not married. Ninety-two of them (62.6%) had reached a maximum of eighth-grade education. One hundred and fourteen (71.7%) had been employed and the majority were laborers. The number of unemployed or retired people was high, reaching a total of 107 (94%). The majority, eighty-five patients (52.5%), lived with their family of origin and seventeen (10.5%) in social agencies of some type. Thirty-five (23%) had a history of mental illness in their family.

As far as diagnostics were concerned, ninety-three patients (55%) were diagnosed as schizophrenic syndromes, five (3%) as depressed, six (3.6%) as suffering from organic psychosis, and sixty-five (38.4%) as having a personality disorder. Only fifty-nine (43.4%) were in remission. The authors found that thirty-eight of the 149 patients (25.5%) had previous legal charges. Their study shows that the most frequent crimes committed by the psychiatric patients were assault and substantial battery (seventy-one or 66.3%), while the cases of homicide or attempted homicide were less frequent (four or 3.7%). The non-psychotic mentally ill, instead, had a higher number of homicides or attempted homicides (46 or 9.7%). In the final analysis, of 169 psychiatric patients who committed crimes of legal importance only ten of those crimes (5.9%) were serious in nature.

The above study reaches conclusions similar to a study conducted during a period of three consecutive years (1988-1990) on 272 inmates examined for competency in an American county jail with a total jail population ranging between 900 and 1,000 inmates (Palermo et al., 1992b). The two samples are culturally different; however, a comparative analysis may still be relevant. In the 1990 American study, schizophrenia was reported in 103 (37.87%) of the offenders examined, compared to 93 (55%) in the Italian study. The personality disorders totaled eighty-nine (32.62%) in the American study and sixty-five (38.4%) in the Italian study. Nevertheless, the cultural differences aside, the American study, even though derived from a different setting, also concluded that serious crimes committed by the mentally ill were few in number compared to the large number of misdemeanors and were primarily due to psychotic behavior. Of the 272 offenders, 67.28 percent were charged with a misdemeanor and 32.72 percent with a felony. The cases of homicide or attempted homicide were eight, the majority of felonies being aggravated battery/assault, rape, reckless endangering and burglary. The similarity between the results of the Italian and the American study of the demographic data of the mentally ill offenders is striking.

In our experience, the results coincide with the demographics of the non-psychiatric offenders that we see. They are young—between twenty-five and forty-five years of age—mostly male, not married or divorced, with a low level of education. They are usually unemployed or laborers. Their living conditions are generally marginal and they often return to their parental home for short or long periods of time. There is a fairly positive history of psychiatric problems in the family of origin. We find, however, that in the American study the presence of a gun as a weapon during the criminal offenses perpetrated by the mentally ill is very frequent; in the Italian study, instead, a knife or a blunt weapon was frequently employed.

More recently, Monahan (1996) reports that one study, not limited to incarcerated or institutionalized persons, found that "3 percent of the variance in violent behavior in the United States is attributable to mental disorder" (p. 1). The above report showed a modest but statistically significant relationship between mental disorder and violence. That mentally ill people are possibly more prone to violent behavior is also reported by an English study. In one London district, "compared with controls, men with schizophrenia were found to have a 3.9 times greater risk, and women with schizophrenia a 5.3 times greater risk, for conviction on charges of assault and serious violence" (Torrey, 1996, p. 46).

One study compared people released from mental hospitals in New York City's Washington Heights with people never treated for mental illness. The study addressed violence, and the researchers found that the three following symptoms, "feeling that others wished one harm, that one's mind was dominated by forces beyond one's control, and that other's thoughts were being put into one's head," could be associated with violent behavior (Monahan, citing research by Link and Stueve, 1996, p. 2).

The above-reported studies support a relationship between mental illness and criminal behavior. However, Palermo and colleagues (1992a) stated that "[m]ental illness per se is not synonymous with violence prone behavior. Usually, aggressive, socially disruptive behavior by the mentally ill is the result of the typology of their mental illness: a reactive behavior to impaired cognition [volition], and/or suspicion/persecutory ideas" (p. 56). Torrey (1996) well described the violent mentally ill as walking time bombs because of their unpredictable violent behavior, possibly due to the presence of delusions of persecution or command hallucinations. These offenders/patients do not belong either in the streets or in a correctional institution; they belong in a psychiatric hospital. It is only there that their problems can be addressed.

Anxiety and depression are frequently seen in inmates. Some researchers have "found that almost half the inmates were experiencing problems with depression, anxiety and sleep one month into their sentence. More than one-third of the sample had clinically significant levels of hopelessness" (Smith et al., 1994, p. 359). We have witnessed the above among a large population of inmates of correctional institutions who often reacted to the impact of incarceration with a depressive symptomatology, at times suicidal in nature. Some of the inmates experienced severe panic attacks and needed prompt pharmacological treatment, in addition to supportive psychotherapy. Anxiety and depression are also, at times, part of a predischarge reaction. Mental illness is not a static state of mind but undergoes fluctuations, manifesting itself in different ways at different times. We are of the opinion that these mentally ill offenders do not belong in a jail/prison setting where they are exposed to all types of abuse, ranging from simple misunderstanding to battery and sexual assault. Nevertheless, at times they choose not to reveal their mental illness for fear of being stigmatized by it, preferring to accept criminalization and avoid psychiatrization. The fact is that their judgment is often impaired. Their presence in the midst of hard-core criminals is not conducive to good therapy, and this is one of the reasons why the ambience of the jail/prison is not favorable to rehabilitation.

The police acquired new roles following the deinstitutionalization of the mentally ill. Police officers frequently "[come] into contact with individuals suffering from mental illness" (Wachholz & Mullaly, 1995, p. 285). Arresting officers, who are frequently untrained in detecting mental illness, instead of directing the mentally disturbed offenders to a mental hospital, take them to the county jail via the police district. A process of criminalization of the mentally ill then takes place. Police officers are often inadequately trained to deal with the disturbed mentally ill offenders, and the understaffed mental health units in the jails are inadequate to properly deal with them. The changes in mental health policy have created a problematic situation wherein the mentally ill as a group are shifted among the judicial system and various rejecting institutions. "Some contend that the tightening of commitment standards has led the police to readily arrest mentally ill individuals as a means to simply remove them from the community" (Wachholz & Mullaly, 1995, p. 287).

Nevertheless, even though the concept of psychiatric insanity is different from that of legal insanity—the latter addressing specifically the culpability and responsibility of the offender/defendant at the time of the offense—one encounters offenders who acted antisocially due to their mental confusion and disorganized behavior, part of an untreated mental illness.

OLDER OFFENDERS

Older people are represented among prisoners first because some offenders grow older in prison during a long prison term or a life term and, second, because crime by older or elderly people is on the rise. Even if the older population is increasing in our society, the overall arrests of older people is not increasing proportionately. And since older people are not arrested or imprisoned for minor offenses, most of the arrestees are those who commit major offenses. At times, they are arrested for aggravated battery in the course of domestic violence. Their domestic misbehavior is usually due to poor interpersonal relationships, diminished interaction outside the home, their less flexible type of thinking, demanding attitudes, unrealistic expectations, and depression with paranoid features or paranoia (Sapp, 1989). In 1978, D. Shichor and S. Kahrin reported that "aggravated assault accounted for about 80 percent of all violent offenses for which older persons were arrested; Alan Malinchak reported the same percentage" (cited in Sapp, 1989, p. 27). Because of poor economic conditions, an increasing number of older people are arrested for larceny and theft. The above statistics refer to prisoners in their late fifties to middle sixties.

The most common criminal acts committed by the older offender (age 70+) are indecent exposure and indecent liberty with minors (ages 7 to 13 in our experience), usually girls and often grandchildren. At times, alcohol is a co-factor in this type of behavior, superimposed on depression, beginning Alzheimer's disease, or impotence. A study by Carl Brahce and Donald Bachand (1989) reported the following observations: "The criminal activity of the older arrestees involves serious infractions. Both those who were involved in some criminal activity early in life and those who only were first arrested in their later years after retiring were charged with violent crimes" (p. 55). Serious criminal activities were also present in people arrested in their forties and fifties. Alcohol, a common factor in both the habitual and non-habitual older offenders, was not usually present "in the arrest pattern of the retired group" (p. 55). In addition to being charged with crimes against others, "retirees were arrested for possession of drugs, larceny, and arson" (p. 55).

Brahce and Bachand also report studies that found that homicide perpetrated by older people usually took place in the home, was intra-racial, and perpetrated by males. In our experience, it is usually the result of a paranoid condition of the jealous type, or an organic mental confusion with superimposed depression.

Retirement may be, at times, a source of frustration and a stressful period which unsettles the older person's self-concept, creating problems of adjustment and a tendency to irritability, anger and impulsive behavior. In such a situation, older people may lose control of their emotions more easily than younger adults, leading to offensive behavior and possible incarceration. In addition, serious illness in themselves or their spouses may lead to altruistic homicide, with abortive suicide attempts. The older offenders are usually resentful at being jailed; however, as time goes on, their adaptation to the prison system and their behavior are, as a rule, better than that of imprisoned younger offenders.

Regarding their demographic data, Patricia Washington (1989) reported that mature, mentally ill offenders (50+ years) in a California jail were "single (73.4%), with a mean educational level of 10.22 years, the majority were white (57.8%), nearly a quarter had been arrested for drunk driving (24.2%), most were employed (65.%) at the time of arrest and an overwhelming majority were recidivists" (p. 164). The above paralleled national statistics. Also, the majority of the mentally disordered older offenders were diagnosed as having personality disorders (76.9%) and 15.4 percent had a diagnosis of neurotic depression (p. 165). More than 15 percent (15.4%) were found to be schizophrenic. The above correlates with the Italian and Milwaukee statistics reported in the section considering the mentally ill offenders.

Estimates of the frequency of the crime rate perpetrated by older people in 1989 were reported as quite varied (Turner & Champion, 1989), however, they were estimated to range between 300,000 to 500,000 per year. Gerri Turner and Gene Champion (1989) reported in their study that felony probation for these older offenders was frequently adopted by the courts, because "confining an elderly offender for any prolonged period taxes most jail and prison systems...[because] jails and prisons are designed for more youthful offenders" (p. 126). We fully agree with this type of probation except in those rare cases of paranoid psychosis in the older offender which would pose a risk to society. In addition, Turner and Champion stated, because of age-related physical changes, the older offenders may not be able to adapt well to a jail/prison routine, and they may need medical attention for various ailments that cannot be offered in a correctional institution. They may also need a differently structured prison geared to their physical and mental limitations, their slowness, their desire for isolation, and an ambience which offers different recreational activities than those for younger inmates. The older prisoners often express their disappointment in being with noisy, unruly and disrespectful young offenders, or "punks" as they call them.

GANGS

Gang members are highly represented in the jail/prison community of inmates. "A gang, after all, is still a community or a group, and better than the total isolation that is a living form of the grave" (Gaylin, 1991, p. 261). Gangs are usually formed by people committed to criminal activities, frequently underprivileged and streetwise, whose personalities can be classified as belonging to the antisocial type—self-centered, aggressive, remorseless, amoral. The youths who experienced lack of affectionate bonding with parents, who offended at an early age (below fifteen) or experienced institutional or probation placement, poor school attendance, drug use, and sexually deviant behavior were at high risk for delinquency (Towberman, 1994, p. 163). Gaylin (1991) asserted:

> The roots of antisocial behavior are set in childhood. The antisocial behavior is our due payment for our neglect of the *biologically determined* [emphasis in original] needs of the dependent child. Care is his natural right. We dare not deprive him of his most basic due, his very birthright. If the neglect and deprivation are severe enough, the developing adult may become an antisocial individual [at times] immune to any corrections except those of fear, punishment, confinement, and aging. Street crime is the avocation and occupation of the young. (p. 262.)

Indeed, many gangs originate in public schools where the youths may be intimidated, coerced or extorted by the gang members. They recruit their members from a younger generation of adolescents (usually ages ten to eighteen) with conduct disorders or who are in need of acceptance because of feelings of rejection and lack of self-esteem. They are young people who crave for higher sensory stimuli. They usually show traits that are frequently associated with victimful criminal behavior which can be listed as follows: resistance to conditioning, defiance of punishment; poor achievement in school, performance below their intellectual capability; impulsivity, and lack of completion of tasks assigned and coordinated by others; hyperactivity during childhood; general risk-taking and excitement-seeking; recreational drug use and, particularly, excessive use of alcohol; a preference for social interactions which is active, often chaotic in type; and "a preference for promiscuous and/or diverse sexual activity" (Ellis, 1990, p. 46). Among the demographic variables of gang members are the following: intactness or not of parent's marital bond; number of siblings or half-siblings; race (African-Americans higher); social status (generally low social status); urban/rural residency (higher in urban areas); age (10-35 year age bracket); sex (males) (Ellis, 1990). It is well known that they may show anxiety, obsessive-compulsive disorders, post-traumatic stress disorder, hyperactivity, substance abuse, passive-aggressive borderline and paranoid personalities (Burkett & Myers, 1995).

Gangs are usually "organized along ethnic lines," have their own rituals and interests, and assemble in specific locations—what they term "turf"—where their crimes are usually perpetrated. The major gangs are African-Americans, Asian, Chinese, Hispanic, Jamaican, and Caucasian. African-American gangs have formed hundreds of sub-groups in different cities. They usually have several types of identi-fiers. Street gangs are known by what they wear, often by their hats and shoes, and by the way in which they wear it; wearing the wrong clothing can be very dangerous. At times, product logos on name-brand sportswear is used as a gang insignia. Almost every sports cap is used as a gang identifier. Gangs have a style of their own, and when recruitment is completed one may observe an increase in the number of gang caps being worn.

Asian street gangs show a great deal of mobility and avoid exter-nal notoriety. Indeed, "members tend not to dress in a distinctive manner, display colors, bear tattoos (with the exception of the Japanese Yakuza), or adopt other visible indicia of gang membership" (BJA, 1997, p. 50). Their behavior is the behavior thought to be typi-cal of the oriental—unassuming, taciturn, non-revealing, distant. They commit crime against property, are involved in drug trafficking, and in the intimidation of people in business for extortion.

Within the large group of Hispanic gangs are sub-gangs from vari-ous Hispanic origins, such as persons from Cuba, Mexico, Puerto Rico, or other Central American or West Indies countries. They have a tendency to exhibitionism and braggadocio. Their attire tends to distinguish them because it is colorful. They use nicknames, bear tat-toos and make use of graffiti in order to communicate at times. They are loyal, are duty bound to the rules of the gang, or better, to the macho rules of the gang, and they keep a strict rule of silence—no informing, no squealing to the police if they want to stay alive.

At times, inmates fear retaliation from gang members if they report them to the correctional authorities, as did the following inmate who talked about a "Willie" who "brutally stabbed me in the head and it may be due to others." Ever fearful of gang retaliation against himself and his family because "Willie is a strong leader in his gang," he added, "I would testify if my family's and my welfare safety would be secured from this day on because these gang members are known for awaiting for awhile and then all of sudden one day someone comes up hurt to the point they are near death, paralyzed or dead."

Gang members are turf oriented, as above stated, take over a district of a city, and often the initiate has to perpetrate a serious offense or even homicide in order to qualify for membership. They are involved in killing, robbery, assault, drug trafficking, hit-and-run home invasion, auto theft—the latter being extremely frequent, and even terrorist acts.

Among the largest and most important gangs are the Crips and the Bloods. They originated in Los Angeles and are neighborhood gangs. Both groups often identify themselves by hand symbols resembling sign language. "Typically, members dress in a distinctive fashion, display colors (with blue associated with Crips and red with Bloods), use monikers, sometimes display gang names or monikers on clothing and communicate through graffiti (BJA, 1997, p. 50). They are frequently involved in selling cocaine in grand style.

The Jamaican Posses, consisting of about 22,000 members, are usually illegal aliens and operate in thirty-five states. Originally from Kingston (Jamaica), they subdivided themselves into the Rat Posse, involved in the killing of police officers; the Hotsteppers, comprising people convicted for capital offenses but escapees; and the Shower Posse, deriving its name from their habit of showering victims with bullets. "Between 1985 and 1992, more than 4,000 U.S. homicides were attributed to Jamaican gangs" (BJA, 1997, p. 52). Drug trafficking is their major activity, followed by trafficking in firearms, and a vast gamut ranging from shoplifting to murder.

There are several street gangs in Chicago including the Disciples (BGD), the Manic Latin Disciples, El Rukns, the Latin Kings, and the Vice Lords. The Latin Kings, the Vice Lords, and El Rukns are mostly present in the Midwest. They are primarily involved in drug trafficking, responsible for 75 percent of their members' arrests.

The Vice Lords are subdivided into Conservative Vice Lords, Unknown Vice Lords, Cicero Insane Vice Lords, Executioner Vice Lords, Traveling Vice Lords, Imperial Insane Vice Lords, Undertaker

Vice Lords, and Renegade Vice Lords. All of the above groups employ various tattoos. Those of the Vice Lords, for example, range from a dollar sign to a rabbit. Those of the Disciples include, among others, the "5 P's" (proper preparation prevents poor performance); a six-pointed star in which each point has a meaning from the top going to the right (love, life, loyalty, knowledge, wisdom and understanding); and the "3 L's" (life, love, loyalty). The open teardrop tattoo of a Latin King member means that the person has killed a member of an opposing gang, while a sold teardrop means a death of a close family member. Among their other tattoos are those representing an eagle's head (Latin Eagles), a halo (Latin Souls), and a heart with wings, horns and a crown (Latin Lovers).

El Rukns, originally the Black Stone Rangers, is more similar to organized crime than to just a street gang. They invest their profits in real estate and businesses and at times have been involved in international criminal activities. The El Rukns' tattoo of an eye with a pyramid teardrop represents the tears they shed for their brothers. Other El Rukns' tattoos include a pyramid (representing peace in all four corners of the universe), a sword (representing the wrath of Allah), and the rising sun (meaning that a new day will come, and representing the lifting of all mankind).

There are other groups, in addition to those named above, scattered throughout the United States and primarily formed of Caucasian members with a particular affinity for music (punk and heavy metal). Among these groups are supremacist groups, neo-Nazis, and skinheads, skinhead style; Northern Hammer Skinheads; outlaw motorcycle and biker gangs. They are usually involved in drugs, weapons trafficking, rape, burglary, vandalism, petty theft, and even violent crimes like murder. An identifier of the Northern Hammer Skinheads consists a male figure in a Nazi salute superimposed upon a swastika, within a circle, topped by a Nazi eagle. Skinheads began in England in the sixties as a rebellious group of youths against the "mod scene," mostly formed by working class people and adopting factory clothing as a uniform. The group became an alternative of the punk rockers. Eventually, they added Nazi symbolism, sympathizing with the White Racist National Front.

Los Angeles County has seen epidemic proportions of gang-related homicides, reaching the point that "a total of 7,288 gang-related homicides occurred [there] from 1979 through 1994" (Hutson et al.,

1996, p. 1031). Of those homicides, 5,541 took place in the city of Los Angeles. Undoubtedly, this has become a major public health problem and has overcrowded the California jail/prison system.

The tragedy of the following young inmate who came to our attention is vividly described in his letter to the judge in which he pleads for mercy: "In 1959, my mother was brutally murdered, shot 52 times with an uzi and threw [sic] down by the lakefront, because a gang member got killed on my front porch and they thought I had done it. I left town. They were still looking for me, breaking both of my jaws and knocking me into a coma. I was innocent. I am diagnosed with traumatic brain injury. Incarceration helped me. I am not using drugs anymore."

Graffiti on the walls of detention cells express the inmates' culture, sentiments, anger, and distrust of the system. "Whenever the average human being is secluded for any considerable length of time from his fellows, he experiences the need of embodying some literary or artistic expression of himself.... There is no vanity here, and it is an instinct from which no individual, whatever his degree of culture, is exempt" (Ellis [1890] 1973, p. 211).

Ellis ([1890] 1973) stated, "The child loves to speak to himself.... The criminal keeps silent his most intimate thoughts.... It is for himself, for himself alone, that he writes what he cannot or dare not say.... His desires and lusts, his aspirations, his coarse satires and imprecations, his bitter reflections, his judgments of life, are all recorded in these prison inscriptions on whitewashed walls, cell doors, margins of books, tin knives, and the bottoms of skilly cans and dinner tins" (p. 212). He also wrote that "[h]igher emotions always play a considerable part [in tattooing]" and "erotic passion is a very...frequent cause of tattooing" (p. 195)

Tattoos, as reported above, are a means of gang identification. They portray their beliefs and their messages. Most gang members will have their gang name and affiliation tattooed on their arms, hands, chest, or back. Gang members take great pride in these tattoos, some of which may be extremely small, a dot in the web of the hand, while others may cover the entire back or chest. What is seen in graffiti is also seen in the tattoo. The practice of tattooing is very common among criminals, with the percentage fluctuating between 15 to 32 percent in early studies. The designs vary, but certain emblems are frequently repeated, such as love, war, religion, occupation, obscene practices, also mermaids, nude women, initials, transfixed heart, swords. Wachtler (1997) wrote that they are the mark of a professional convict.

> ...the dagger dripping blood, or the swastika; the skull, serpent or spider; the roses and crosses; the teardrop under the eye–all can be supplied by a fellow inmate using tattoo guns made from motors stolen from tape players, paper clips, wire snipped off guitar strings–need ink? You can always get the blue ink used for printing prison forms by boiling the forms and distilling the ink. If you want black ink, burn some Styrofoam; the ash is perfect. Need a stove? Take an electric wire with a plug. Split the wire on the opposite end, and attach each end to the ends of a metal spoon. Put the metal spoon in the substance to be heated, put in the plug, and you will find out how well a "stinger" works. (p. 239.)

Most of the tattooed criminals belong to gangs, but tattooed persons certainly are not always criminals. Tattooing may be used to cover up their inadequacy, as a sign of belonging to a group, or as a fashion statement. Berté (cited in Ellis [1890], 1973) believed the impulse to tattooing to be a momentary whim, "favored by imitation, the prolonged idleness of the sea, the barracks, the prison, and the hospital.... [It seems] to become irresistible" and is often found in persons with a neurotic, restless character (p. 200). "The greater number of tattooed criminals are naturally found among recidivists and instinctive criminals, especially those who have committed crimes against the person," wrote Ellis ([1890] 1973, p. 194).

Other methods of identification of gang members while in the correctional setting are their medallions, their hairstyles, the shape of their eyebrows, the manner in which they fold under the collar of their uniform, or in which the right side of their uniform is pleated to accent the right side of the body where their affiliation tattoo may be. Their trouser leg may be rolled up or tucked into their socks, or the pants pockets on the back of the jail uniform may be ripped down either the right side or the left side.

It must be recognized that many of the gang members come from ghetto areas of the cities. "The ghetto residents are aliens, forced to live in an alien world. The street is not 'theirs,' and they have no identification with it. The garbage is in the street not just because there is poorer collection service, although God knows that is true, but also because slums create slum attitudes and slum despair, and these in turn are capable of creating more slums and more people with slum mentalities" (Gaylin, 1991, p. 261). These young people are deprived of an equal share of self-pride and self-respect, and the independence and power that issue from such positive identification, and "[a]ll the research indicates that boys in father-absent homes have great difficulty with sex roles and what's called gender identification" (Pothrow-Stith, 1991, p. 79). No doubt, during their growth they were unable to form necessary virtuous, moral character, as demonstrated in a 1996 study of Richard Craig and Kenneth Truitt. Their study seems to confirm the relationship between moral cognition and moral action—already demonstrated by other authors (Campagna & Harter, 1975; Deardorff & Finch, 1975; Berkowitz et al., 1986). The inmates they studied at the Patuxent Institution in Jessup, Maryland showed that such a relationship exists. In other words, institutional infractions are usually a good reflection not only of an inmate's adjustment level to the institution but of his moral conduct. Their study seems to reflect the ideas of Jean-Jacques Rousseau ([1762] 1968), who stated that people's mature behavior should be driven by their morality and that "to be governed by appetite alone is slavery, while obedience to a law one prescribes to oneself is freedom" (p. 65).

Chapter 5

LETTERS FROM PRISON

*Just the thought of being taken from my family scares me. I am
afraid of prison, I'm afraid of the state of mind that I will end
up with after an extended period of incarceration.*

A prisoner

INTRODUCTION

More than a century ago, Cesare Lombroso ([1888] 1996) published a book, entitled, *Palimpsests from Prison* (*Palimsesti del
Carcere*). Lombroso should need no introduction. Nevertheless, for
those who are not acquainted with him, he was a nineteenth-century
psychiatrist and professor of anthropology at the University of Turin,
Italy, seen by many as the founder of criminal anthropology and who,
together with Enrico Ferri, was one of the most important criminologists of the Italian positivistic school of criminology. He is most well
known for his 1876 book, *Criminal Man*, in which he presented his theory regarding the characteristics of what he termed the *born criminal.*
The theory, based on his lengthy and minute observations of "degen-
erative signs" in the thousands of criminals examined by him, has
been both accepted and rejected during the past century.

Lombroso was not alien to the rehabilitation of the offenders and
was an acute observer of inmate behavior. *Palimpsests from Prison* is a
collection of stories, messages, writings, and graffiti of Turin, Italy
prison inmates around and about the end of the last century. The collection of their communications demonstrates not only Lombroso's
interest in the subject and in the inmates as individuals but reflects a
reality that is not bound by limits of time: the humanness of the prisoners, themselves, subjected at that time to a strict carceral discipline
and crying out for freedom. In England, Horsley, in *Jottings from Jail,*

and Davitt, in *Leaves from a Prison Diary*, also collected a good number of these inscriptions. Today's prisoners, finding themselves in a generally more permissive carceral system with easier access to means of communication, rather than through graffiti on their cell walls as in the past, are more likely to voice their feelings, reflections, hopes and fears directly to families, judges, lawyers, doctors, and, at times, even to members of the media. The prisoners whom we will present belong to that relatively small group of offenders—part of that vast silent majority—who have the capacity and desire to communicate their feelings. Their letters reflect not only their inner conflict and struggle in accepting incarceration but their search for an explanation for their uncivilized and offensive conduct, their remorse, and their desire to be understood, their hope for forgiveness, and for judicial clemency. Even though we are quite aware of, and briefly report, the inscriptions and graffiti present on the cell walls of present-day inmates and the many symbolic messages portrayed in tattoos, we have limited our analysis mostly to the microautobiographical stories of letters from inmates which were addressed to us or to others unrelated to the offender but connected to the judicial system or the media. Indeed, while prisoners often express their thoughts and worries by writing on the walls of their cells or on their bunk beds, at times carving out the letters, the most frequent means of communication today, as stated above, is through their letters. Their communications are not really palimpsests, since they are not written on previously used manuscripts, but are letters written by the inmates on ordinary paper, in simple English, and reveal with simple candor their microcosm, their pain, suffering and hopes. Their letters reflect the simple but human feelings of people who are aware of the deprivation of their freedom, who ask for understanding and leniency, express ambivalent feelings, love and hate, insecurity and determination, self-pity and accusatory projections, and, most importantly, demand justice. Their *j'accuse* is against what they consider to be the power system and their inhuman, discriminating punishment. Their cry for help is almost obsessive and cliché-like, and their justifications for their offenses bring into discussion dysfunctional upbringing, lack of parenting, poverty, and their inability to find a niche in a society that they feel has extruded them. They frequently write, "Give me a chance," the chance they feel they never had.

Our interest in reporting these letters is to add a human dimension to these prisoners, to present the inmate's side, in order to appreciate their view of what justice is and what justice they expect from the bench, from their attorneys, and from the mental health experts with whom they come in contact. Our hope is to put into evidence the humanness of the offenders, of those offenders willing to talk and able to do so, of those who speak for all of them, and to try and assess them within the context of contemporary society. We believe that these written messages may help us in better dealing with them and with people like them in the future.

We subdivided the several hundred letters we perused into various topics and, in reporting them, will obviously keep the identity of the writers anonymous. We generally left uncorrected the writers' misspelled words and incorrect punctuation because they are intrinsic to his or her self.

LETTERS ADDRESSING PERSONAL ISSUES

The main object of a first group of miscellaneous letters was to plead for leniency, and within these letters some statements are quite interesting. One inmate, awaiting sentencing, wrote to the judge: "My life is in the third-quarter of a four-quarter game, with no time outs left. Sometimes it takes something like this to bring a person around.... I feel much older and I am ready to take responsibility for what I have done. Just give me a jump start or a running start your Honor." The comparison made to sport competition while referring to his life vividly and simply portrays this inmate's plight. Another wrote to a judge about being scared "of the prison environment that I have put myself into. This is not for me." The same inmate raises a frequent theme found in many of the letters: "My children need a father figure to keep them in [sic] the right track. I myself feel that if I had a Father figure I would probably not have to appear before you." The following inmate brings a vivid touch of human love and caring in his writing to the judge: "I think I can deal with jail or prison better knowing my kids still love me. My daughter wrote me and told me, 'Daddy, I will always be there for you, I love you, just call me.' She is only 8 years old. I am not a brave man or a bad man. If one of your children wrote you and told you that, don't you think you could go through anything too?" Feeling that they are still loved by their spouse or children and not an object of rejection certainly helps many inmates to get through their months or years of incarceration.

"I have a beautiful supporting family that loves me. I have two lovely kids that I have to nourish, provide for, clothe and be their supportive compassionate father," says another inmate, who ends his letter to the judge saying: "Sir, I am not a bad person, yes, I'm human and I make mistakes." Not too many inmates speak of their family supporting them; however, some express gratitude towards parents as in the following letter: "I have no charges as a minor, and because I think I was raised buy [sic] two of the best parents their [sic] are in the world. My mother told me when I was 14 to behave well, otherwise I would go to jail." Another inmate wrote to the judge: "Your Honor, I have always been in trouble only because I have never had a mother figure as well as a father."

Another group of letters discusses at length illness of family members and their concern about them. Several addressed their innocence and stated, "I told my attorney I would be willing to take a lie-detector test." Several write of wanting to sue their attorneys because they feel they were poorly represented, and one threatened to sue the judge for not allowing him to fire his attorney: "Please help me, judge, otherwise I will have to start a suit against you, the DA's office and that two-bit attorney you wouldn't allow me to fire." One who testified for the state cried out for help: "My life is in danger due to the two murder cases I testified for the state," and further added, "Yesterday my mother's home burned down. It was on the news."

Suicide attempts are frequent in jail or prison. The following excerpts are from the letter of an inmate, addicted to cocaine, who committed his offense while under the effect of drug-induced hallucinosis of a command type and who, in the silence of his cell and free from drugs, reflects on his life: "That cocaine is something. I hope that whoever is doing it will stop it today. It is mean, it is not good in the eyes of the Lord, it will kill who does it.... I have never hurt anyone, just the things that I did to myself, try to kill myself 5 or 6 times cutting my arms with razors or walk in front of a bus or taking a lot of pills."

Jail may be a terrible experience but still a place where one may learn something about himself as stated by another inmate: "Coming to jail has been a learning experience I will take with me always, and even though this was the last place I ever wanted to be, I have learned the real meaning of love and joy through studying the word of God, and I am very anxious to share this with my family and with people I will be in contact with. I am not a saint, but I am looking forward to a new life."

One inmate, who had worked in the correctional system, charged with indecent liberty with a minor, a person in his family, claimed to suffer from panic attacks and fear of being mistreated because of being recognized by another inmate: "I was harassed as a child molester while incarcerated, having pictures of children ripped out of magazines and put on my bed when I was not there, threats of being killed or seriously hurt." He further wrote, "It was even mentioned that I could meet the same fate as Jeffrey Dahmer or Jesse Anderson." (The first was a serial killer and the second a man convicted of murdering his wife who had accused two black men of having perpetrated the crime. Both were found dead in a prison section with their heads smashed by another inmate.) He wrote of his personal feelings and stated, "I am very remorseful and apologetic to everyone. I am living in shame here in front of people I used to work and associate with. I am embarrassed with my friends, family, attorney and the D.A." He ends his letter pleading for compassion from the judge. The above case points out the occurrence of feelings of shame, not frequently verbalized by inmates, and the presence of the inmates' "moral" code. There are certain crimes that inmates believe need to be punished—crimes against children and serial killing.

In asking for understanding, another inmate pleads for forgiveness for his crime, because he is ashamed, hurt, and emotionally disturbed by it. "I am grieving remorsefully over making this major mistake. This is a shadow over my life, not only will I bare [sic] this on record, but also in my mind for the rest of my life."

When asking for clemency, some inmates bring into their letters past memory and express gratitude, even to police officers or detectives, as in the following letter from an inmate who had tried to overdose himself with heroin and cocaine: "The night of my arrest I met a man who was more concerned about the scab of the wounds on my inner elbow, this man was Detective.... He touched my heart and changed my life, because if it was not for him, I would most surely be dead. He cared and wanted to know why I had attempted suicide." While assuming responsibility for his offenses and decrying his suicidal attempt, he stated, "When an addict finally convinces himself that death is the only means of escape from his mental health problems he adds idiocy to his stupidity, because there is another way. Escape can be achieved by simply changing masters. The person must realize that every living person serves a master, each of us serves either God or Satan...in my case it was Satan."

Some prisoners claim innocence and sincerity in their new outlook on life, their newly found moral code, or good behavior plans, which are often supported by their assertion that they have found God. They write that they would like to do community work, enroll in school, search for employment: "I am not a ward of the Court and this is my 1st brush with the justice system.... I am able to perform community service hours. I admit of the acts I have done and I am sorry and I would like to apologize to all involved.... I am asking for a chance at my career and life." This phrase, "Give me a chance to prove myself," is encountered frequently in reading the prisoners' letters. Many are given a chance by the courts; however, many come back either because of a similar crime or a more serious one. Others are revoked from probation or parole, as a matter-of-fact, for minimal infractions or for official decisions that do not take into account the facts and give in to an established correctional routine which may be questionable.

Some offenders' letters are pitiful because they not only are difficult to read but reveal the borderline psychopathology of the writers, who often medicated their illness with illicit drugs or alcohol: "I am a nice child, I stay away from trouble and all it is in here [the jail] is trouble. They yell out their doors all night.... When my attorney comes too [sic] talk to me I still don't understand what he is saying to me.... I am scared...forgive me for lying.... I just don't fit in these types of places when I was in the outside I mostly use [sic] to be in the house listening too my radio if you don't believe me call my Grandma that who I lives with [sic] and she can tell you that."

Some inmates believe themselves to have been framed and plead for justice: "The D.A. is taking full advantage of my misfortunes due to my past record and drug addiction. I do admit that I have burglarized in the past and have always been in complete cooperation with the authorities. I never took a case to trial if I knew I was guilty.... I believe I am paying for those things now the wrong things I did in the past." Others raise doubts about the charges against them: "I feel I was wrongly charged with these offenses. There is a copy of the charges that I should be charged with, enclosed in the letter.... I also sent a copy to my attorney."

Besides the case in which someone wants to bargain his way out of a long sentence due to him because of his offense, how does one act if accused of a crime never committed? How do defendants feel when they find that they are being charged with a crime while incarcerated as the next inmate wrote? "At that time [a battery case] I was at the House of Correction. I did not get out until June 26th." It may be difficult to trust a felon, but it should not be difficult to trust dates.

It is interesting to realize that some inmates, frequently litigious paranoids, have a fairly good knowledge of legal issues and at times create some genuine professional embarrassment for their own attorneys who may have been negligent in handling their cases. The following excerpts are from an inmate's letter requesting to point out the evidence against him in an indictment against his representing attorney: "My new attorney didn't seem as though he wanted to fight my case, curiously it did not shock me knowing this, but also he took part of my discovery material. Please request that the P/Defend and DA send me all statements made, interviews, fingerprint results, report of marked money before leaving the police station, all audio occurrences. Thank you!" Yet another inmate wrote to the judge and stated that he was not read his Miranda rights prior to his confession. Actually, he stated that he was in a state of mind that he "did not knowingly understand my constitutional rights, I was not properly apprised of said rights as enunciated in the Miranda decision." He further mentions the Fourth, Fifth, Sixth and Fourteenth Amendments to the United States Constitution in support of his request. We have seen prisoners act as their own attorneys, representing themselves and questioning their previous public defender. Some of these offenders appeared to be well prepared and extremely capable. Other prisoners are poorly educated but streetwise. They accumulate a fair legal knowledge by talking with older inmates, reading legal books in the prison library or being exposed frequently to debates in the courtroom.

At times, sentences are severe and prisoners have great difficulty in accepting them. Occasionally, their resentment and hostility against the sentencing judge is at the basis of a threat of suicide. They write to the judge about what they have in mind to do: "I just want to tell you that with each passing day I think of killing myself right here in this cell." Is this an unconscious (or conscious) attempt to make the judge feel guilty?

The inmates, even though deferential towards the judges to whom they write asking to reconsider their cases, very rarely express gratitude towards them as did the following inmate who wrote, "I want to thank you again for giving me a chance to be a mother to grow. Right now I am in parenting classes.... I have learned how to make the right decision for me and my family. I have learned that every decision I make whether good or bad will affect me and my kids."

These letters are a means of communication for the inmates. By writing, they try to fill a gap which exists because of the often dehumanized way in which they are treated, either because of lack of time, overcrowding in the correctional system, the strict rules of due process, or even negligence. They want to introduce themselves as one human being to another, or to the person who is about to decide, or just decided, their future. At times, in their simple ways, they even call the judge by his or her first name, perhaps believing that the familiarity will bring about more compassion or understanding. "I am looking sir to give you just a little bit more of the type of person that I really am other than what you read and see off the Police Criminal Complaint," wrote one offender. He then continues in a clear demonstration of his insight into his poor decision to overcome his plight: "I realized I did not have a lot of education. I left school at the 8th grade. I could not find jobs. I saw my brother last year gunned down right in my place, in my face. I felt helpless. I looked for some type of 'release.' My mistake, judge, was to pick up the wrong type of release– 'drugs.'"

Another inmate expressed his thoughts along the same line, even though he realized that "sinful acts like crimes have to be punished." He stated, "There are many factors contributing to these sinful acts which does not justify by any means these wrongdoings, but will give birth to this distasteful nature as well as the fall of a man." The same defendant stated that without considering the contributing factors, no judge could pass a fair judgment. He wrote of becoming addicted to cocaine, owing money to peddlers, pleading for some time, and being told, "If you don't come up with the money, we'll kill you." Because of fear, he ended up in robbing his place of work, and the next day told his boss what he had done. He added: "Drugs are a destroyer of people and families.... This cocaine is nothing but a demon spirit and has caused a spiritual warfare. I am better confined here than in the streets, Your Honor." He ended his letter asking for help.

Also on the theme of addiction, a 33-year-old female inmate wrote, "Two years ago, I was a nice decent caring productive person, however since I started on heroin—it changed me—heroin makes you sick and you have to support that terrible habit." The ravages of drug addiction are widespread. "I am ashamed and I regret my distasteful choice of being addicted to drugs which put me in bad positions.... Only now do I realize that life consists of choices (the right choices)...a normal life and a productive life in the community," wrote another inmate.

Letters may be deeply moving, such as that from an inmate diagnosed with a terminal malignancy who clearly stated that he could never have gotten the same medical attention on the outside as he receives at the nearby university medical center through the prison doctor. He wrote of wanting to become a born-again Christian and of making his pre-funeral arrangements because "I don't want to bother my daughter with that."

Soul searching while incarcerated goes on uninterruptedly for some inmates. It brings about shame, remorse, new projects and plans. It stimulates resiliency in some prisoners and they bounce back—a flight into wellness—but it does not happen often. Remorse was expressed by one 19-year-old inmate who was charged with being party to a crime in a murder case: "I am deeply sorry.... I was at the scene when the incident occurred, but I did not do the shooting.... I am guilty of stupidity because I allowed myself to be a follower when I have leadership abilities.... My heart goes out to the family of the victim, losing someone that you love and care about is always hard. I just pray that they'll forgive me for being involved." Remorse and shame for the wrong deeds is expressed in the following note: "I sit in my room and constantly look at how I've changed other people's lives because of my actions." Another inmate wrote to the judge: "I feel very embarrassed when I step foot in your courtroom. I felt especially lousy one time the court was filled with young kids and they called me in and read my charges. I also feel that I let down my race and the community."

Snitching, as the inmates call informing, is occasionally encountered. At times, the accusations against people, both in custody and free, are well-outlined. Among the letters is one from a prisoner who claims to want to "redirect my life in the positive way," and would like to report the names of some people whose crimes have not been solved "in exchange of some help in my behalf." *Do ut des*, Machiavelli would say.

One of the frequent statements we read in these letters is, "I was involved with the wrong people," or "I made a mistake for not getting treatment for my drug addiction because I did not want anybody to know about it," or "what I am charged with is totally out of character for me." The above come from a long letter written by a 28-year-old inmate who recounts the escalation of his criminal activity over a ten-year-period to feed and cover up his drug/cocaine addiction. Writing of his many burglaries, he stated, "The amount of time I am facing is just.... I can't take what I did but I can make sure that I do all it takes to deal with the addiction." Then, after making a social statement: "I knew what I was coming into. The system has changed a lot in the past 4-to-5 years. The city has gang problems, not to mention our murder rate and serious crime rate, but it is very seldom if ever that any of those people are trying to pursue a decent life. Instead I knew I was, because I was going to school, working etc. while I was pushed and driven by something I had no control over." He ends his letter by stating: "I can only hope that you see me as a person who got side-tracked. Give me another chance–something to shoot for."

The following letter is from a 23-year-old male who was charged with first-degree reckless homicide while armed. He not only asks for forgiveness, but adds, "I am not a bad man but a human who made a terrible mistake and a bad judgment in life." Throughout his letter he portrays his life difficulties, his feeling different, his many rejections, and he asks for clemency, understanding and reconciliation. Reconciliation is thought by some to be a deterrent to future offenses and the best approach to anger. Even though one can understand its purpose, it is not easy for many people to reconcile with someone who killed their loved one.

One young inmate, who in his simplicity addresses the judge man-to-man, talks about his despondent self during his childhood and adolescence, with a "diabolic stepfather–[who physically abused] all the time, me and my mother." He is proud of his high school diploma and comes to the conclusion that even if he did wrong, there are many good things about himself.

A long letter from a woman charged with carrying a concealed weapon bespeaks the high degree of dysfunction in her family. She writes that she was sexually molested by her next-door neighbor, beaten up by her mother who she claims was jealous of her father's attention to her, and of "his putting his hand over my mouth while doing what he wanted with me." She writes of carrying a gun because she was afraid of her violent boyfriend and of being found with the gun when visiting a friend at the penitentiary. (A socially disrupted upbringing brings about poor judgment.) She ends her letter by asking for help and asks not to be separated from her daughter.

What inmates do about their sexual urges and their loving feelings is not often talked about. However, these feelings are present and at times erupt in homosexual assaults within their cells, especially when the person is not capable of channeling them into creative and spiritual activities, as did one prisoner in the form of a poem and an attached love letter that defy any introduction and that convey his psychosexual craving for his girlfriend and his anticipation of a joyous re-encounter when he is released from jail:

Sin is a prison
that many can't see,
and Satan is the jailer
who has captured me.

I committed no crime
to create my sin.
this is a prison
that I was born within.

It's so dark in this prison
that the bars can't be seen,
tho I bathe in the sunlight
my soul is unclean.

This prison is spiritual
and my sentence is death,
unless I find Jesus
before my last breath.

He is the light
that allows me to see
the bondage of sin
and my captivity.

Jesus is the "way"
the "truth" and the light,
only He can give
me spiritual sight.

> Only he has the key
> to unlock the door,
> that will set me free
> forever more.
>
> You too can be free
> from your spiritual prison
> if you accept Jesus
> as your Saviour, arisen.

The same prisoner also wrote to a friend: "...I just wrote to let you know Im thinking of you, and a terrible storm is going to blow me your way next month so be able to except [sic] me as a friend and not a lover so dont let me interfere in your personal life because I have my own. But still in all I still love you as friend and always will." To his girlfriend he wrote:

> ...I miss you boy and all of our lovemaking. Please forgive me for all my wrong doing and all the hurt I put you through. But believe me all of that is in the past and I have plans for you and believe me for now on the only thing matters now is you being happy.... I've realized...your not happy and thats my fault.... When I get out they have to pay me and the first thing Im going to do is take you to the mall and to the movies and then out to eat.... I do want you to be my wife and have my baby as long as I've been with you...I've grown to love you more.... [The correctional agency] will have me a job as soon as I get out and I'm gonna work my ass off.... I don't want you to leave me boy and I love you and I need you in my life. So please put away your doubts about me and have faith in the man that loves you and that's me of course. Because true love is so hard to find especially one like yours. So hold on to your love and don't be afraid of the way you feel because its real love.... When I get out were going to spend as much time together as we can and your gonna be the happiest woman ever and Ill make sure of that.... I think of you every night and I must say without you in my life I dont even want to be here on this earth.... I'll never put anything before you again. And I promise on my Grandfather's Grave.... When I get out, just tell me what you want me to do.... I fell in love with you the first time I saw you in the laundry mat.... You really are a very smart and intelligent lady and Im gonna make you my wife just watch and see. P.S. Take the pink slip to [police station] and get my property you can have everything.

The chaplains in a correctional setting often receive letters from inmates. They counsel the inmates about practical life issues within a religious context, and through their interaction with them while passing on the word of God, friendship at times develops. "You are a man of God. You showed me hope, when there was despair," wrote one inmate, while another expressed his gratitude to the chaplain by saying: "I am thankful to God and everyone else who have made it possible for me to turn my life around. I feel so much better about myself and my entire outlook on life has completely changed.... Now I honestly believe I can do anything I want, with my limitation, and with the help of God." Another prisoner who encountered difficulties in communication with a correctional officer wrote to a chaplain saying: "I can't seem to find the trust and understanding with these people [in the prison] like I could with you." He then voices his past fear of being killed in jail by someone "who put the word out among the prisoners to have me killed" and the way he faced the situation: "I faced 2 of them and I told them what they had coming if they chose to mess with me" and added, "That was the first and only run-in I had here." Then, after stating that he is six-feet tall and weighs 250 pounds and that people want to be with him because they consider him a "Big-Brother–Protector," especially of the sixteen and seventeen-year-old inmates, he adds: "I am a nice guy and just hate to see young guys get bullied around or steered into the gang-banger life style because that's just a troublesome way that goes on here. So I do what I can to look out for them...so I find myself giving advice and keep these young guys on a positive path so they can work on getting out."

Emotional, friendly ties are often established between the chaplain and the inmates because, as one inmate who thought a judge was too hard on him wrote, "When a person is behind these doors of total confinement there is nothing like hearing from you, brother, a good friend." He wrote that the judge "had it for me...and I gave in to a promise of a 20 y. sentence to run concurrently with another case, a promise not kept because I had a lawyer who was not in my corner." The prisoner had been sentenced to ninety years in a maximum-security prison.

The importance of the chaplaincy in the prison is vouched for by many of the letters we read, such as the following one. "I was going thru a rough time and I felt encouraged and comforted after our discussion.... There is so much darkness in here. People are blinded of the ways of God. I pray they may have eyes to see." Another inmate wrote, "I will be released. I wanted to thank you for everything you've done for me. You have helped me tremendously." Another letter tells a bit about the overcrowding in the jails/prisons. "I am here, in this different jail, because they don't have any room for people in the institution. Isn't that sad? There are so many people locked up that they don't even have room to *store* them." He adds, "Well, I thank God that I am on my way home. They are sending me home on the D.I.S. Bracelet. It's not the best thing in the world "The Bracelet" but it sure beats being locked up." He ends his letter writing, "I thank God for this experience. Through his grace I am saved. I do need your prayers, brother, because the Adversary is trying harder than ever to take me down because of the closeness of Jesus and I...I have done some witnessing here to a few of these guys, but it seems as if they just aren't ready." At times, in fact, wives write the chaplains about being afraid that their husbands, once released, may continue the same abusive behavior for which they were incarcerated. "I am fearful and confused. I remember his domestic abuse," wrote one.

A prison, even when well run, appears to be a sad place of confinement where the pensive expression and the slow psychomotor activity of the prisoners alternate with the loudness and crying out of their blaspheming and utterances for help. Some inmates make the best of these dreary places. They work, keep busy within the confining walls, divert their attention to less important things, avoiding continuous rumination about their unpleasant conditions. "I need a job in order not to think too much about myself and my family," stated one mature offender.

At times, the letters show not only surprise but despair. "My mandatory release date is 2,058, this is crazy, if I don't get my time run together I will die in here, for a crime that don't even call for a death sentence." And then a lighter and more hopeful note: "The system will place me at.... They have some programs there I want to take advantage of. I should be going there within the next week or so," followed by the stark realization of the necessity of learning how to break the "endless circle of coming back to prison."

Indeed, recidivism is quite high. Obviously, one cannot tackle recidivism among offenders/inmates unless the basic roots of crime are addressed. An addict who begs the judge for clemency, when recognizing that because of his drug addiction he is also addicted to stealing, ends his letter by saying: "I know that for the first nineteen years of my life I have not been the greatest person. I know I am a wrong doer and I knew I would have to face the consequences," and then he sadly writes, "My life is in your hands, your honor."

Feelings of depression and "being stressed out," an inability to find a job, life in a dysfunctional family, are frequently given as co-factors in their offenses by a large number of inmates. One female inmate wrote to the district attorney that she was not willing to press charges against her brother, on whom she had called the police, because, she said, she was able to straighten out her conflict with him.

"Give me a chance for such foolish stuff I did," is frequently voiced, and "Allow me to continue my studies," is occasionally requested in these letters. Some letters are replete with thoughts concerning being frightened of the district attorney, of being poorly represented by their public defender leading to plea bargaining for offenses not committed. One offender wrote the judge in a strong statement: "I told my lawyer I am not going to accept a plea for something I did not do," which, together with the one by another inmate, "I am not getting proper representation and I wanna take my guilty plea back and take this all to trial before I am railroaded to prison," bespeaks their dilemma. The inmates who write seem to understand, but not appreciate, what has been done to them: "If I would not go along with that, the DA would raise the charges from possession to possession to deliver," and that would call for a longer period of incarceration.

People are temperamental, and impulsivity and loss of control often lead to crime. This fact was acknowledged by one young inmate who wrote to the judge: "I now realize that I must learn to control my temper." "I lost the most precious person that meant the world to me, my mother," wrote an addict who admitted to his impulsivity. "I did this crime on impulse, due to drugs and alcohol and now I have been hit with reality. I have known for some time that I need medical help." Pleading for clemency on the part of people addicted to drugs is frequent, as is the claim that their children need them at home. One wonders how they suddenly recognize their responsibility to their children when for years they have been negligent in their care of them. One prisoner wrote, "I am 23 years old. I have completed 12 years of school and about 2 years of college. I have 5 beautiful children who have been experiencing a very tragic stage in their life.... My wife...is currently trying to maintain a stable situation for them during my incarceration. They need, your Honor, a steady income. I have many different job opportunities and I plan to become again a good father and become a major part of my community. I am begging you even for intensive probation if you have to."

One prisoner claimed to have been assaulted by a detention guard and added, "Out of all the years that I have been coming to jail, I haven't seen a guard conduct himself in this kind of manner." The guards, too, are human and at times, under pressure, they may lose control. Overcrowding and conditioning affect them as well as the offenders.

Some people look at their prison programs as a way to get their GED and eventually go to college. "I chose to be positive and use this time and these programs to my advantage. I am grateful," wrote one.

At times, parents are the center of the writing of the inmates, especially the female inmates, as in the following excerpts from the letter of a woman writing for a bail review who obviously cares a great deal about her father: "I am not a bad person. I worked since the age of 14. My father has been my role model. I am his baby girl. I don't want him to sell his things to help me. I am 35 y old and he still feels that he has to do it for me and if I say no that would brake [sic] his heart." She ends her letter by saying, "Please consider the fact that I was never in jail before and 'I am not a risk.'"

One offender who sexually assaulted a minor seems to be remorseful and quite aware of the damage he has done (assuming that he is telling the truth): "I was absolutely wrong for committing this crime. For it showed disrespect for the law and most of all, for...my victim, as a human being. I hope [her mother and she] will find it in their hearts to forgive me.... I never done anything like this before, not to anyone. [I] showed a betrayal of trust not only with [the victim] herself but with her mother, the rest of her family, her friends and to the community.... I have a parole eligibility date with the prospect of getting out of prison. I have come to realize that [she] does not. For she will always be in prison because of the mental affects [sic] of the crime that I selfishly and disrespectfully committed against her.... I can not forgive myself for [this].... I always pray to God [on her] behalf, to give her strength to make it through each painful day of her life."

One young man wrote to a psychiatrist asking for understanding in his suggestions to the judge: "Keep me here, otherwise I will not be able to see my parents. Don't send me away." Loneliness and nostalgia are expressed by a female inmate when she writes to the judge in her short letter: "I miss my son, help me." Another says, "I am ready to accept responsibility for my actions. I have a loving and caring family that supports me that will help me lead a law abiding life." Another, too, wrote to the judge: "I learned my lesson. I would like to apologize. I take full responsibility for driving the car. I am glad nobody got killed." The following young inmate also accepted his responsibility for his offense and then said, "I believe when one makes a mistake he should be punished, and should be able to correct his mistakes, not to make the mistakes again and also teach others about not doing what he did." Yet another wrote, "It is very embarrassing to me. I have repeatedly made bad choices—use and sell drugs. I got to get out and start a new life—be productive...be lenient with me."

A drug addict charged with two counts of armed robbery states: "I was not what you would call a bad child to my parent. I went to school everyday, brought home good grade's, then, I met a guy who was cool, exleast [sic] that's what I thought until one day, I woke up and found myself doing things that, I shouldn't of been doing.... I'm not trying to say that my habits are what made me do the things that I've done, but that they do play a big part of things in my life. I know what I done was wrong, and I would true like to say that I'm very sorry for my action and would do anything that I can to show those that I hurt that I'm not a (bad) [sic] guy."

A female offender who knifed her boyfriend wrote, "I knew he is an obsessive person, I knew that he would harm me which he has done before. I was not only in fear for myself but also for my son." There is no domestic tranquility in many of these homes, disrupted by alcohol, anger, rivalry and drugs, and often the lack of a strong father figure. Domestic violence is not only between man and woman, however, at times two women are involved. "Yes, I did fight this woman, but only with my bare hands," said one female inmate, while another, who stabbed her own mother, stated that she did so while under the effect of delusional ideas and prey to auditory hallucinations. "What I need is treatment," said this young inmate, "as an inpatient—and in a long term place."

One female inmate who admits to using drugs and to prostituting herself to get the money for them begs for understanding from the bench when saying: "I am willing to swear under oath or the Bible or take a lie detector test as to my innocence [of the crime committed]. I am not proud of using [drugs] but I don't want to be labeled a pusher—it has destroyed my life and many more." Another female offender pleaded guilty to her offense but at the same time accused the police officers of throwing her against a wall, and "next day I was throwing up blood and I miscarried my baby."

One offender wanted to communicate to a judge what he considers to be the real facts in the offense of first-degree reckless homicide of which he was found guilty and sentenced when requesting a sentence modification. After stating that his victim was on cocaine and jealous of him and had beaten him with a baseball bat, he asserted that wanting to defend himself, he found a .380 handgun in the trunk of his car (instead of the crowbar he had intended to get) and claimed that during the struggle the gun went off accidentally. He claimed that "had my father been in the house while I was growing up, I believe I would not have gotten away with near as much as I did. This would have taught me a level of discipline that would have carried on into adulthood. A father figure is crucial to growing up." In his letter he expresses his fear of retaliation and asks for a transfer to another state. "The victim had friends and family who would definitely be disturbed by my presence in the community. I do not know how far they would go to seek revenge. I don't want any further confrontation," he wrote. Stating that he is not worried about finding a job, he wrote, "The job market appears to be tough, which is a myth.... The unemployment rate is so high because people don't want to work anymore. I will do any kind of work." He ends his letter by stating: "I am afraid of prison, I am afraid of the state of mind that I would end up with after an extended period of incarceration." The above are very important reflections. They are, unfortunately, post-offense reflections!

The following are the thoughts from confinement of an "unpretentious," as he calls himself, 30-year-old felon who believes himself to be rehabilitated and states:

> Since my transformation into the new self, each morning I look into the mirror glancing at one who loves, has joy, peace, mercy, kindness, self-control, practical wisdom, and has self-rehabilitated himself. I need to be in society providing human resources for schools and other agencies assisting in the development of young teens in the inner cities, and offering any testimony to the lost souls on drugs and other addictive substances.... After countless trials, testings and tribulations in my 30 years of life I finally found a hope, a purpose, a point. This Spirit tells me to "Love thy neighbor as they self." Therefore there is no room for immorality, impurity, sensuality, enmities, strife, jealousy, outbursts of anger, disputes, dissension, enving, drunkeness, carousing, murder or attempt.

Another prisoner, convicted of forgery, communicating with the judge, wrote extensively about helping others, his feelings at the loss of several close family members, and finding new hope.

Most of all [I'm] looking to be loved by my family who playes with my emotions, and who also loves power, and control.... Today i'm a man first, and, secondly a man child with a lot of inner child that's comes out. I never truly had a real child-hood being that I had adult responsabities...help taking care of my grand-parents as well as my baby brother who's handicap.... I'm worried "yes I'm worried" and, scared to death this time more so than ever before.... But I realize that I'm criminal still. But willing to make the complete turn in my life. I do take full responsibility for my past, and present actions. I knew I had choices but to only choose wrong over right, just because my family wouldn't except [sic] me. I should have love myself first, just wanting to be excepted [sic].... From [year] to [year] it's been one hell of a nightmare, just like being condem was like an eternal punishment.... But through it all I was smart enough to get my diploma. I got my G.E.D. General Education Diploma.... I do have my carpentry, and, masonary certification along with survival skill self-help, and, many other academic courses of studies doing [sic] my periods of being incarcerated.... I went through a truly real extreme intense drug, and, alcohol treatment program for 90 days.... I went to [a local technical college]...only to fall short by half a semester...due to people pleasing and overextending my hand being more help to others than I was to myself.... I got married [and] I've gotten lost in trying to help my soon to be ex-wife. She had so many demands of me, and, not only that she took me through the ringer as well.... Doing this time I was a full time student...in the evening I was running drug, and, alcohol classes, and, teaching sober living skills to those in the halfway house 3-times a week.... I was a volunteer board member for project return along with weekend meeting and a basket-ball player for [another] halfway house. The lost of my grand-mother that hurted because we were closer than my mother, and, I. Then I had an uncle who was ill, and, unable to care for himself so I took it upon myself to care for him giving my best.... But then...I lost my uncle and, I was very angry "but at who?" Now I begain to find myself, wanting to fall back into those old patterns, but something wouldn't allow me to. That's when I begain to go back to meetings, and, more meetings just to keep my head on straight.... Then my wife moves her brothers in our house, both of her brother is gang relates.... And now our marriage is getting rockey but through it all I stay clean, and, free.... My wife was still drinking, and, doing drugs.... I just had found out that my favorite aunt was dying.... I was the son she never had, and, she was the mother to me I never had...so I left school to help take care of her.... I started back drinking heavily trying to hide my hurt, and, pain. Then...drugs begain to come in...[and] the only thing I had was my wife and she didn't make matters any better.... One night while leaving my aunt's house I was shot twice...[and] I still have a bullet...but..I thank god for blessing me to live because the doctors told me that I wouldn't be able to work again because where the bullet lays.... Later...I had to be rushed back into the hospital [for surgery].... My wife was unable to take care for me because of the alcohol, and, drugs. So I had to return home with my mom for awhile.... I had to start making the correct choices in my life.... I started worked for the city...and still is a [work supervisor].... I met a beautiful person...a christian person.... I was a strong man...but I never had a strong woman to stand with me, and having good qualities. She just made me complete.... An what makes my life even better is because I know god [by her] helping me showing me the way god has truly made the difference in my life [ellipses in original].

One inmate echoes a theme that has a lot of truth: "Unlike my father, I want to take care of my children, if you give me a chance," adding that he is not a risk. Another explains the reason why some inmates accept plea bargaining.

I've never in my life been involved in a situation such as this one in my intire life. Your honor sir I've never been involved in any case where there was bodily harm or a threat to do so to any human being in today's society. Sir I've never even owned a weapon in my life, because of the fact that I do not like that type of life style where there is a need of such violence. Sir I am a high school graduate, and has had a lot of experience in jobs, educational skills and so forth. Your honor sir, I truly want to make it in this world and be something positive to me, my family and also in today's society. You honor I would truly like to prove my family that I...can be a positive role model in this state and in my community.... Because of today's younger generation no one seem's to have strong trust in today's young men. Sir I was so afraid of the outcome of this case that I took a plea bargin for something that I truly *did not do.* Your honor sir I was afraid to face a jury because I've been in trouble before, but sir never an incedent such as this.... I truly hate to be another satistic in the [state] prison system.... If I must go to prison [I ask] that I be sentence with a sentence that will allow me to return to society at a young man's age where I'll still have a chance to set a positive goal in my life and pursue in some type of career where my family con look a me and say look at [name] he sure has got his self together.

I had a chance but I blew it, says one inmate.

I do not blame any one by my self...for my violating one of my DIS rules.... I was going thru a lot of family problem's.... I use the only resource I know by running away from the problem insteady of asking for help.... I have been involve with a program call Partnership here...which helps you deal with problem that may arrive while out on DIS.... If a problem arrives I need to deal with the problem insteady of running off.... Since being place on DIS I have became a father and I have became a better person with in my self.... At night I lay in my bed and wish and pray that I had the chance to start my life over again, to be a man, that was helping buld in the commiuty insteady of being lock away from the commiuty.... I'm asking for that chance to be a responable man...too become once again a tax paying

citzen.... I can be one of law abideng citzen. I promise this day as a man
and Father, that I will never brake the law for any reason.... I come to realize that by me braking the law, I'm hurting more than just my self, I'm hurting my son, because the he has know father to talk too, I'm hurting my wife
to be, because the man she love is not there to support her, I'm hurting my
mother because the son she brought to the world to be some one is lock up.
Your Honor I'm asking you to look in to your heart and help this black man
to be some one, that the world will be proud of...please give me that chance
by giving me probation.

Gangs are present in some neighborhoods and people often fear
for their lives. The fear of becoming a victim is given by some inmates
as the cause of their homicides. One young male stated, "I am not a
killer, Your Honor, my action was motivated by fear–fear of becoming another black victim in the streets of the city." Several offenders
plead fear and self-defense, as in the following letter: "They began
shooting and I ran for cover. I was afraid. The phone was upstairs.
The only thing I could do is to shoot back." Another stated, "I bought
a gun because me and my wife and kids moved to a bad neighborhood
and I felt like I needed it for protection. I was drunk and on drugs at
the time of the shooting," and then added: "I want to be a father to
my kids and a husband to my wife. Give me a chance, please!"
Another younger inmate also writes about how difficult it is to live in
a community filled with sudden, unexpected criminal behavior. "I
live in a dangerous neighborhood and have a young wife and 2 little
girls who are dependent upon me. So, at the time, I felt it was necessary to own a gun." While assuming the responsibility for having committed his felonious crime, as did the previous offender, he admitted
to being intoxicated during the period of his offense. He described the
offense accurately down to the last detail in his attempt to prove his
lack of intention to shoot and to show the provocation on the part of
the victim. He stated, "I should know better than playing with guns.
This is a senseless tragedy. I am not placing all the blame on alcohol,
it was my stupidity. I am a young man and young people often forget
their responsibility." Yet another young defendant, admitting to being
guilty of armed robbery, wrote interestingly to the judge: "I am guilty
of first-degree stupidity."

A nineteen-year-old defendant charged with first-degree intentional homicide and attempted first-degree intentional homicide wrote to
the judge prior to sentencing about his dysfunctional upbringing and
his constant fear of being killed in jail. "I come from a Single-parent

household. My mother was involved in an affair or relationship with a person who was very abusive and took things from the house.... I tried to do anything I could to help her in that situation. I eventually pulled out of school in the 10th grade and took a job to help her with food and bills. I understand I'm going to go to prison and I will use that time to complete my education. I want you to know that I am very sorry and I regret even being in a situation like this.... I wanted her [the mother of the victim] to clearly understand that I was acting in self defense, for fear of my life. I was constantly being confronted at Gun Point by these men. I new sooner or later I would either wound up severely hurt or dead. That last incident they came armed to rob or kill me.... I ask that you please give me a chance to prove myself worthy of living a productive citizen in the community. I have found God and God has found me and I know he will strengthen me." He ended by expressing his fear that the same men might try to kill him in jail.

Some inmates have good insight into the consequences of their conduct on their family: "My brothers and sisters have given up on me because of my past. I believe they are carrying around my sins, and not forgiving me. That is their choice since that is the way they feel. I know I have let them down many times–thru my previous incarcerations. I guess they want to see my actions and not lip service as my sister says."

Prison life is not an easy one. Many inmates write about the inter-personal difficulties they encounter. "I am having a hard time making it day by day in here, because I don't belong to a gang, or have any war stories of how many people I shot, or how much dope I sold, I don't fit in," wrote one man.

The following is the sad story written to a judge by a man charged with battery:

> My wife and I have been together for 22 years. Her parents died when she was 6 years old. So me and my peoples were like her family. Me and her started getting on each other nerves when she was about 13 years of age because she had a problem running off with strangers and staying gone for weeks at a time.... We started living together when she was 18, she still would run off. I use to tell her that she could get hert running around in the streets.... I have slapped her a few times and she would call the Police on me, but a few other times she called the Police on me just to get rid of me.... I just didn't want anything to happin to her in them streets.... I'm in jail now because I came home from work one day, and some guy called for her and

I ask him what was his reason for wanting my wife and he told me F me and hung up. So I ask my wife about it and she jumped in my face and told me don't worry about hew it was, I pushed her back off me, She grabbed me and we started restling and we fell and she hit her head on the window seel.... It was my falt...[but] I just don't won't you to think I was just beating her. She use to call the Police on me and tell them I did something to her just to get me out the house.... We got married...and had three girls hew I realy love. Shes with onther guy now agin but this time I'm going to get a Divorce and let her live her life.... I wrote you because I know once I got in front of you I would have got tong tied so Thank You for hearing me out."

An electronic bracelet is sometimes requested on the basis of a family's medical need, as by the following inmate who says: "The reason I solicit the electronic bracelet is because my wife is in poor health, actually very ill and when she goes to the doctor and she does that frequently, she has no one to look after the 2 very young children." But children, illness and family dysfunction are not justifications for granting special requests, even though such decisions may face the family of the inmate with problems of a practical nature. These same factors may have contributed to the inmate's behavior.

Even though inmates never express satisfaction with their being confined, at times, when incarceration is not too long, for some of them it appears to be a kind of respite from their homelessness, their continuous rejection by society, their fear of being mugged, assaulted or killed, and their fear of behaving criminally because of hunger, illicit drug or alcohol use, or their deep hostility. One offender who admitted to using drugs on the outside and had been charged with battery to a police officer wrote, "Basically, I have no one to look after if I am released onto the streets again. I have been getting raped by men—and women have been trying.... My mother has a bad heart and my sisters constantly kick me out of the house because they do drugs and drink.... I am very safe in here and they have all the facilities I need, doctors, lawyers, nurses, and the most important *my medication!*"

Throughout the many letters we reviewed we found frequent reference to the offenders' mothers. The mothers seem to be very close and dear to them, and rarely are they thought of as "no good." For many prisoners, their mother or grandmother or aunt are important persons who tried to buffer the consequences of their clash with societal rules. This is how one of them expresses it: "Judge, I am embarassed and ashamed of myself in the eyes of my relatives, the Great Spirit, and most of all, my mother. My mother did not raise me to turn out the way I did. I feel I have disgraced her with my failures."

Occasionally, one encounters a person who can be considered a real smooth psychopath who nevertheless has some insight into the importance and the negative effect of his dysfunctional family upbringing.

> My mother knew I was different as a child and she did all that she could to help me, but my learning problem was too much for her. As time went on we grew apart and the only person who really understood me did not know me anymore. This really hurt! So I used drugs until I really hit the bottom of my life. I became sick and denied my problems. I asked God to help me to get off drugs and to help me in winning back my mother's love. I took time, but eventually she became to trust me and even depend on me. I can't tell you how good that made me feel.... My biggest concern in life is being a loving and honest son to my mother and a loving and devoted father to my children.

Beautiful words that, unfortunately, are not integrated into the offender's personality and behavior, because, he writes: "The salesman let me test drive the car. The car ran out of gas. While at a gas station the car was stolen. I had left the keys in.... I was afraid to call and tell the car owner or the police what had happened." In the last words, he crystallizes his psychopathic behavior: "I acted without thinking. This has been one of the biggest problems in my life. I have always found it easier to run and hide from my feelings.... I have been lying, pretending and being dishonest since I was a kid."

The last seven letters that we report almost in their entirety belong to people ranging in age from fifteen to twenty-three years who have been charged with first-degree intentional homicide while armed, contributing to the delinquency of a child, death as consequence of first-degree reckless homicide while armed, second-degree reckless homicide while armed, and causing the death of a girlfriend by drenching her body with gasoline and setting her on fire. The letters address their feelings of shame or remorse (one for having killed his adopted son), their thoughts and feelings about their mothers, the defense of their mothers for their upbringing, their apologies to the mothers of their victims, their feelings of guilt, their acceptance of due punishment, their not wanting to become a statistic, their assumption of their responsibility, their thoughts about the jail/prison and imprisonment, the gun jungle in which they lived, their illicit drug and alcohol addiction. As previously, we have left the following letters as written by the prisoners, without corrections.

A fifteen-year-old drug house lookout who murdered for his boss and who was sentenced to life imprisonment without parole eligibility until December 2025 wrote:

First of all I want to say to the Family & Friends of [the victim] that I can't find the words to let you know how sorry I am for the pain & souffering I have caused you bey committing this needless act. I can now understand how deeply you must miss talking to him, laughing with him, hugging and crying with him. For this I am sorry And I hope that you and god will forgive me I pray that god will comfort you & will ease the pain that I have caused you.

I am speaking out of my hart that what I done was verey stupid. I would like to say that I am sorry for what I done and being in here for 8 months made me think that what I done was wrong. I am not trying to convince you to letting me out on the streets this day but I am trying to convince you into letting me have a chance to start a new life.

I have never denied my involvement in this. You see I could not Live with myself Knowing I was responsible for taking the life of someone. My guilt was responsible for me turning myself in and cooperating with the Authorities. And though I dread this moment, I am grateful to god for giving me a conscience. Looking back, there are many things I would have done differently, & Avoiding drugs & my so-called friends would be first on the list.

At night I can't sleep I tose and turn thinking about that night over and over again. I hope the victoms family forgives me for what I have done. But now all I can do is accept the penalty for the crime I committed.

I am so verey sorry!!

An inmate convicted of contributing to the delinquency of a child leading to his death wrote the following letter:

Dear Honorable Judge:

I am writing to say I'm sorry for what has happened. The lost of my friend has affect me in more way than one, I hate that this incident ever happened. But now that it has, I have to take my punishment like a man.

The time that I have spent in the...jail has made me realize, what my faults were and that I have to improve myself before I become another statistic. I am ready to turn my life around totally for my child. I want to be a postive role model for my unborn child. While here I have enroled myself into G.E.D. After receiving my G.E.D. I am going to take courses in social work. I have choosen this career because I want to help other young men and women like me. If our youth can see that someones cares and they see someone who has been through the same things they are going through it might help. To make a differences in someone's life.

I believe by turning myself in has proving to myself and every one else that our responsibilites are our own, they just won't disappear. While in jail I have gotten to know God and to depend on him more. I now see where the streets can get you. I guess I had to learn the hard way and now I see I am just hurting myself and my love ones.

I am ready to be a man and do manly things. I now see to get treated like a man you have to behave like a man. To think and act like one. I am going to take a active role in my child life, to be more postive and I now realize that there is no drug on the street that can uplift me like God. I'm going to leave drugs and alcohol alone for my and my child's sake. I am determined to be a good father.

I feel one of the reasons that I was out in the streets is because I had no father to look up to. I'm not trying to blame my father its partialy my fault becaus of poor judgment. But if my father would have been a good role model been there for me I wouldn't be suffering the way that I am. My child doesn't have to look else where for comfort because I will be there.

The following letter was written by an inmate convicted of first-degree reckless homicide while armed.

Dear Judge:

As I sit here in the...jail, I contemplate my Life & realize how easily things can happen; & lives can be changed. I am deeply remorseful for everyone concerned, the vicitm & the family of the vicitm as well as mine. While I know, I cannot undo what is done, I can try to mold my life, and correct the error of my past. With positive thoughts and thinking things over, I feel very sorry for what has happened, and I pray and ask for forgiveness the whole situation Caught me by surprise, if I have ever regretted anything in life. God only know, that what has me standing in your presence today, is truly a mistake and was in no way planned that is the truth so help me God. I've asked God to forgive me & I ask this court to have mercy on me. With respect, I humble myself & ask meekly for some consideration and guided direction.

The following letter was written by an offender convicted of second-degree reckless homicide while using a weapon.

Dear Judge:

I am writing this letter to let you know how I feel about the victim and the seriousness of the crime. I am very apolgatic that this took place and someone was killed due to my reckless conduct. I am sorry that [the victim] was taken away from her love ones and doesn't have a chance at life or to see her babies grow up. I am also sorry for all the pain and sorrow and tears that I have made her mother and love ones shed in the past few month's due to my misconduct and carelesness. [The victim] was a close friend of mine's and I have felt'ed a lot of pain and sorrow since her death also. I have also lost'ed a lot of rest and shed many tears knowing that, I have took another human being life plus a close friend. I know I have not shed'ed as many tears or felt'ed as much pain as her family has thoe but I have felt'ed some. I also am sorry to my mama and family for putting them thru all the pain and tears I have made them shed over the last 5 months. They have not felt the same pain that [the victim's] family has felt'ed but they have felt the pain of losing someone also. I have hurt many people that did not deserve to be hurt. My mother and family lost their love one me to a prison cell due to my reckless behavior. I know that this would never happen if I would have never been drinking and smoking weed cause I would'nt had the Gun and would had took it out. I know that this type of Accident will never happen again. When I get out prison or in Life cause I am never using alcohol or drugs again. This offense has taught me How thoe's two things can destroy your life. Another reason that it won't happen again cause I am not going to put myself in this type of situation or the type of crowd who get involve in thoes type of things anymore. I will like to close this by saying I am sorry that [the victim] is not here and I am the cause of that and if I could give up my life to brings her back I will do that in a heart beat. I apologize for this offense happening.

The next letter was written by a man convicted of first-degree intentional homicide, and being party to a crime.

Judge...,

First of all I would like to apolize to the [victim's] family & friends I'm so sorry I did not leave home to hurt anyone I don't know why it just happen. Please please forgive me.

To you Judge I would like to said I don't know what happen me and two friends left my home at.... I did not carry a gun with me my friend had it. We went to [an area in the city] to buy drugs. When we bought the drugs and began to leave all these boys start rushing us. I don't know who fired the first shot but I remember my friend throwing the gun to me. I do know that I did fired that gun.

If I could turn back the hands of time I would have listen to mother never would have let my friends move into my home. She told me not too but I didn't listen. I thought she just wanted me to stay home with her. Everyone wants to blame my mother for what I did but Judge my mother worked all her life to give me the better things in life. We had our own home car best of clothes and I never went hungry or was without food to eat. She kept trying to talk to me and my brother but a hard heads leaves you to where I'm at now. I know that I hurt the [victim's] family. But not half as much as I hurt my mother. She age ten year losing weight and tell me she's not sleeping. Please tell my mother I'm so sorry.

I guess my trouble started when I drop out of school but where ever I go the first thing I want to do is to go back to school. Maybe learn how to grow up. Maybe all those thing my mother try to teach me will help me up there. You know Judge I've never stole anything in my life. I've never hurt anyone knowing. I love my family and I know they will be there for me even in jail. My mother told me she love me and she's going to be there for me that's all I need.

To you judge and the [victim's] family I'm sorry what happen to there son but if [my coactors] tell the truth they will tell you I wasn't there. [Compare this with his admission of having had the gun thrown to him.] I do know who was there But since you not going to have the person that was with me on the [second victim's case] stand trial. That means you only wanted me. Because not one person ever asked my antying really but my lawyer. Police just told me I would neve see the out side again. They told me that five min after my step father bought me down there.

I know that my [relative] will be in court will you please tell her how sorry I am. Some one shot up my house she lost her eye she's only fourteen years old. So you see Judge how many people I hurt. But please tell the [two victims'] family I'm sorry and that I'm hurting just as much. I'll never be a father I'll never see my mother everyday my [relatives] until visiting day. Tell my brother... to please listen to mama. I don't want him here that would kill mama. Tell [my male friend] thanks for being there for me. Tell...that try to be a father to me I wish I would have listen to him.

Please I know it's a lot to ask you. But I'm asking you to please run all my time together. I'll leave it to you for the time I just hope its not life. I've never been really in troubel except for not going to school

Thank you for listening,

The next letter was written by an inmate convicted of first-degree reckless homicide while armed and being party to a crime.

I no I did wrong, but I promise I'll never do wrong again. Something told me not to go that way. I didn't no that was going to happen. I guess being with the wrong people can get you in the wrong place. All I wanted is some gas for my car...and as we was walking past them they started to shot at us, but they really was shoting at [my coactor].

I ran behind a car, and [my coactor] continue to shot back.... I'm real sorry that a person died and for the family that raised him. You have to understand that I don't want my family to see me like this. It's like my whole family been in and out of jail. I don't want to be like them. If you this (sic) give me another chance I promise you'll never see me again. I promise and I'm beging you. (please). I'm not a bad person. I was just with a bad person. This is a serious case. So I want lie to you, I did have a gun, but I did not shot it. [My coactor] have a shot gun he shot it one time. I guess he had bad luck. By he only shoting one time. I don't think [he] killed that person from one shot. I think they shot they own friend. They was shoting like five or more guns at us. but if you do give me alot of time, I no that's the law, and that's the way life is. But I'm still leting you no that I can do better. So I pray to God that you'll never see me never again. My first case and it had to be something serious. I no you have alot of letters from other people to read, so please don't think of me like other people,

some people just write just to be doing something and they no they did it. So I need you to look at me diffent then all the other.
Please think about it, I don't belong behind glass window.
Sincerity, Your's

The following excerpts are from a letter written by an offender convicted of causing death by drenching his girlfriend's body with gasoline and setting her on fire.

Dear [Victim's Mother]: I'm writing this letter praying that God will unharden your heart and allow you to forgive me for what I had done and appreciate what I have become, A CHILD OF GOD!!.... Not a day has gone by that I have not prayed for you and your family and for [the victim] to hear my prayers. [The victim] and I were trying to change our lives but we kept procrastinating and would not let God enter into our lives. As I look back and reflect on the past, I wish that when I first met you I would have taken heed to your prayers.... I do want you to know that I am not nor have been a violent person. When you are on drugs, you tend to react in a different way. There are the times when [the victim] and I had misunderstandings. Our relationship for the most part was based on drugs. As we began to know one another, we became inseparable, we became attached; WE WERE IN LOVE.... I prayed each and every day that the time would come when I could write and apologize for my actions on the night of [the offense]. I want you to know that I have remorse for what I did and I'm taking on the responsibility for my actions. Also, I did not have a jury trial so that you and your family could be spared continued suffering.

An offender, physically abused as a child and guilty of having killed his adopted son wrote a lengthy letter to the judge in an attempt to explain his actions. Some excerpts are reported below. The ellipses are in the original.

I've never wrote anyone a letter before.... I'm very afraid and very remorseful for what I did.... I never meant to.... What happend that day makes me more than sick, it makes me feel like dying. Not to escape punishment, but to stop the pain.... I never considered myself suicidal.... I had to live thru my mothers many suicide attempts, and I'll never forget how sad that made me. But now, I feel exactly what she went thru. I never imagined how many people actually thought that I hated my little boy.... I didn't spoil him, because he was a boy, And I cant believe that ws mistaking for hatred.... I took him everywhere with me...I was proud to have him as a son. My friends would say to me, Why are you bringing him, why are you taking care of the next mans kid, and why would you go and have a baby with someone who already has a kid by someone else. I loved [my son] so much, that what they said never bothered me....
When I close my eyes, I see my little boy just lying there, with me

breathing in him, reliving how scared I was, how sorry I was.... None of the pain [suffered in my lifetime] even combined compares to what I go thru daily because of this.... People say I hated my son...who never had even one conversation with me.... When I was asked I use to say, This is my little boy, not, this is my girlfriends little boy, but my little boy.... It took me almost a whole year before I confessed to my mother he wasnt.... It felt bad to lie to my mother, so one day I told her the turh,...and said no,...but he was.... I keep thinking my little boy will never grow up. How I put him in a cold dark place, when I was suppose to protect him.... I keep thinking how could this happen to my little boy, after all I went thru and swore not to do to my kids. When I was very little...my father left me at the hands of my mother.... I still love my mother very much. But from then until I met [the boy'-mother] my life was pure hell. It started with my grandmother and uncle beating me and my brother. My grandmother use to ask me if I had done something wrong that day, and I'd say no.... Then she'd beat my anyway, and say, that because we both know you will. I hated my grandmother for a long time.... At the funeral I remember thinking, I'm probably the only one here who isn't crying because she's gone!... I cried because I hated seeing my mother so hurt.... I just couldnt bring myself to feel anything for her, it was to hard.... One time...[my grandmother] told my uncle to whoop me after she had whooped me.... When he went to hit me a second time...I tried to snatch away and he hit me in the private.... He...said he was sorry, and I forgave him, but I never forgot.... My grandmother was the worse, she'd hit you with what ever she had in her hands, or...the extention cord...or the swicth, or the belt.... The beatings lasted a few more years, but her mental abuse...until she died.... My family didnt stick by my mother after what happened to my father.... They would call her a Killer...and she would try to kill herself.... I hated how they did my momma. She didn't deserve that.... Someone...used to come in my room at night and say, "Your dadds gonna get'cha." Id start screaming, jump out of bed an run for the door, but they would hold it shut...until I kept screaming and my mother would get up.... My mother thinks I hate her...but...I love her more than anything.... Whenever [my mother] was left alone she would try [suicide].... Sometimes I would just sit and cry and watch her sleep...[and] everyone use to say to me..."Except my Mother."...that I was going to grow up to be a fag if I kept crying so much.... I started to skip school. My family said it was because I was lazy, My grandmother said I just need a whooping. But...there were no gangs, or drugs that I knew of [then], or even other kids skipping school, it was just me.... I was ten years old.... All I could think about was my momma. And that was more important to me than school. But when I did go I got good grades.... [Holidays] I spent at home.... [My family] would come together for one day of pretending,... I wasn't going to be apart of it. I continued to skip school. My first day back...the teacher [told] the other kids...to feel sorry for me because I had lost my dad. Then...they would make fun of me.... When I got to the seventh grade,...I didn't even know

how to do the work.... The teacher said,...What am I going to do with you....
I couldn't believe a techer had actually embarrassed me like that.
Everybody laught at me...and it hurted. I never forgot it, or botherd to
come back.... They tried everything to get me back interested in school....
I really tried, but I could not do it.... I didn't know anything.... If it wasnt
for my mother needing me, I would have left this hell along time ago....
After my dad passed we...moved to an all white community.... [Our friend]s
parents didnt like us.... I talked proper...called talking white...so [the new
black kids] beat me up, and pick on my [semi retarded] brother....
[Mamma's] protecting me made things even worse.... Id rather get beaten
up than [get called sissy, momma's boy, etc].... I made friends with...a real
trouble maker. I was a kid, so I was no angel myself...but things I did...hurt
myself. But things he liked to do hurt other people...[and] he would blame
it on me.... Rumors started to surface, about me being the neighborhood
hoodlum...."

The offender gives a lenghthy account of his troubled youth leading to the day when his mother caught him in the house with a girlfriend and "for the first time in life,...I spoke back.... She came around
the corner and up the stairs with a knife in her hand.... I was scared....
She had never done anything like this to me before...." He ran out but
then turned back:

> Everything I had ever did for my mother came back. All the times my
> grandmother beat me and I didnt say nothing 'cause that was her mother.
> All the times they would call her a murderer and I'd say, I still love my
> momma. All the times I stayed up crying, holding empty pill bottles beg-
> gin her to just wake up.... All the times I watcher her scream and cry her-
> self to sleep and would crawl into bed with her so she wouldnt have to cry
> alone. All the times I got beaten up because of what happenen to my own
> dad!!!! And didn't say nothing because it would have made her relapse.
> The education I started throwing away in the fifth grade, just to be at home
> to protect her from herself.

The prisoner continues at length in recounting the teasing, ridicule
and beatings that he was subjected to while growing up, and then
states:

> I hit her, I hated it and myself. I dont care what she did to me or what she
> tried to do thats still my mother and I love her very much.... That happend
> over eight years ago and I still wake up at night asking God to forgive me.
> After that happend I became a loner.... I use to just let people say anything
> [to ridicule me] or stand there and let people beat on me and hit on me....
> [but] I seemed I was always getting used and I hated it.... [Then] I became
> mean just to keep a girl [not physically mean].... Worse I acted the more
> they like me...[but] it was a lie not the real me. You cant live a lie forever....

Things never were the same between me and my mother. I remember how I felt the second after I hit her. I wanted to grab her and tell her how sorry I was. I just wanted to die because we had been thru so much. I felt as if for the first time, I was letting go of her hand and turning on her to stand and say with all our other family members,... "You Killer!!.... You Murderer!!!...." I actually said those things to her. Not because I wanted to, but because she had hurt me so bad.... I didnt mind taking care of my mother...but living with my [step] father was different.... The roaches were so bad you had to plug up your ears at night. They were real bad at night, they would get in the refrigerator, jump off the ceiling, get in the boxes of cereal, when you would get up at night to go the bathroom there would be so many on the floor they would cruch under your feet. When you wake up in the morning they would have gotten tangled in your hair.... On my twenty third birthday I was jumped and beat up pretty bad by some friends.... They claimed...they never liked me.... I told my family...I fell.... I couldn't go back to hangin with my old friends...because they all had familys.... They had grown up, while I was just becoming a kid. By the time I had met...my sons mother, I was three...but by the time she had got me there was really nothing to get.... [Her son] was around from the beginning.... I had never dated someone with a kid because of jealous fathers. And I wasn't about to trust [my girlfriend] because I had heard it all before.... I wasn't about to get fooled again. But [she] was different.... She had also been abused.

He describes his girlfriend's sexual abuse while she was growing up and their life together. Then, he wrote:

I told my mother everything [my girlfriend] and myself had been thru.... Me and my mother talk every day now!!!! And that really hurts. It took the death of my son at my hands to get back something I lost because of the same damned hands!!! [You don't know]...how scary it is...not to stop looking at your hands thinking about what you've done, and at the very same time not wanting to be condemned to prison for a major, major, horrible incorrectable accident!!!!!!!!!!!!!!... How can I be mad at [my girlfriend] for lying, When at first I didnt even have the courage to say I lost it, and that how my little baby boy died, I just lost it.... I've been a...coward all my life, and you have no idea what it feels like not to be able to stand up and say "This is what happend to my son." [I] was afraid to take my anger out on people who hurt me so I kept it all in until I lost it on my very innocent little boy.... My mother keeps saying God has the last and final say, and if its his will the truth will come out in the end.... [My girlfriend said] she knows in her heart that what happend was an accident."

He then writes of how his girlfriend came to visit him and told him how her family cannot understand how she can forgive him and still talk to him. He then adds:

The same family that didn't, couldn't protect her from her own father for over 11 years. Then force her not to press charge's, and then used the bible to make her forgive him.... Her mother talks about I hated my son,...but she never kept him. She acted as if it was [my girlfriend's] fault for getting raped by her dad and felt that it was a possiblility [the baby] could have been [her] Dad's.... Before [our daughter] was born I told her no matter if a boy or a girl, I would have rights as a parent and she or he would never go around her father, ever. She said...she would tell her father he could never keep are newest child.

He then describes how his girlfriend's father wanted to keep their baby girl and how he felt that she had broken a promise to him and was not trying to protect the children. But he couldn't stop the little boy from going over and he reports on how he would return home showing signs of abuse. He then describes his own physical abuse of the crying child:

I was under a lot of stress...and I told him to shut up and kicked him with the side of my foot. Nothing had ever happend like that before and never happend again. But every time he fell after that, every stratch, every nic, everyone thought I was beating him.... And when he got burnt that day...that really did it...that I would intentionally burn my own little boy.... Even what my mother said was twisted and distorted to be used against me.... I've been dealing with pain since before I learned how to walk.... They're even trying to say because of what I did Im also responsible for my little girls injury's.... People always assume because you did this, you must have done that! Or people who hurt there children hate them. Only because its easier to understand. I will never say I hated my kids, just so someone else can understand why this happend. I love both my kids, my mother and [my girlfriend] more than myself. The most honest explanation I can give is, everything in me, I mean all the stuff I had came out in just a few seconds.... I loved being a father...but I didnt know how to be the perfect dad. I had no parenting skills at all. I just tried to remember how my grandmother would handle the sittuation, and do the opposite.... What happend wasn't done out of malice of intentional, I just couldnt get my thinking back, it was like it was gone!! My self control was gone.... He kept screaming...he never cried when we were alone. I asked him I asked him to please stop, whats wrong?!! He just kept screaming...he kept screaming!!!... He kept screaming!!!... He still kept screaming....I said, be quiet.... God make him stop!!!... I said,...shut up!!!... I know I finished what I was saying I just couldn't hear anymore.... I could see him and he was still crying but I couldnt hear him. I dropped to my knees and I couldn't even feel myself hitting...all I know is that I didnt hit him in the face.... I wasnt trying to discipline him scare him or kill him, I was trying really hard to gain my control back. It took me only seconds,...but that was to long.... I had never felt like I just lost it..... I didnt even know I was crying.... The little boy I was suppose to protect, raise and teach was just laying there.... Why couldnt it come out on all those people who gave me all that stuff in the first place. Why take it out on my mother, even tho she hit me first or on my son just because he kept screaming. You see...there is always some excuse, I say well this or that happend thats why I had no control but...Im really scared and Im begging you to help me. I talk to the other people in here and they say it doesnt bother them that they've killed someone, that its a way of life to sell dope or rob somebodys momma even to kill or be killed doesnt scare them.

They say its no problem to do 2 to 3 years. Two people said they could do it standing on there heads. I met a man who says this is his fourth time going to prison. He asked me if this was my first time I said yeah, he said dont worry youll get use to it. As if I had made plans for the future to just give up and throw my life away.... I envy those who dont feel because it hurt real bad when you do.... I remember thinking a lot, "I wish I had somebody to listen to me. So...those people didnt have to say all those lies to hurt me or claim that I hated my son.... Sometimes tho...when I feel the world thinks I did, I wish that I did, so the hurt would go away, but I hurt everday all day long. You can break out of jail and run, but if all of the pain and punishment is right there inside you, where on earth can you run to.

Some time later, the same prisoner wrote another brief note to the judge:

Im writing to say Im going to school now!!! My Teacher's said Im real smart and I do good work.... I have to admit the other letter about me, my son and what happend was my very first letter to someone and I used a dictionary to help me spell some of, a lot of the words.... I tried to teach myself at home.... I learned what I could but without a teacher to explain some of it was really hard.... Im not saying Im glad I came to jail or anything stupid like that, but it feels good to be in some kind of school again.... There was a guy who didnt even know as much as I, so I helped him out!!!! Now that felt really nice.... Ive got to help myself so I'll be able to help others someday.... Ive never been to prison, its real scary to think about. People say you come out worse than when you went it. Is that true?... Will I get messed up in there?.... Please Please dont think Im bad or that I cant change. Because I think I can. No I know I can. Please dont give up on me now!!!! Help me please!! I'll do what ever you say just please get me some help. I should have asked for help a long time ago. But how many kids tell that there being abused and many of those are believed?!! Now imagine a grown 25 year old man saying I was abused. And who could I have told? My mother? She had enough problems. My teachers? I wasnt in school long enough.... When I say there was no one to tell I mean there was no one believe me please. There isnt always an immediate solution to big family problems. And the longer you keep a secret the harder it is to tell. I'll forever be sorry for what happend to my son, but for his and my daughter sake I cant just give up!

Finally, a prisoner found guilty of first-degree reckless homicide while armed wrote to the judge pleading for forgiveness, stating:

I'm not a bad man but a human that made a terrible mistake and bad judgment in life, that I'm realy sorry for and regret will all my heart. First of all I'll like to apologize to the [victim's family] for all the heart ach I cause & pain for one day they can reconcile with me and hope for forgiveness. Because the Lord knows I didn't mean to cause harm on anyone. My heart goes out to you all and May God bless you.

I was born...with a birth defect witch cause me to lose one kidney. I survived the operation leaving me the right one. Most of the time I spent in the hospital when I was home I didn't get to play as the other kids because I had to steady watch my side.... I grew up the youngest of six. I went to school as much as I could.... At 3rd grade I was placed on a LD class and that made thing even harder because people in school just look at you funny like you were an alien or something as I got in high school I learn how to hide until the bell rang for people wouldn't know were I was.... Some [classes] were ok but two I never got to ecept was math. soc.st. I told the teachers I wasn't good in math or soc. st. But every time I went in there they pick on me to do something I couldn't do or read. One day she call on me and I just got up and walk out and never returned because it seen like she like imbarassing me in front of all thoes people. It was easy for some people but hard for me. And they used to call me stupid or a learning dummy.... I went through a lot with the second youngest of my brothers he would always jump on me when my mother wasn't around because she would be at work or just out. He used to tease me an say I was adopted and I wasn't one of them he used to say can't you see you don't look like us or act like us time an time again he used to say that.... As years past my mother finaly told me the man she said was my father was realy my stepfather. Man why did she have to tell me that for it hurted me worse not know what my brother used to say I felt she had let me down the one I turned to the most. As time went on my stepfather left town and my father started coming around. I didn't know how to act because I was used to call the other man dady. My mother used to say act diffirent towers him because he is your father. But I was so used to my stepfather. As I got to know my father I found out he drank alot an that drew us father apart.... I couldn't come to him because he was drunk most of the time.... Time went so fast I found myself at his bedside of his death. I had pick him up at a tavern and gave him his car because he had just flew back in town from being down South at one of his family funeral. Two days later he was in the hospital with pneumonia.... I stayed at the hospital waiting for a change for him to come around. When he did...I look in his eyes and all you could see was a gaze over his eyes and darkness. It was like stairing in the eyes of death. Wich

I was an didn't know. All I can remember was holding his hand and him telling me he love me and that I was his only son. The monita went off...and 15-20 min later they came out and sayed he had past away.... I tryed to suport my mother but I just didn't know how to ecept death. Now time got rougher my father side didn't ecept me at all.... At the funeral...everone sits in the front they made me sit in the back.... It is realy hurts. Just knowing none of them realy cared.... It bad enough growing up without a father and when I finly got to get myelf together at the time I had 3 kids now I have four [children], a loving wife and mother. I saw how shot life realy was. I had to do my best to help my kids in every way I could. Spending more time with them teaching them right from wrong. My wife help me through all my rough times.... We been together now for six years very happy ones. She encourage me to do my best and not let other people get me down. The only thing I kept from her was that I was in a LD class that was because when we go by my cousin house to visit her little brother is in LD and she teases him be calling him a learning dummy. And I didn't want my wife to look at me funny.... I held down job after job trying to provide the best for my family. I made an oath to my wife and kids to stay away from trouble an jail. For I can always be there when they needed me. My wife also kept me out of trouble.... We started doing more family thing together...because I know I didn't get to know my father and I wasn't about to do the same to my kids.

Your Honor I never in my life tryed or wanted to hurt anyone. All I tryed to do was provide for my family an strive to be a better father to my children. I stop hanging around sertand people and with the help of my wife I keep out of the streets. Trouble every day I wake up wondering why me.... The Bible sayes God has a different call for everyone. Why did my calling have to be as serouse as this. God could have put me in a fatal car crash or I could have been born blind or pairlize.... The Lord says every problem in life has a meaning. But I see no meaning for this. My mother always tought me from right & wrong sence then I been doing to do what's right. I just wish I wouldn't have woke up that day of the accident. It hard to live with myself. First I like to deeply apolize to the [victim's] family for the wrong doing I have done an all the hurt and pain there going through. And if I had the power I would change things because I never ment to cause harm on him or anyone else. I used to watch the news and say to my wife I wonder what this world is comeing too. I tell my people to stay out of trouble now look at me. Because I know no mater what happens people are going to look down on me.... My wife says as long as the lord forgevess you everything is fine and you have to forgive your self. There's not a day that I don't hate myself for what has happen.... I know how bad it feel's in side to hurt.... I wake up crying wishing I was dead instead of [the victim].... I would have gaven my life for that day....

It all started when I woke up. I drop my wife off at work took my daughter to her grandmothers house and went back home to clean up.

About time I got through takeing a bath and cleaning up. It was time for me to pick my wife up from work on the way I ran in to my cousin and he ask for a ride over to our other cousin house. I said "ok" because it was on the way to pick my wife up.... What started out as droppen someone off ended up in a shooting. What started off as a conversation got out of hand. I got scared and afraid after that things happen so fast it was like time had speeded up. All I rember was I was walking down the street holding my head down shakeing my head.... I couldn't tell [my wife] what had happen because I didn't know. For months I couldn't eat sleep or talk to any one. All I kept doing was praying this was a nightmare. After I found out he had died I wanted to turn myself in but I was scared and afraid and sick.... All I could do is pray day & night for forgiveness. And please alow me to see the birth of my son and God can take it fom there....

I work all my life for me an my family to have something for I can give my kids the thing my father never gave me. All in 15 min everything I ever work for was gone.... Your honor I'm *very sorry* for what I *done*. Words can't exspain it at the time I was scared for me and my family all I could have known it could have been my wife, kids or even me who had got shot.... I can't talke to my wife because she can't handle it. I'm scared to tell my mother because she might fell bad. I fell ashame. She also might fell she didn't do a good job of raising me. All I do is pray to the Lord and ask for forgiveness and repentance. Deliverance. *There so many people down here on shooting cases and I can't belive I'm one of them. Some people think this is a joke or summer camp. But it's not. This is hard life, a wake up call an some too blind to see it.* [Emphasis added.] Most people in the justice systems are tired or just bent out about others that they don't care because the herd so many cases that they think everyone is the same. When some one comes in front of them they don't get a fair change because they let the personal feelings got in the way. We all are not just a number but humans that made a mistake. Some people in life don't get a secound change they just get lock up on the key gets thrown away.

Even Moses, Paul took a down fall an God still forgave them and gave them a scound change and made them great.... We all have fallen short of the Glory of God. So people say think before you act. Sometimes you don't have time to think.... I'm deeply sorry. I'm also sorry for bring this case infront of the judges, lawers, DA's. I deeply sorry. Please reconcile with me.... Please give me another change in life.... Please don't keep me from my kids for the rest of my life. Please alow me to give them some type of fathering. I know in life I wasn't perfect, but I never was the uncareing type nether.... All the hard work I done I pray this is not my pay. I let the community down, my family and every one else that belive in me. My father is dead and I still bring shame on his name.... My Apology and Heart goes out to the [victim's] family. Please forgive me for the heart ach I cause. Amen.

LETTERS ADDRESSING SOCIAL ISSUES

Even though the above letters occasionally touched upon cogent social issues, the following letters are almost totally concerned with social issues and their relationship to crimes and prisonization. Many of them are concerned with what is felt by the prisoners to be the inequality of treatment because of "skin color." Most of these excerpts are from letters to journalists, and their content is obviously different from those written to persons in the law enforcement or judicial fields. The authors shows good insight and interesting ideas, even though obviously one-sided at times. One of them, whose writing is quite well researched, also writes poetry. The ellipses are in the original.

I'm a black male in my early thirties, and yes, today I find myself enslaved in the midst of this world of new industrialized industries of human warehousing known as correctional institutions.... But this correspondence is about a problem which is plaguing society and literally destroying and wasting lives. Our politicians's, leaders and governors of these states have sought to cure this problem and epidemic by building more prisons and longer sentences of incarceration which are primarily directed to the African-American race.... Whenever the issue is brought forth of the double standard of how black Americans are sentence in criminal matters as opposed to their white bretherens its immediately down played by smooth talking politics, though the reality is blacks are punished more harsher.... I'm sadden, hurt, and filled with grief to encounter daily many young 15, 16, 17, 18 year old boys who have been sentence to life terms in these facilities with a chance of parole in 50, 60, 70 years, and now they want to send 10 year old kids to prison for life.... The mere word correctional derived from the word correct, which means to (change or modify a mistake) or a wrong decision one made in life.... In closing this correspondence...I would like to start a program that will help deter many of us from ever having to wake up in my present situation.... I believe people will tend to listen to real experiences especially when the person speaking of it is actually living it and they see its not just a story. I want to help my brothers and sisters find that lost respect for themselves, that dignity, morals, and principle. I want to help them find that love in their hearts for oneself and get back that self esteem removing the substance and material values from their lives.... For a whole year I tried killing myself. I even tied my sheets in the vents and about my neck and jumped to hang me, because I was tired of hurting and tired of hurting others through my actions and let downs—but God would not allow it.... [Please don't use my name] for fear of reprisal against me by the prison staff here in speaking out on how these facilities are built around black bodies and souls but run overwhelmingly by whites and subjected to racial overtones daily.

Another prisoner wrote:

As a black man who has been incarcerated for the past thirteen years I've had a unique view of the world I am no longer a part of, like that of an out-of-body experience.... Drugs have become America's most lucrative import and their impact on the black community has been like that of a nuclear explosion; crime—a mere radioactive fallout.... Both businesses [the war on drugs and selling drugs] need each other for their survival. The government needs drugs and the effects of drugs on a portion of American society to justify billion dollar crime bills. While drug lords need a government of indifference to ensure that *they* stay in business.... We've gone from cotton fields to billion dollar crime bills. From plantations to mass incarceration. Where we once picked cotton so that whites could earn a living today we merely need fill a prison bed two hundred miles away from home in America's neo-plantation.... How can we as intelligent people intelligently expect the police...to honestly give a damn about us killing each other and rigorously police our neighborhoods like that of their own when by doing so would inevitably lead to lay-offs in their department and empty prison beds that America has invested so much money in?...We have to take back our community businesses by boycotting any business that isn't black owned until the foreign owners get the message that *we're taking control. No more free rides!*...We need to police our own community.... We can start raiding *two* drug houses a *day* and not sit around and wait months while drug dealers are poisoning our kids and destroying our future. Until people get the message that this is destroying our future. Until people get the message that this will not be tolerated any longer. Unlike now the message is that one can get rich if you sell drugs in the black community *only*.

The following inmate entitled his note, "Is The Black Man Really An Endangered Species?"

I'm an African-American prisoner...[and] have been incarcerated for nearly fourteen continuous years.... I have routinely told people that "I am an endangered species,"...but, I don't think Black men and Black women can afford to think of each other as "separate entities."...As far as [the White majority] is concerned, we are a bunch of drug dealers and gang members, and should be locked away. That's why the government passes multi-billion dollar crime bills. So they can build these African reservations (its euphemism being "prisons") to put us away...forever.... Even Black people have gotten in the act...lamenting America's favorite campaign of "More jails! Longer sentences! More police!!!" But, you'll never hear such cries where white collar crimes are concerned.... Building more prisons will not solve America's crimes woes. And, politicians know this is not going to stem the wave of crime. But, as long as American thinks the "band-aid" effect' is the cure, they will continue to heed its cries.... "We're killing ourselves." ...How doomed are we as a people when we use lower forms of life to describe each other.... I can't even recall the last time a White man called me "nigga." But, I can barely have a conversation with a Black man without him referring to me as a "nigga." I am so weary of admonishing people not to call me "nigga," that I'm at my wits end. And, because of my protest, they always assume I'm a Muslim, and I'm not. As if Muslims are the only ones who have any sense. Its not White men who have to be fathers to our children. It is we...who need to take control of our total existence.... Because, the "war on drugs is a joke. It doesn't exist!" ...It would be simple to line our border with our Navy ships and patrol our skies with sophisticated planes, and virtually end the influx of drugs into our country. But...if drugs aren't permitted into this country, a lot of people would be out of work and very unhappy.... Police do not have to sit outside of a suspected drug house for nine months of surveillance before making a drug bust...giving the drug dealers time to poison the community and flaunt their wealth.... Within nine months, [the dealer] will have impressed the neighborhood kids so much with his pretty cars, etc., that they will gladly take his place once he is arrested.... This happens to dozens of kids every day.... Surely [the government] can afford to create some jobs and programs to eliminate the need for these fetters [prisons] in the first place.... Everyone knows that an oppressed and financially depressed society, confined to a segregated community will eventually turn on itself. So, it shouldn't be too shocking to suspect White America of a huge conspiracy to destroy a population.... But...I am a realist. And, I realize that we have to stop looking outside our communities for help that doesn't exist. The answer to our problems are in our own hands.... This is partially why I always say that I'm an "endangered species," because I'm intelligent, childless, drug-free, worship Black women and have a long list of talents. And, we need a lot of "me's."

Another letter stated:

Today our younger generation are following the footsteps of the wrong doers and getting...involved in serious crimes and unrighteous infractions...hoping to find riches in selling drugs, stealing personal property...and breaking into one' homes and businesses. These young people have been misled by older groups of individuals that once exercised the aforementioned illegal activities.... It is time for our youths to act as if they are going to be important in the...future...and they must start preparing themselves for this cause, because if they aren't educated and don't meet certain requirements, they are going to be facing some harsh times and experiences.... We shouldn't give up our hope towards them! We must motivate them to do these things and to help them reach their goals and help them find out what their cosmic mind holds for them within. They may hold a treasureous talent within themselves and we are needed to help them bring it out, by offering some kind of programs that includes music, art, poetry writing, creative writing, sports and gymnastics and physical education. This type of program would encourage the youths to do what they do best and would keep them away from committing crimes.... They choose to do wrong because they feel they are being robbed our of their creativeness, talents and inner abilities that would be a great factor in their lives. We must show and help these young people, and help ease the violence that erupts our communities. And as a young adult, I can encourage those that have a problem with chemical substances, to seek help in our communities, because there are some good resources available for those that are in need of them.... Don't feed your fellow brothers and sisters of all races the chemicals of destruction. Give them a chance to be somebody. Let them acknowledge what life is all about and learn our purposes and values of being upon this earth When you use drugs, you kills the mind and the life within you. Wake up my people and live to be free and live your life in harmony.

The above writer ends his letter with a poem:

Don't believe the pipe
It is not right
It is only a five minute hipe—
That would keep you smoking it all day
And night!
It would also make you live your life in strife
And even take away your life.
The pipe is dangerous
And it kills the brain
So say "NO" to those that try to get you
To use the little white grains!
The pipe will keep you broke at all times
Because you chose to use it after—
You've first used the little white lines.
The pipe would take food out of a child's life—
When the parents is on the freebase hipes.
I pray that the pipe would perish
And decay forever
So that my brothers
And sisters could live their lives better;
And together.
My brothers and sisters it is not right
So please take heed and don't believe the pipe!

In another letter, a prisoner wrote about African-American women.

Now that African Women have stood up for equal job opportunities, equal justice, equal rights, our own culture are beginning to shoot knives at those who are striving to achieve success and show leadership amongst our culture. We must be conscious of the positions African Women are assigned to uphold in America. Historically, African Women were aware of the positions they held in their slave-master's houses and knew they were used to dominate their men; and it is not that way today. But...the matter is still being debated by the younger generation. From the grass roots, looking at the African Women in high job positions, some men feel they shouldn't have the position, because power belong to the man and they should be the decision makes in our economy. I totally disagree, because professional women have been taught to make good decisions!

One inmate wrote during the period of the Gulf War: "It is a must that we begin to save our babies from the AIDS VIRUS, Street Gangs, The Prison System, cause if we refuse to act, the...homicides and the death rate of African Americans will skyhigh upon the earth...or the prison systems will be packed! We are fighting in the Gulf over money and land instead of cleaning up our own backyards filled with crimes."

One prisoner entitled his topic, "Party to a Crime," and commented on reports of police brutality in Los Angeles and New York. He stated:

> The public need to be aware of the focus point that surrounds the beating of the African American that took place...in which police brutality have been shield.! Thus, PTAC which have not been fully explain in depth.... Everyone of the officers that were on the scene should be charged with party to a crime, because they did not try to prevent it and knowingly knew what was going on! If all the officers...are not indicted...then 80% of the African Males and Females who were charged unlawfully under the Party To A Crime confined throughout the penal system should be released from prison in the name of Justice.

He then describes the circumstances of the crime of which he was convicted, "Armed Robbery and First Degree Murder as wit PTAC," and cites several legal decisions which he feels put him in the same situation as that of the above-mentioned police officers, i.e., that he was present at the scene but did not actually commit the crime.

Also writing of police brutality, a prisoner stated, "It is cruel to chain a man, shoot him with a shock-gun and beat him as if he was an untamed animal! And people say the color of our skin have nothing to do with the beatings, injustice, cruelty imposed upon the African Race. It is blatant that our skin color is a big factor all over the world." Another letter states:

> Many of us know that a lot of police brutality inflicted upon the African-Americans goes on without being reported in society! Yes, in prisons and therein society!... The excessive force used on a "African Individual" is still the sign of the slave-masters lashing the whip on the "Negros" and "African Slaves" 100 years ago.... Don't take things out of their proper context, because we do have some good police officers working in every police

department; and you must remember, not all police officers are bad cops!...
When excessive police brutality is used against African-Americans, some of
us enhanced the fear that we have observed from movies, seeing police officers stopping drug dealers, pimps, people with dirty dirty laundry money....
We all must learn to put our differences to the side as a race of people and
live in harmony. We must begin to follow the laws of Moses! We also must
be aware that police brutality causes people to organize street gangs and
powerful organizations. We don't need these type of problems in our communities! If we begin to live out the love we have for our parents and children, we can make our society a better place to live in. In concluding, the
police officers who are upholding law and order...without unnecessary
excessive force...continue to service our communities with justice for all!

The prisoners frequently wrote of the necessity for black males to
respect black females. The following excerpts are from a letter written by the above prisoner and is devoted to the subject.

...We quickly realize that our African Women are a sweet smelling bed of
roses, covered with fresh morning dew glistening on the petals like dia-
monds in the bright morning sun.... Brothers must become conscious and
aware of all the beauty our African Women possess physically and mentally! Stop taking on the slave-master's roles!... Cease enslaving them to the
street corners making them sell their precious bodys.... Restore their love
to forever love our race of people! Stop shooting drugs into their arms and
turning them onto [other drugs].... When you kill one of our African
Females, you have killed nine or ten of our African Babies; babies that could
have taken many of our people away from the slums and held a important
place in politics.... They could have been the next messengers from God!
African Women are tired of being mistreated by our strong hands. It is a
sign of weakness.... Never in history our African Goddesses gave birth to
Crack Babies! Never in history our African Women crawled on their
knees...begging [for drugs]. Never in history our Beautiful Sisters were
thrown into the cold...or left their babies on another person's house-steps
abandoning the future! Never in history our African Women were afraid of
their African Men!... Without having love, knowledge, wisdom and understanding about our culture love, you will always find yourself disrespecting
the pearls of the worlds!... Love is life and loving yourself is loving someone else. History asserts we are the empires of live, and until we begin to
rebuild the love that is lost amongst our people, how can we love thyself?...
Please be aware, I love all people of colors.

One prisoner requests a transfer to a minimum security setting so
that he can enroll in the university to further his education. If that possibility is denied him he asks to obtain work release "so I may save up
some money to pay for my school entry and college courses." He
claims that in order to enter recommended programs as told by the

clemency and parole board he must plead guilty to crimes he claims he did not commit and to which he pleaded not guilty. At the same time, he states:

> [I am willing] to participate in programs that will benefit me and help me move through the system, so I can return home to my family.... I sincerely understand the crimes that I am convicted of are violent and serious. Please take into count that all the codefendants who were convicted of the same crimes and had their sentence reduced are living in society.... Throughout the years of my confinement prison officials have accused me of being a gang leader because I have been seen talking and walking with inmates that prison officials designated as being gang members.... I am not a gang member. When I entered the prison system I did not know that gangs existed here in America. I entered the prison system by myself and will leave by myself. I am not a trouble maker. I was trained professionally in the communication of art and the legal arena to communicate with prisoners from all walks of life. It is wrong for people to pre-judge a man by his color of his skin instead of judging him on his character and beliefs.... I don't want to spend the rest of my life in prison! I want a chance to show everyone who does not believe in me that I can make it in society; and really want to assist politicians in saving our communities from drugs, gangs and violent crimes. All I need is one more chance to return back to society. By allowing me to transfer through the prison system it will give me the opportunity to return home to my family and become that good product I see myself as being.... If you deny me minimum placement, allow me to transfer to [a neighboring state prison] where I can enroll into some college programs. I do believe this type of transfer can be permitted through the Interstate Compact Agreement.

The following letter from the same inmate seems to show that discrimination also exists in a prison. It is a part of life. He writes:

> In order for me to receive minimum placement and the right to return home, I must admit my guilt.... Before the Program Review Committee [I was] repeatedly asked...to admit my guilt in order to become a candidate for the treatment programs offered.... I conveyed to the Committee Members: "If I plead guilty to the crimes that I did not commit, will this committee transfer me to a minimum security and will I be able to return home?" One of the gentleman said, "There is no guarantee," and agreed that I am in a "Catch 22 Situation" because I refuse to admit guilt.

The offender encloses his curriculum vitae and then describes the jobs he has applied for after completing various educational programs, and continues:

> I have been denied the opportunity to exercise my paralegal skills.... The administration filled all the clerk positions with white inmates! All except

the law library job position that was filled by an elderly African Male. I was told that my skills are needed in law firms in society; and that is what amazes me.... I was [there] before any of the white inmates that were assigned to [the] jobs. The administration would rather see me waxing and shining floors.... They gave me a janitor job and refused to send me to a camp to obtain school release. [They have] nothing else to offer me in the educational arena!" He ends his letter with a common complaint: "Because of my poverty I am unable to petition the court at this time...." It must be noted when a person is poor that person will not receive any justice according to the law of this land!

Another prisoner writes that he is "so accustomed to failure," that he is in "new waters" because help has been offered to him to become "a successful poet." He adds:

"My manuscript...[is] a part of my soul—the very essence of my being—that I will have entrusted to you to nourish."
In an earlier letter, he had written, I want to share something with you. I think it's the secret to creative genius. My personal belief is that God's gift to each and every human being is a piece of Himself. That piece is our soul. What makes us a lot like God are the characteristics of love, kindness, peacefulness, gentleness, and joy. These are the qualities that every human being longs for. Though we live in a cruel world, it is because people feel threatened, when they don't receive love that they become distant. So, it is up to those who are blessed with insight to give them hope.... I love to grow in God.

A black prisoner exhorted his fellow African-American men to regain the moral highground and do what is right. He ends his letter with an eloquent poem.

Wake up and look at our African Family Structure and realize we must take on our responsibilities that will keep our family together! Then we will find peace again. This law of tranquility is rooted and derived from the origins of our ancestors.
When we, the African Men impregnates our African Queens. We must take care of our babies and stop breaking up our family structure.
African men you must understand that we are survivors; creative; ambitious; heros; good fathers; hard workers; smart and emperors of our kingdom (household!) In the past decades we were the sole breadwinners and made sure our children were taken care of in every hour of the day; and it is evident that we are not taking on the male responsibilities. If so, there would be less killing in society; our children would be an A or B Student in school; our children wouldn't be a part of street gangs; our children would never disrespect their parents; our children would know how to read (Frederick Douglass known as Frederick Augustus Washington Bailey, born

in 1817,) stated in one of his great speeches: *reading is the road to freedom.* thus, our children wouldn't be consuming drugs into their body; they would be the future (great men of science) that we are praying to see in our communities! But, our mothers are still crying and wishing for the strong hands to rule our children, again!

African men, it is time for us to bring back our African Unity and rule our children with an iron fist; and return them to the blackboards; giving them the full package to be a man taking on responsibilities. Martin Luther King Jr., said, "We got some difficult days ahead of us." and wanted our tribes of people come into unity. Inside the home is where things can begin! Brothers, we must stop using the word "Nigger" and any other fould [sic] names toward our people. When we can do this, we will begin to respect ourselves and become ministers!

African Men it is time for you and I to own some businesses and to employ the younger generations. We must begin to set responsibilities for them instead of making our society a prison!

To everyone that can hear my deeply felt message, you must stop the child abuse; misusing and abusing our women; turning our back on education and trying to make excuses on how we don't need it! Our homes are indeed a Yale, Harvard and Tuskegee University!

History tells us wars and revolutions bring changes to reality, but to change into a spiritual, educated and righteous male to lead our children, no bloodshed is needed. We must move the stumbling blocks in our path and stop digging our own pitfalls.

The prisoner then wrote the following poem:

African men when I stare at pyramids
I think of you
You stood strong throughout all the cold wind...
You are immortal–
Aging slowly in time
You are my history being repeated–*
In society some of us asserts we have been cheated–*
When you stare at me
You see our lost history
And pure wisdom coming out thee–
How long will it take before you can see your responsibilities?
Inside your mind you must take away the chains
And learn to live free!
African men when I stare at pyramids
I see the valley of darkness
And the greatest knowledge in time...Become great men of science!
Teach our children how to survive...
Open up your eyes and stop the war against our people!

The same offender, who is very proud of his heritage, during Black History Month writes of many of the noteworthy blacks in his community and in the United States.

This is African History Month and we must make homage to Charles Hamilton Houston who challenged many of the Jim Crow Laws which still exist today. The 1859 Jim Crow legacy seems like it will never die!

We must also remember Micheal Kern who faught [sic] hard to keep drugs out of our communities. His efforts in combating drug trafficking in the African's Communities remind me of three great women...three African Women [who] are constantly trying to wake up the African Race and our poor neighboring friends from all walks of life, by announcing, stop killing yourself with drugs; stop shooting each other; stop committing crimes against human beings and educate yourself for today, tomorrow and the future.

No matter how they are aging beautifully with a legacy in life. They will always find themselves appearing before a panel of people or a judicial committee speaking brilliantly–like John H. Rock. He was the first African Lawyer in the United States.

No one has taken out the time to salute our great voices in our communities, so I want the world to know they have earned their place in the African History Books! Even though not all the African Americans will be like Richard T. Greener (the first African Male to graduate from Harvard University) [politicians must] continue to stress the need that our younger generations need to be fighters like Charles H. Houston, George H. White, Frederick Douglas and Harriet Tubman (Sojourner Truth). Keep on setting precedents within the political arena like Charles Summer. He set a precedent in 1855 fighting against the elites who were excluding people from public schools on the grounds of their race and religious opinions.

All of [a local journalist's] newspaper articles centering on our African Culture is the truth. Some of us know the truth hurts in many situations and are afraid to acknowledge the African's Voice Of Truth! Your voice is a powerful spirit to the African's Culture, and we as a people must never give up our quest for equality and leadership. You must continue to pass on your wisdom to make champions listen to your heartbeat like Rosa Parks made the elites and our culture listen to her in 1955 when she refused to sit in the back of a bus in Montgomery, Alabama. When we give good education to our race it is like giving good jazz to their ears like Duke Ellington executed brilliantly. You are a good writer revealing the essence of our African History and the destruction of our civilization all over the world.

[A female African-American preacher should] continue to preach to the mass of people and keep them aware of their spiritual nature. [Her] voice reminds me of my very own mother and Reverend Richard Allen's powerful spiritual messages. Richard Allen became the first Bishop in Philadelphia of the African Methodist Episcopal Denomination. From my perspective, you will always hit home runs like Jackie Robinson and so many people will remember you, also. The Most High will always lead you to the roads of victory saving our younger generations. Continue to let your workshop be a symbol of the Tuskegee Institute that was founded in 1881 by Booker T. Washington and his friends.

In concluding, we must never forget about Ida B. Wells, W.E.B. Du Bois, A. Leon Higginbotham Jr., Martin L. King Jr., Elijah Muhammad, Malcolm S, the Buffalo Soldiers who faught [sic] in the Civil War and all the Great Leaders fighting for our Civil Rights in Babylon and on the grounds of Zion!

I salute all the mothers and fathers across the world and pray that you will continue to tell the Pharaohs (our own people) set our children free from drugs, street gangs and violent crimes. Let it remain your song, "Go Down Moses, Way Down in Egypt Land Tell Old Pharoah To Let My People Go."

CONCLUSION

These letters face us with a stark reality. They are frequently repetitious in their similarity of expression and statement of facts, to the point of making one think that the writers are psychological clones of either the Lombrosian born criminal or are victims of a shared human/social rejection. The text of their letters is extremely simple, as the people who write them usually are. However, it is their simplicity that allows one to *feel* their feelings, because in order to understand, one does not have to penetrate through the meandering expressions of a sophisticated human being. What they say is clear, so clear and to the point that it hits one hard and demands reflection. What is wrong with them? What is wrong with us? Are the ways of present-day social living right? Wrong? Just and useful for everyone? Are these people so bad, and if so, whose fault is it?

The letters from the prisoners that we reviewed are a microhistory of the prisoners themselves. They range in length from one page to numerous pages. They are addressed to persons in the judicial system or the media with the intent to explain to them what led to their offenses, their loss of freedom, and their frustration with the system. Occasionally, they thank the recipient for the help they received. They often write of their disadvantaged youth, their dysfunctional families, their unsuccessful attempts to pull away of their addiction to drugs and alcohol. One offender wrote, "You know, there are people who are addicted to drugs. I, instead, am addicted to stealing."

Even though the prisoners usually bring into their narratives other important figures, such as parents, girlfriends and boyfriends, children—often children out of wedlock—and other friends, they generally talk about themselves in other terms: the difficulties they encountered in their lives and the rejection and the debasement they experienced in a society that is felt by them to be unjust. Their unadorned narrative frequently shows their lack of education; but their words, even though often misspelled, are clear, plain but incisive, and they seem to come from an inner world, their world, which is contained by the inner-city ghetto where many of them lived. Their letters are human documents of carceral correspondence. But even though simple words are used, their letters are not superficial. They touch not only the reality of their existence but also delve into their socio-psychological problems. One has a feeling that they have been prisoners all their lives, even when not incarcerated: prisoners of their handicaps, social prejudices, hatred, passive-aggressive attitudes, and chained by a socioeconomic, technological period that is enslaving them more and more, and in the process impedes their wholesome natural growth.

In his introduction to the latest edition of Lombroso's book, *Palimpsests from Prison*, Giuseppe Zaccaria wrote that during their carceral detention, while brooding and reflecting on their offenses and their fear of sentencing, the prisoners described by Lombroso looked forward with anxious expectation to the possibility of clemency or even freedom. These feelings are still seen in present-day prisoners, even though society has changed. This is frequently expressed in their letters and graffiti, expressions of what prisoners have always felt. It seems that after all, incarceration promotes reflection, brings about remorse and new wholesome plans for many of the prisoners. But, alas, not too many of them are able to keep their plans; indeed, many come back to jail or prison. Could it be that possibly they did not totally appreciate their personal inadequacies in the protective ambience of the correctional institutions? And, when confronted with the crude reality of their unhealthy homes, the chains of discrimination, and the lack of training for the competitive world outside, after realizing their incapacity to make their dreams a reality, out of despair and anger they reverted to their previous antisocial, but mostly "antiself" behavior. Life in prison is stressful, but the stress of "real" life is not felt in a prison cell. There is a different type of stress: how to make it through the day; how to adapt to and maneuver in the present reality. It is the stressful events on the outside that bring them there, to that constricted, at times hellish, atmosphere of the prison cell. There, in prison, in the "here and now," the person's imagination is free, to dream and to project about the "there and then" of what they will do when released. In their desire to do well, their projects for the future, their many promises to themselves and to others, they underestimate the negative contingency of their lives. As Lombroso realized while writing his book, we too realize that the population of correctional institutions and jails/prisons is not silent, inexpressive, and detached, but highly charged with human feelings, with sarcasm, frustration and hope.

The letters seem to attempt a kind of mediation for justice in punishment. A striking fact is that only lip service is given to their victims. They are rarely remembered by their victimizers. The prisoners' cries for help are visible in each of their letters, in the graffiti on the walls of their cells, and in the statements they make when interviewed, as well as from their cells. A confusion of noise and feelings of frustration are carried by their voices. At times those voices cross the walls of their cells, or through the grates flood the surrounding ambience, like a repetitive tam-tam, a lament, a *j'accuse*, or just a reminder that they do not want to be forgotten. This is Hell, they seem to say, and we are burning in the fire of justice!

Their letters seem to be concerned not only with their guilt or their innocence, not only with their attempts to explain their behavior in simple terms, but also with their awareness that while in prison they may be exposed to and conditioned by older, more experienced inmates to the ways of making their criminal activities more successful—"During our incarceration we learn new tricks," and, as another inmate stated, "You ask me what I have learned by being incarcerated. I will tell you. I learned how not to be caught." The stark reality that life in jail/prison may be conducive to more and bigger crimes is well-known and should be given strong consideration in formulating judicial policies, because common offenders, conditioned by experienced criminals, may direct their resentment towards the law-abiding society.

Chapter 6

PRISONIZATION

It's the law of the jungle here, fellows. But even here you can live.

Alexander Solzhenitsyn,
One Day in the Life of Ivan Denisovich

INTRODUCTION

The first book of the *Divine Comedy*, of Dante Alighieri is entitled *Inferno*. The inferno, or hell, is where those persons whose behavior was antisocial, sinful, or unacceptable to society were sent to do penance. While visiting jails or prisons, observing their architecture and the precautionary systems against unruly behavior or escape, at times one has the depressive feeling that the loudness of the inmates, their ejaculatory blasphemous words, their cry for help, their attempt to exchange words with someone from another cell are similar to Dante's description of hell. At times passing close to the prison confines, one can hear the calls of the inmates as they try to catch the attention of a passerby who, by his mere shadowy distant presence, breaks the monotonous routine of their life. That may remind the prisoners that they are still human beings.

These prisoners are eager to talk, and their words seem to indicate their need for hope: hope to leave prison, hope to start a new life, hope to regain their total freedom. In Canto III of the *Inferno*, the words of Dante ([1307 ca.] 1982) seem to fit beautifully with what the inmates may feel when entering a jail or prison. He wrote:

> Through me [the gate of hell] the way into the suffering city
> Through me the way to the eternal pain
> Through me the way that runs among the lost...
> Abandon every hope, who enter here.

154

Dante's damned people, because of their violence, had not only to expiate the sins of their offensive behavior against neighbors or people in general but those against God's dictates and nature itself, in the infernal place, in their afterlife portrayed in the "Seventh Circle" of the *Inferno.* Contrary to those persons, the prisoners in today's jails, or inmates in prisons, are alive and in a better place than hell. Many of them, as Dante's damned people did, still retain the hope for forgiveness and also for a new life.

Being imprisoned is shocking not only for the criminal offender but for any person who may be incarcerated. "When Dostoevsky wrote of his years in prison in Siberia, he called it the *House of the Dead.* The title told the story. Living there was like death.... He wrote that if he died and awoke in hell, he would expect it to be no worse" (Clark, 1972, p. 15). This feeling is also expressed eloquently by the many imprisoned writers whose suffering and endurance are immortalized in the book, *This Prison Where I Live* (Dowd, 1996). The prisoner loses his freedom of movement, he finds himself part of a rigid structure within which he loses his identity and falls captive to a system he does not totally understand. It is no wonder that at times a few imprisoned offenders completely lose their sanity, become confused and bizarre in their behavior, and manifest Ganser syndrome, or prison psychosis. The shock of incarceration has been reported by them to be unbearable and they unconsciously had a flight into illness.

THEORIES AND STUDIES

Prisonization can be thought of as a functional survival form of adaptation to an environment that is viewed by the prisoner as depriving him of his self-esteem, of his personal relationships, of his privacy. However, since many prisoners subjected to the above limitations of freedom and loss of personal identity do not assume prisonized behavior, one may argue that prisonization may be the outcome of a combination of the prisoner's reaction, character, pre-prison experience, and his realistic or non-realistic perception of the carceral system.

Gresham Sykes (1958) and S. Wheeler supported the idea that the carceral culture is the outcome of the strict and dehumanizing rules of jails/prisons, and viewed it as a defensive collective reaction which originates in the prison itself. David Ward and Gene Kassebaum

(1965), Marvin Wolfgang and Franco Ferracuti (1967), and C. Welford (cited in Piperno, 1989) were of the opinion, instead, that the carceral culture is brought into the prison by those offenders who belonged to the subculture of violence and that prisonization intensifies the criminal tendencies of offenders. Neither theory has the prerogative of explaining the process of prisonization; both are equally important for obvious reasons. Any offender comes into the prison with his own cultural baggage. Within the prison many of them find a culture which at times is in some ways similar to their own and which reinforces their disregard for society, their impulsive offending, and their desire not to change their behavior, even though often claims to the contrary are made in an attempt to manipulate the system. There is no doubt that the interchange between the outside society and the inmates, and among the inmates themselves, may bring about various degrees of prisonization. It is difficult to prove whether the culture outside the prison or that existing within the prison is the basic factor in the production of prisonization (Ellis et al., 1989).

It is interesting to note that already 110 years ago, Cesare Lombroso found on the walls of the prison in Torino not only statements condemning the justice system of that period but also suggestions on how to make one's prison term more acceptable: "Make a mock suicide attempt, they will send you to the infirmary, there you'll not be alone anymore, you'll eat better and they will treat you more humanly" (Lombroso, 1996, p. 109). Today's prisoners, not secluded as inmates were at those times, are well aware of the above technique which they also pass on to others by word of mouth.

In an attempt to explain prisonization, deprivation and importation are the two major theories originally proposed by Donald Clemmer (1940) who described it as the process by which the inmate makes his own the prevailing customs and habits within the carceral situation. This was further elaborated by Hans Toch (1969) and Paul Hofer (1988). Wheeler (1961) supported the functional aspect of prisonization since the prisoners he had examined and followed through their incarceration period reverted to "conventional social values just prior to release from prison" (p. 95). We, too, have frequently noticed the above shifting of prisoners' attitudes and values from those of prisonization to more acceptable social conduct values a few months before discharge. It may be argued that many inmate attitudes acquired during incarceration are just a facade, a survival maneuver, an adaptation to the code of the inmates, and not integrated into their personalities—out of resentment towards authority at first, out of fear of other inmates later. Just before decarceration, this behavior, antagonistic towards prison rules and the guards, undergoes further elaboration by the inmate who reassesses it on the basis of a confrontation with the more acceptable conduct of the outside society, his family, relatives, friends and past employers.

Hans Toch and colleagues (1989) described a transitional period of shock sustained by inmates early in their sentences that may require hospitalization and is identifiable as depression, anxiety or panic and, in some mentally ill people, a reacutization of their psychiatric syndromes. It is also worth mentioning that the paranoid/psychopath, finding him or herself in detention, frequently develops a more evident paranoid symptomatology.

The study by Wheeler (1961) is interesting because it indicated that prisonization does not linearly increase during the period of incarceration but assumes an upside-down U-shaped curve, in which the highest level of prisonization is reached during the middle period of incarceration, with a low level of prisonization, due to the influence of socio-emotional ties with family and friends, at the time of incarceration and prior to the time of release. According to this study, the offender/inmate initially rejects the carceral environment, then adapts to it, and again, prior to release, wants to leave it behind.

The process of prisonization is also influenced by the age of the prisoner, the length of incarceration, the type of jail or prison, and the alienation from the outside world. "Studies focusing on the generalized psychological effects of imprisonment have found that inmates experience the most difficulty in the beginning of their sentences" (Smith et al., 1994, p. 358). The prisoner's personality greatly contributes to his adaptation or lack thereof to the new prison culture. As a rule, his personality affects his acceptance or refusal of the rules of the prison. His adaptation also depends on his relationship with the other inmates and whether or not he becomes affiliated with a primary or semi-primary group. At times, a placement in a gang, or with a cell mate who belongs to a gang, will influence his adjustment to the prison environment. "Inmates with histories of drug use, particularly major illicit drugs such as cocaine and opiates, showed deeper penetration into the prison sub-culture, greater rejection of staff, and higher levels of institutional maladjustment" (Winfree et al., 1994, p. 281).

Daniel Glaser (cited in Piperno, 1989) believed that stricter discipline in prison is conducive to a progressive increase in prisonization even to the time of discharge, while a more lenient type of incarceration tends to progressively diminish the height of the inverted U-curve prior to discharge. However, while strict discipline is still present and necessary in the carceral system, during the past twenty years, the ambience and discipline of correctional institutions have drastically changed. In most jails/prisons not only is there more respect for the prisoner as a human being but his life within the prison is more liveable. He can associate with other prisoners (and that may be positive or negative), have frequent visits with family or friends, is exposed to some remedial school courses if interested, and has access to pastoral counseling, social worker consultation, or psychiatric/psychological assistance when requested. The inmates are not in prison to be punished—the loss of their liberty is their punishment (East, 1951), and within the prison their human needs and their rehabilitation are increasingly being addressed. The strict isolation of inmates at the time of the Quakers is long past. Indeed, we would like to emphasize the point: *prisoners are in prison because prison itself is the punishment.*

Rates of recidivism and reincarceration are very high. "Two-thirds of all persons entering prison [in 1991] for the first time had a prior sentence to probation and a third had been sentenced to a local jail or served time in a juvenile facility" (Bonczar & Beck, 1997, p. 5). Bruce Wright (1993) wrote: "The vast majority of prisons that exist today do little more than increase the census of an ever-increasing hostile underclass channeled periodically back among (not into) society" (p. 209). Can it be theorized that the offender's return to prison is due not only to the realistic offenses in which drug addiction, lack of job training and unemployment, and ghetto life play a large part but, also, to an unconscious wish to work out and through his childhood-frustrated dependency on his non-giving mother?

Paul Hofer (1988) applied the dynamics of splitting—well known in psychiatry—in attempting to explain the inmates' behavior. His basic intuition that the mother's failings are at the roots of the criminal's antisocial behavior is certainly interesting. "The father serves as a vessel containing projections of glaring maternal shortcomings," he wrote (p. 99). Hofer's insightful dynamics into the motivation of prisonization and recidivism could actually be carried a bit further in order to shed more light on the recidivistic behavior of many offenders. Are inmates mature adults or should they be considered as immature persons reverting to a childhood stage when confined to jails/prisons? Can the offender's acting out against society be viewed as an acting out against an emotionally frustrating mother and a non-present father or, when present, a non-role-model father? Does he indict society for his family's and his own failure to thrive and grow out of indigence and for not giving him a chance? It is quite possible that the recidivist wants to return temporarily to a dependency state. The prison environment, even though unsatisfactory, may be a practical solution (three meals a day, a bed, and some medical care) in exchange for an unproductive freedom. In a prison, practicality and conflict dynamics may be at work at the same time.

It is a fact, borne out by experience, that repression of feelings is frequent among inmates. They almost never speak in derogatory terms of their mothers and most of the time have little to say about their fathers. They see the authority figures around them with the same eyes with which they saw their own father when they were young, and by an unconscious or subconscious process of generalization/association, they perceive them as ungiving, punitive figures, as their fathers were, and, unconsciously rebelling against them, they strike back against the authority figures around them in order to get that attention they never had. They often ventilate their hostility in a destructive way, repeating it over and over *ad infinitum*, until they either obtain the help they crave for and solutions to their inner emotional conflicts or the continuous abreactive process burns out their hostility and acting-out behavior. Acting out against other inmates or the guards, with the possible consequence of ending in a segregated cell, in restraints or strips, could be viewed as the work of the unconscious mind of the prisoner who, like a person in analysis, has his ups and downs during the reshuffling of his conflictual self. In his case, however, his behavioral reaction is usually not understood and an attempt to correct it is not made by an experienced psychotherapist; it is viewed by the correctional officers as plain uncooperative or uncontrollable behavior. This type of behavior within a prison system is frequently observed in borderline, recidivistic offenders who, as part of their psychopathic selves, do not learn from experience and impulsively give vent to their feelings of hostility.

Charles Thomas (1973) wrote that "most prison inmates do not become completely or uniformly assimilated into the inmate society," and reported that in his study of 276 adult male inmates, "only 32.6 percent...showed high degrees of prisonization" (p. 21). He further added that too strict prison discipline promotes isolation and endangers the resocialization of discharged inmates. In subscribing to the importance of the importation model in prisonization and subsequent resocialization he concluded by stating what he considers to be the variables the prisoner takes with him when incarcerated, important for his adaptation to the carceral life: "social clan of origin, social class of attainment, pre-prison involvement in criminality, extent of contact with the larger society during confinement, and the inmates' perceptions of their post-prison life-chances" (p. 13).

Prisonization and effective resocialization are strictly related. The length of incarceration, interpersonal ties with other inmates, the proportion of the sentence served, the social role adaptation of the inmate within the prison, his degree of alienation from the institution, his self-concept, his post-release expectations and his degree of alienation from the larger society have been the focus of research in attempting to demonstrate their relationship to the resocialization of prisoners. The suggestion to be drawn from the multifactoriality in prisonization is that "prisonization will have a significant impact on the inmate, an impact that is not conducive to effective resocialization" (Zingraff, 1975, p. 368). In our experience, this has been the case with the vast majority of those offenders/inmates we have seen.

The stressful process of imprisonment affects inmates in various degrees, depending not only on the culture of the jail/prison but also on the inmate's reaction to it, as previously stated. The inmate suddenly finds himself in a dependent, receptive position. He is given food that he may not like. He dresses in jail/prison garb which depersonalizes him. He sleeps next to people he does not know; at times he may work for a pittance. He acquires a new jargon and is required to behave like an automaton with duties and expectations that often make him resentful. A certain type of conduct, a duty-bound behavior, is expected of him—frequently a person with no sense of duty, either toward himself or towards others. At times, this behavior—compulsive in type, as in a boot camp—is expected of people who, by and large, never followed any family or social rules. David Abrahamsen (1952) aptly stated, "If freedom were the only thing a prisoner lost when he entered prison, it would probably not be so bad, even though losing freedom is sometimes more than a person can bear. Added to this is a loss of prestige, status; there is a feeling on the part of the prisoner that he has been rejected, put away for a long time...[and] in addition all the possibilities for a normal sexual outlet for the prisoners are eliminated" (p. 219).

For John Faine (1973), prisonization, intended as "the inmate's degree of participation in the prison social system" (p. 576), is chiefly due to the inmate's self-concept and antecedent incarceration. His study of 257 male inmates suggested that "self-concept plays a crucial role in defining both the likelihood and form of attitude change following imprisonment" (p. 576).

The interplay of the above diverse factors may make the inmate one of many exteriorly and behaviorally well-adapted individuals in the carceral regime. Doubtless, prisoners respond differently to incarceration depending on the meaning that the jail/prison assumes for them. Some of them, indeed, seem to be quite accepting of the routine of incarceration, actually viewing it as a place where they feel protected from the stress of outside life, the temptation of drugs, alcohol, and criminal behavior, almost as if it were a place of respite. Others do not fit well within the prison setting. They are no longer themselves, they have lost their identity, and at times their rebellious behavior within the institution is due to nothing other than the sudden realization of becoming an automaton, a non-entity. At times the hole—the segregated cell—is a negative way to escape from an unbearable routine; becoming closer to the chaplain, on the other hand, is a more positive way to elude a monotonous repetitive way of life in prison.

Responding to a chaplain's query as to what the prison is like, a prisoner wrote:

> Well, it is over packed, with men waiting to go to other prisons, depending on the amount of time you have been sentenced to. I don't know how they can handle all these problems. This place looks like an old eighteenth century castle, decaying, dirty, depressive and dangerous. I sit here deep in the bowels of the joint, refusing to submit to the prison disease. I try to stay in tune with the reality of the world, but prison holds a whole different reality for its captives. We are not here to survive this setup, we are here to go insane and be a broken man, die a coward. I stand on my square and I strive for perfection. One looks forward for continual peace.

Another inmate addressed his denial, pride and shame when writing to the chaplain about missing his (the chaplain's) presence, missing his mother, missing his freedom. Another wrote to the chaplain about the jail environment—the fights among the inmates: "I am sitting here working on this letter, a fight broke out and these two dudes are really going on at it. The only guard who is present is a female and she looks like she is in shock—she called for back up.... There was a few moments the female guard was without help and she could have been hurt trying to stop this fight." After expressing his concern for the guard, the inmate went on to say. "Later she asked me if I would have helped her in case of further trouble. My answer was she was on her own, because in this environment I have to be aware of the fact what side I must be on to make it here in this jungle."

The inmates group together, show solidarity, reject the system or put up with it, identify with one another in a common plight: "survival" and the hope for discharge—early discharge—and looking forward to the cherished freedom they lost. What happens to incarcerated persons is more or less what happens to any individual who is institutionalized. One is reminded of the chronic schizophrenics in the large mental institutions of the 1950s who had lost their schizophrenic symptoms after years of institutionalization and had, instead, assumed the passivity and lack of motivation which ensues after years of routine life. They also had, like many prisoners, a pre-discharge anxiety, and many of them were unable to adapt to a "free" life outside the institution. It is quite possible that a factor in recidivism among some offenders is due to their inability to adapt to a free, responsible life when released after years of incarceration. Indeed, it is difficult to change from a passive, receptive routine to an active, responsible one!

IS THE PRISON CULTURE A SUBCULTURE OR A PARACULTURE?

We prefer to call the culture present in the prison a paraculture, a culture that developed and continues to sharpen itself as a defensive, surviving *modus operandi*, in reaction to the emargination from society and the obvious necessity to get along with the correctional officers and the group of inmates. Fear is a common feeling among many inmates—fear of other inmates and fear of retaliation from correctional officers.

Can the jail/prison augment the criminal tendencies of an inmate? The way the system handles imprisoned persons is most probably often inappropriate and inadequate and does not address the basic issues. In fact, writing in 1993, Bruce Wright stated, "The latest statistics reveal that most of those arrested, tried, and convicted have been repeaters and persistently involved in careers of crime" (p. 202). Does the supportive, large community of inmates influence the negativity of an offender's future behavior? Clemmer (1940) believed that prison life is fundamentally a learning process but that it breeds crime, even though it may retrain some prisoners and frighten a few of them. In fact, as Ramsey Clark (1972) stated, "Jails and prisons in the United States today are more often than not manufacturers of crime" (p. 15). Presently, between 40 and 80 percent of inmates are returned to prison for additional offenses. Ten to 20 percent of inmates placed on parole violate it, and the recidivistic offenders' crimes are frequently more sophisticated and appalling than their previous ones.

It is possible to theorize that the communal life of the microcosmic ambience of the subculture of violence finds in the prison a codification of a paraculture of violence. The jail/prison may become a place of indoctrination/confirmation and support for non-socially acceptable behavior: a school for violence. Indeed, a prison is a community of persons of the same sex that is stigmatized by the broad society. Many of the prisoners have or had attitudes of a predatory sexual nature. Their conduct was also unacceptable and generally assaultive. Within the prison, these people are concentrated in small areas, with no privacy and limited interaction with outside people. The inmates live together, eat together, have recreational time in common. They exchange thoughts, feelings and behavior customs with one another. They are bound to influence one another. Their world is a confused world, often filled with dishonesty, in which they feel dominated by others to whom they must submit. The composition of the prison society is a depersonalized community microstructure of its own, with myriad values and conflicting attitudes, no communal goals, where egoism and self-reliance are at a maximum, and where the individual is more important than the group.

The prisons today have assumed a new role, and a process of transinstitutionalization has taken place. At times they seem to be the *dépendance* of many minority communities, and the way of life and the facilities offered to many inmates is only minimally punitive, rehabilitation is almost nil, and crime indoctrination is rampant. "What did you learn during your incarceration?" one inmate was asked. "How not to get caught," he replied. As a result of transinstitutionalization, the outside community is represented in the jail—a microcommunity of victim-victimizers. This is probably the reason why many of the prisoners are apparently unaffected by their prisonization, appear to be rather alert and gregarious, and communicate among themselves, almost oblivious to the fact that they are in prison. Indeed, for them, the carceral institutions are divested of negative connotations. It seems as though they are going through a rite of passage that at times repeats itself *ad nauseam.* Is this due to the fact that the prisoner's philosophy of life includes time in prison as a part of his life, something that cannot be avoided and that, by being so common and frequent, loses its meaning, and that they are able to strip from it any negative feelings? The jail/prison seems to be a place of respite for some of them, while their feelings of the injustice they believe they have been subjected to are submersed in their subconscious. One could argue that without a conscious realization, they use incarceration as a means to get even with a rejecting society, as if crying out like an ancient Greek chorus: "Take care of us—you, who have forgotten us."

Even though the above may be thought of as a generalization of a group reaction to what may occur in many jail/prison settings, at an individual level each of the inmates also reacts in his own way. One sees the square John, a model prisoner; the right guy, defensive of his rights and acclaimed by fellow prisoner; the outlaw and the politician, whose attitudes towards incarceration distinguish them one from another and who undergo different levels of prisonization (Glaser, cited in Piperno, 1989).

DEINSTITUTIONALIZATION AND INCARCERATION

The process of deinstitutionalization of the mentally ill in the early 1960s and even a later (1978) well-funded, well-serviced mandated deinstitutionalization effort in one region of Massachusetts never fully achieved their desired goals. Many of the deinstitutionalized mentally ill have not been able or willing to accept outpatient psychiatric care. The result of the above has been a deterioration of their social behavior, and "a large number of socially marginal people have been cast adrift, free to roam the streets, occupy steam vents, invade public facilities and businesses [and disrupt] the regular modus vivendi" (Palermo et al., 1991a, p. 98). This behavior has often led to their incarceration and has added to the problem of the overcrowding of the carceral system. "It is, indeed, ironic that in our so-called progressive society...the jails and the streets have become repositories of the mentally ill" (Palermo, 1994b, p. 141). The majority of the mentally ill offenders are misdemeanants, but because the security of the mental institution is no longer available, either for the patient or for society, "dealing with the social disturbance of the mentally ill is left, by default, to the criminal justice system" (Palermo et al., 1991a, p. 98).

EFFECTS OF INCARCERATION:
COGNITIVE, EMOTIONAL AND BEHAVIORAL

Incarceration may have acute or chronic effects on the emotional, cognitive and behavioral self of the prisoner. Anxiety is frequently encountered in first-time imprisoned individuals. At times the shock may be so disruptive that the individual becomes mentally confused, as previously described, and/or exhibits the syndrome of Ganser, in other words, he undergoes an unconsciously determined process of ego dissociation. At other times, paranoia sets in, either as a reacutization of a previous delusional tendency or as a new disturbance. Hysterical reactions and frequent masked depression with somatization are also present. Depression, reactive in type, is frequently observed. "It is suggested that the uniquely supportive matching of the penitentiary environment with pathological aspects of the antisocial personality provides an unconscious characterological appeal to many inmates, promoting expression of rebelliousness, prisonized attitudes and increasing the chance of recidivism" (Hofer, 1988, p. 95). In fact, only the callous, recidivistic criminal, who belongs to the antisocial personality disorder (formerly termed "true psychopath") is not, as a rule, affected by the stress of incarceration. He continues, however, to demonstrate a rebellious, manipulative type of behavior.

Incarceration is a traumatic event that deprives an individual of freedom and autonomy. Studies have been done to see if there is any long-term cognitive deterioration due to prolonged incarceration. R. Lazzari and colleagues (cited in Piperno, 1989) studied the effect of incarceration in a group of 150 detainees in an Italian prison. They found that younger inmates underwent a statistically significant cognitive deterioration which the authors believed to be due to the way their personality reacted to imprisonment. In 1961, A. Taylor found that performance on psychological testing (Kohls Block Design and McGill Delta Block Test) showed some deterioration during the first part of incarceration. However, as the inmates adapted to the prison, and possibly overcame the shock/reaction of being confined, their test results improved.

A report of Stanley Cohen and Laurie Taylor (1972), contrary to that of R. Best (cited in Piperno, 1989), showed that the group of inmates to which they were closely associated for a four-year-period in a teacher's role exhibited cognitive deterioration. Their deterioration was positively correlated with the length of incarceration. P. Banister and colleagues (cited in Piperno, 1989) studied 200 inmates whose sentences ranged from ten years to life and who underwent various psychological testing during their incarceration. Their study disclosed not only that the inmates' intellectual capacity but also their perceptive/motoric capacity (in other words, their tempo of executing their performance task) were somewhat slowed down. Contrary to the above, a study by Robert Homant and Douglas Dean (1988) found that "[h]igh SE [self-esteem] and low PRI [prisonization] correlated significantly with higher scores on job planning and job attitudes" (p. 19). The above studies, and a comparative analysis conducted by Simon Dinitz and colleagues (1976) on a sample of 450 Italian and 124 American inmates, did not support Clemmer's assumption that mental deterioration correlates positively with the length of incarceration, even though the index they obtained for mental deterioration in Italian inmates was higher than for the North American inmates. Culture and personality of the inmate, together with the individual's reaction to social deprivation, are no doubt important variables in assessing the effect of incarceration as well as the presence of prisonization.

Kevin Wright (1993) cites Toch's 1977 research conducted with more than 900 inmates who were tested on the importance of prison variables thought by them to be helpful in coping with incarceration. The study reported high scores for privacy, safety, structure, support, emotional feedback, social stimulation, activity and freedom. Because highly structured settings are characterized by clearly articulated rules and scheduled activities which reduces choice and self-determination, they may promote frustration, rebellious attitudes and acting-out behavior. A more flexible climate and a more flexible organization of the prison itself would aid in elimination of behavioral disruptions on the inmates' part. Prisoners are often forced into idleness, in spite of the fact that the main objective of society is to teach them how to become self-supporting. Indeed, one can safely assume that prisons "limit freedom of movement and choice, thus placing residents in subordinate and dependent roles which result in concomitant behavioral responses" (Wright, 1993, p. 93). Wright believes that the inmate should "reside in a setting which allows the expression of choice," since "inmates incarcerated in highly structured facilities are more disruptive and have more stress related sick calls" (p. 108).

There is no doubt that many inmates lived a meaningless life prior to incarceration when viewed by middle-class standard values. However, incarceration further decreases their self-esteem and "prison socialization deëmphasizes and even denigrates legitimate authority and middle class values. Prison-based therapeutic communities are intended to improve the attitudes and orientations of participants" (Peat & Winfree, 1992, p. 206). We believe that prisoners should be helped to develop responsibility for themselves not only because it will benefit the correctional institution but also as anticipatory of discharge. This can be achieved within a climate that allows and supports not only Toch's above-described prisoners' highly scored variables, but tangible, reachable, realistic goals aimed at offering them a different kind of life and different opportunities in the outside community following release. That may contribute to the creation of a purpose in their lives. "If all that can be done to prevent recidivism is done in prison, those who leave the environment are not so dehumanized that their standards for survival are bluntly at odds with those of society on the outside," stated Bruce Wright (1993, p. 208). Incarceration is retributive punishment, but it should also be rehabilitative and remoralizing. That should be not only for altruistic humane concerns but also for, in a sense, selfish reasons, since recidivistic antisocial behavior may be diminished in streets and homes.

It is a fact that prison life does not lead to rehabilitation because prison may lower a persons' self-esteem making rehabilitation impossible and breeding antisocial behavior. In addition, "[w]hile half-way houses are geared to aid in the transition between prison and freedom, ten years of prison life, if spent in inhumane conditions, cannot be undone in a matter of months" (Wright, 1993, p. 208). Alternatives to prison may avoid the prisonization effect and reduce recidivism. Few are the cases in which a prisoner is able and willing to change his behavior when discharged from such an experience. When it does happen, it is only due to the resiliency and strength of his character.

Chapter 7

PUNISHMENT

The people's good is the highest law.
Cicero

HISTORICAL NOTES

Throughout history poets have been highly perceptive in realizing what is not right in a society and have often anticipated social catastrophe, frequently pointing out the way to redress injustice. In Greece, at the time of Homer, the writer of the Iliad and the Odyssey, there was no written law regarding punishment. However, Homer seemed to describe some moral retribution when he writes of Chryses praying to Apollo to vindicate him against Agamemnon for his loss and for his fatherly suffering. He wanted compensation for his grief. During that same period, in the case of a murder, the murderer was allowed to continue to live in society after the victim's family received payment. This offered an opportunity for a more humane understanding of the emotional suffering of the victim. "Chryses' attitude towards his loss [was] one of concern for his own emotions rather than for his daughter; the insult he...suffered assume[d] priority," wrote Henry Sidgwick (1907, p. 77). What occurs between Agamemnon and Chryses appears to be a struggle to save their self-esteem and their dignity.

In Homeric poems there are no crimes as such, because crime involves culpability and culpability or blame is missing in them. There will be no crimes or criminals. In Homer, there was acceptance of responsibility—one was to pay the penalty for his wrongdoing—but not of culpability. That may only mean that at that time the Greeks were not very concerned with the feeling or emotional side of an offense. The offense was limited to the wrong done against someone else or his property, an extension of the self.

169

Following the Homeric period, Greek society viewed punishment differently. The poet Hesiod may be considered the forerunner of Cesare Beccaria (2,000 years later). He complained of unfair judicial decisions and urged that the princes "should pass good straight judgments" (Sidgwick, 1907, p. 88). Men were considered fallible; laws and statutes were recognized and accepted and men empowered to make judgments, to pass sentence or to commute sentences. Hesiod advised the avoidance of violence and injustice, and Solon moralized that he would not want to be rich unjustly because God's punishment would come to him while alive or even after death, a just and infallible punishment. In reflecting on *Diké* (justice) and hubris, Hesiod believed that the just man should receive more reward than the unjust and he portrayed the bad person as a hawk and the good as a nightingale. That is understandable.

Later, Draco recognized that legal authority should be responsible for the punishment of crimes, and suggested a definition of crime, its punishment, and the judges' responsibility for just sentences. People found guilty of breaking their word or of behaving in an immoral manner were banished from Athens. As opposed to the Gods in the archaic period, both the authorities who exacted punishment and the penal authorities were presumed to be impartial. The Gods played a great part in the ancient Greek idea of offense and punishment. Indeed, Zeus rewarded virtue and punished wickedness. In the *Prometheus* Aeschylus pointed out that punishment is at times not fair, and a virtuous man may undergo an incongruously harsh punishment for his actions. Through the works of Homer, Hesiod and Aeschylus and others one can follow the early development of morality and justice.

Herodotus already considered that responsibility only exists when the individual is able to exercise some control over what is occurring. He believed that "limited responsibility engendered limited culpability..." (Sidgwick, 1907, p. 103), and as Sidgwick stated, that "desert should be assessed according to intention..." (p. 106) while taking into consideration responsibility and maturity. In contemporary forensics, in the so-called determination of legal responsibility, a judge will often request that a psychiatrist or psychologist address the intentionality of the offender to offend, and whether he or she possessed substantial mental capacity to intend and understand, and to will the action.

In ancient Greece, that restitution which is often found in contemporary sentencing was also present and was based on the recovery from the aggressor/offender of the loss the victim had sustained. It was the rectification of the offense, almost a commercial transaction, which was superseded in the ensuing years by penalties based on the moral appreciation of crime and congruous de facto condemnation of it. Thus, retribution will take the place of restitution as a better and more complete expression of people's angry/just reaction to an offense received. Punishment comes to be seen as retributive, coming to each man as he deserved, and directed at the perpetuation and assertion of justice.

The views of Plato and Socrates on punishment are also interesting in the discussion of present-day approaches to punishment. Socrates, Plato says, affirmed that no one fails willingly. In supporting the idea that knowledge, accompanying virtue, leads to the right choice, he stated that because of ignorance a person is prone to failure, and that such ignorance is a possible cause for their vices. He added that "mistake, inflated desires, or perverted spirit.... Folly [seen as]...either madness or ignorance impair a person's judgment [and] make him blind to reason" (Sidgwick, 1907, p. 176). He also believed that a diseased criminal was to be pitied and seen in a benevolent manner.

Plato's ideas are similar to the humanistic-humanitarian approach of later times and they are doubtlessly incorporated in the present-day view of punishment in our legal systems. In Plato's *Republic*–the ideal state–citizens do not commit crimes–crimes which would call for punishment. His proposal that various social injustices are at the basis of criminal behavior is also the view of some modern proponents of social reform. Education and restraint were thought by him as necessary to reform the criminal, an approach similar to the Quaker approach to punishment in early America. And he believed that virtue or being virtuous should be the interest of every citizen; this is not only humanistic but also utilitarian. Reforming the criminal is typical of the penology of Plato 2,500 years ago, as it will later be typical of the Philadelphia Quakers. It was believed that the offender should acquire "the habit of virtuous behavior that will eventually lead to possession of justice in full rationality" (Sidgwick, 1907, p. 205); however, it should be acquired through punishment. Deterrence is viewed as useful for society at large–the public good–and for the individual him/herself.

Aristotle (fourth century before Christ) developed a theory of moral accountability formally introduced into jurisprudence by

Pufendorf, in 1660, in his *Elementia Jurisprudentiae Universalis* when he used the term imputability (accountability) meaning that just punishment is congruous with moral culpability, at the basis of which are free choice, free decision and legal responsibility (Morris, 1973).

At the time of the birth of the town, exile and concomitant shame took the place of retaliation. Confinement in a jail or prison subsequently came to be used as punishment, since shame, by pillory or public derision, did not seem to be appropriate or adequate in the anonymous city. Penalties came to be codified only later, after Beccaria, Montesquieu and Voltaire pointed out the inhumanity of indiscriminate punishment. Punishment lost its vengeance and acquired a retributive aspect. Prior to those enlightened ideas, regardless of the quality of the crime, minor or major, the punishment was the same—hard and sometimes capital.

Branding of the offender was used during the Anglo-Saxon period in England between 600 A.D. and 1000 A.D. for those crimes that were grouped as "against the King's peace," (arson, robbery, murder, false coinage, violent crimes). Later, persons guilty of murder were either fined or subjected to short imprisonment, many of them in the Tower of London, one of the most important prisons in England. A recrudescence in the severity of punishment came about after the fifteenth century, and capital punishment was a common occurrence for crimes of treason, heresy, swearing, adultery and witchcraft. Offenders were often imprisoned and frequently subjected to mutilation, death, exile or at times had to pay high fines.

In the seventeenth century moral offenses or vagrancy called for imprisonment. The structure and hygienic conditions of prisons were poor. Offenders, who had to pay for their maintenance, were segregated, severely punished and even tortured before execution.

During the Spanish inquisition people were imprisoned, tortured, and conditioned by pain and fear in the name of God. As reported in the chapter, The Evolution of the Prison, in Italy, people found to be guilty of a crime underwent imprisonment in the name of God. The *poena carceris*, or incarceration, was instituted by Pope Boniface VIII in 1300. During the reign of the Franks people were punished with forced labor, mutilation and capital punishment. Imprisonment was a common form of punishment in 1300 France, and in Paris, until the time of the French Revolution, the Bastille, like the Tower of London, was used as a prison with extremely poor physical conditions. Castel

Sant'Angelo and Le Stinche in Florence began to house prisoners around the thirteenth century, as reported previously. There, they were not only imprisoned, but tortured and their imprisonment was an alternative to execution. European countries such as Spain, Portugal, France and England, as well as Russia, exiled the criminal offenders.

Slowly, by the seventeenth century, the prison became the most common means of punishment, and as Michel Foucault stated, "...the representative institution of industrial society and [the] bourgeois society...." (Morris & Rothman, 1995, p. viii). Workhouses came to light during the seventeenth century and were used to house minor offenders. The hygienic conditions in these institutions was poor, the offenders slept two or three to a bed and each cell housed from four to twelve people. The prison became the place where punishment had to take place. The offenders expiated their crimes with deprivation of personal liberty and lack of humane attention.

New Haven, Connecticut saw the first prison in North America in 1773 and by 1790 prisons had been built in several states. Some were underground—literally; some were located near taverns; men and women were housed together. The sanitary conditions were extremely deficient. Around 1790, almost two decades after a similar experience in a prison in Ghent, Belgium, the Quakers began to operate the Walnut Street Prison in Philadelphia and it became the first prison in the world where radical reforms took place. The Quaker penological rehabilitative philosophy kept the inmates working in isolation, supposedly reflecting on their past, and exposed them to moral indoctrination. Auburn Prison, in New York, opened in 1815 in rivalry with the prison philosophy of the Walnut Street Prison. There were harsh discipline and strong security measures. The offenders were confined in individual cells at night and silence was enforced. A similar type of prison was opened by the Puritans in Boston. The above prisons with their new philosophical approaches to the reformation of offenders, even though not the best, were certainly better than the old English prisons which made no attempt to rehabilitate the inmates. It must be remembered that in England, for over 200 years, capital punishment had been used extensively. In 1760 there were 160 capital crimes, while in 1890 there were two hundred and thirty-three (Foucault, 1979).

The Age of Reason brought many changes to eighteenth century Europe. These changes were in part brought about by the essay of

Cesare Beccaria ([1775] 1993), *On Crimes and Punishments*, written in the second half of the century. Based on his work, the foundations were laid for a new approach to crime and offenders. This was the beginning of the period of the classical school of criminology. In his work, Beccaria denounced numerous laws of the society in which he lived. Many of the laws of his time called for the cruel torment of offenders. Beccaria spoke ardently in favor of reforms in the judiciary, stating especially that "crimes are only to be measured by the injury done to society" (p. 33) and that the security of individuals "being the principal end of all society, and to which every citizen [has] an undoubted right, it becomes indispensably necessary, that to these crimes the greatest of punishments should be assigned" (p. 37). He believed, as did Montesquieu, that punishment which "does not arise from absolute necessity is tyrannical" (p. 17) and that "[i]t is impossible to prevent entirely all the disorders which the passions of mankind cause in society. These disorders increase in proportion of the number of people, and the opposition of private interests" (p. 29). He emphasized that "[t]he more immediately, after the commission of a crime, a punishment is inflicted, the more just and useful it will be" (p. 73) and that " *[t]he degree of punishment, and the consequences of a crime, ought to be so contrived, as to have the greatest possible effect on others, with the least possible pain to the delinquent*" (p. 74) (emphasis in original). Beccaria's views are based on the social contract theory according to which a contract is formed when free and independent individuals unite to form a society by giving up individual freedoms for the benefit of all. His acceptance of the social contract theory is part of the reason he felt so strongly against excessive punishment and more specifically against the death penalty which he viewed as a breaking of society's end of the social contract. He also believed that the death penalty had no deterrent effect. Beccaria's major ideas continue to influence people even today, and as the use of the death penalty is re-evaluated they should be again taken into consideration.

Two important aspects of punishment may be useful in deterrence. One is that punishment be prompt, and it is a fact that delay in punishment creates an ineffective legal system and with little impact on recidivism. The other is that punishment be severe and congruent with the offense. "The loss of liberty," stated Walker, "is aggravated by the physical discomforts and inconveniences of prison, the separation from families and friends, and the monotony of food, work and recreation" (Walker, cited in Zimring & Hawkins, 1973, p. 248). Gregory Zilboorg (1954) wrote, "If it is true that the punishment of the criminal must have a deterrent effect,...why make punishment milder and thus diminish the deterrent effect of punishment?" (p. 78).

Karl Menninger (1968), in his attack on the present-day system of punishment, stated that society makes "a fetish of wreaking punishment...to control crime by deterrence...to keep the legend of primitive justice alive and to keep our jails and prisons, however futile and expensive, crowded and wretched" (p. viii).

Punishment may have preventive effects, may be a deterrent, may reinforce moral inhibitions, and may enhance conformity to socially acceptable behavior. Deterrence may be viewed as a frightening warning. Already Beccaria thought that "the political intent of punishment (is) to instill fear in other men," and Jeremy Bentham defined it as a form of intimidation or the "terror of the law" (Zimring & Hawkins, 1973, p. 75). Similarly, Zilboorg stated (1954), regarding deterrence and its effect, that "[w]e have only our unalienable faith that man can frighten man into decency, goodness, or at least moral neutrality" (p. 27).

Montesquieu ([1748] 1994) pointed out that fluctuations in severity of punishment reflect society's views of personal liberty. He believed that "severity of punishment is fitter for despotic government" (cited in Garland, 1990, p. 11). Foucault (1979), reviewing punishment throughout the centuries, viewed it as an expression of barbarity exceeding in savagery the crime itself and at the service of social powers, and, like Benjamin Rush (1787), saw it as "proof of the feeble influence of reason and religion over the human mind" (p. 10).

Eventually, punishment came to be viewed with humane concern, and successive criminologic and judicial theories formed the foundations of a new social philosophy of crime. Nevertheless, society had to find new ways to deal with the problem of offenders and punishment. As Oliver Wendell Holmes (1895) aptly stated:

> The law, so far as it depends on learning, is indeed, as it has been called, the government of the living by the dead. To a very considerate extent no doubt it is inevitable that the living should be so governed. The past gives us our vocabulary and fixes the limits of our imagination; we cannot get away from it.... But the present has a right to govern itself so far as it can and it ought always to be remembered that historical continuity with the past is not a duty, it is only a necessity.... An ideal system of law should draw its postulates and its legislative justification from science. (Zilboorg, 1954, p. 5.)

Isaac Ray, with his treatise on the medical jurisprudence of insanity (1844), attempted to introduce medical science into the courtroom "seeking thus to avoid emotional decisions which so often appear disguised as judicious decisions" (Zilboorg, 1954, p. 7). Well known is Karl Menninger's (1972) criticism of imprisonment and its rehabilitative shortcomings. He wrote:

> How silly of us to think that we can prepare men for social life by reversing the ordinary process of socialization—silence for the only animal with speech, repressive regimentation of men who are in prison because they need to learn how to exercise their activities in constructive ways; outward conformity to rules which repress all efforts at constructive expression; work without the operation of economic motives, motivation by fear of punishment rather than hope of reward or appeal to their higher motives; cringing rather than growth in manliness.... (p. 54).

VIEWS ON PUNISHMENT

Laws are written to protect the members of society, preserve their property, and promote the smooth functioning of community life. Crime is an act perpetrated against those laws. It is usually an action that encounters the disapproval of society, and in our legal system is classified as a misdemeanor or felony, i.e., a minor or major criminal offense.

The designation of criminal offender implies that a person has broken or maliciously circumvented the law. If he possesses the mental capacity to understand his action and to freely exercise his will, he becomes responsible for his action. Responsibility is "the relationship between the responsible man and his act" while "culpability refers to the relation between the responsible man and our reactions" (Mackenzie, 1981, p. 8). This means that a person is responsible for his action, but it is we, as a society, who judge him culpable. Responsibility, however, is influenced by circumstances, the mental status of an individual, and an assumed moral involvement in any act directly connected with the individual.

Punishment can be classified as: (1) punishment which causes pecuniary loss to the offender; (2) punishment which causes loss of prestige (publication of criminal proceedings in the press); (3) punishment which causes physical suffering; and (4) punishment which causes social restrictions or loss of liberty (East, 1951).

What is punishment? "The very name is rooted in the Latin word that gives us 'penitence.' To seek divine forgiveness, to repent, to be sorry for one's sins, to be alone to contemplate the pity of one's wrongdoing–this was the theory, if not the practice, of early penitentiary" (Clark, 1972, p. 20). The word punishment may also derive from an Indo-European root meaning to make one pay. It is a penalty deliberately inflicted by a legally recognized authority upon an individual who has committed an infraction of the law and who has been found responsible and imputable for the act. Punishment implies the presence of a legal justice system and a codified definition of crime. Emmanuel Kant subscribed to the idea that the law concerning punishment is "a categorical imperative," and that *poena forensis* or judicial punishment is the consequence of the fact that someone has "willed a punishable action" ([1797] 1985), p. 21, 23). Emile Durkheim viewed punishment as an expression of the collective social conscience which "reaffirms group solidarities and restores the sacred moral order violated by the criminal" (Garland, 1990, p. 26).

Some persons favor severity in punishment. Professor Singer, for example (cited by Zimring & Hawkins, 1973), stated that "the empirical facts...are quite clear. Punishment can effectively suppress behavior, provided it is sufficiently severe," and "for maximum punishment effectiveness we should not permit parole," and "[in cases of recidivism] make repeated punishments...not only progressively more severe but progressively much more severe" (p. 239).

Thomas Szasz (1963) held the opinion that sentencing a person to an indeterminate term in a correctional institution is a restriction of liberty akin to a form of cruel punishment. He applied the same reasoning for people who may be confined to a mental institution against their will, even though due process of law was followed, and viewed their confinement as an undue restriction of their right to liberty. Herbert Morris (1985), on the other hand, upholding an holistic concept of humankind, believes that "we have a right to punishment,..that this right derives from a fundamental human right to be treated as a person... that this fundamental right is a natural, inalienable and absolute right...and...the denial of this right implies the denial of all moral rights and duties" (p. 25). Gregory Zilboorg (1954) seemed to side with those who consider punishment in a negative way, either because it may represent "a true manifestation of that revengeful power-seeking, that instinct of domination which society may adapt as a form of rationalized self protection" (p. 97) or because "those who condemn and sentence feel somewhere within themselves rather burdened" (p. 91). He feared that it may lead to the "diminution of those healthy, auto-punitive, restorative trends in man, which alone make man capable of inwardly accepting punishment and making salutary use of it" (p. 106). He believed in "the will to resocialization or reintegration, or to reincorporation into oneself of certain standards so that they become one's own (p. 98). The detractors of punishment believe that it serves to unburden society of its inner guilt. Ideally, the offender's healthy reactions should be awakened and not stifled by the act of punishment, and the offender should be helped to improve his social-moral self.

To react in an emotional way to someone who has committed a crime appears to be a rather natural act, almost like a reaction to a stimulus. However, punishment should be "distributed according to criteria of justice" and it should be based both on utilitarianism and retribution, says Mackenzie (1981, p. 13). Even though grounded on a predictable penal system individualized for each offense, punishment should be dispensed in a flexible manner, with equanimity and moral ethics at the discretion of the judge who may interpret the law and its guidelines in view of the offense and of the offender's personality. The authority dispensing the punishment should be impersonal and impartial and should interpret the law in an objective manner so that even the offenders are not victimized.

WHY DO WE PUNISH?

There are various theories that attempt to explain the rationale behind punishment. Herbert Hart (cited by Zimring & Hawkins, 1973) stated that "any theory of punishment purporting to be relevant to a modern system of criminal law must allot an important place to the utilitarian conception that the institution of criminal punishment is to be justified as a method of preventing harmful crime, even if the mechanism of prevention is fear rather than the reinforcement of moral inhibition" (p. 34).

Max Grünhut (cited in Morris, 1973) wrote that "[t]hough our 'idea of punishment has deep irrational roots,' and though 'psychology claims to detect unconscious motives for the demand for punishment in man's fear, in his insecurity and even in a sense of guilt which seeks satisfaction in the vicarious suffering of the convicted criminal'" (p. 14). Malinowski found that punishment was consciously employed to serve the needs of social cohesion within the group among Melanesians (Morris, 1973). Sutherland (cited in Morris, 1973) contends that "respect for law grows largely out of opposition to those who violate the law. The public hates the criminal, and this hatred is expressed in the form of punishment. In standing together against the enemy of their values, they develop group solidarity and respect for the orders of the group'" (pp. 14-15). Kant (cited in Zimring & Hawkins, 1973), on the other hand, stated that "[p]unishment can never be administered merely as a means for promoting another good.... For one man ought never be dealt with merely as a means subservient to the purpose of another" (p. 36).

Punishment can be discussed along different lines—historical, judicial and societal—but for mnemonic purposes the main theories can be designated as what we refer to as the 4-R theory: (1) revenge/retaliation; (2) restitution; (3) retribution; (4) rehabilitation.

Retaliation, part of the blood feud, is the oldest human way of dealing with an offense of which one has been the victim. It was regarded as an acceptable form of punishment in ancient societies, and the *lex talionis* consisted in exactly that: equal punishment for the offense suffered. The biblical "eye for an eye, tooth for a tooth," is perhaps the most well-known example in Western society. This is a primitive means of revenge or retaliation which in itself upholds a simple type of justice—that which people today would refer to as "gut reaction justice."

Ancient tribes dispensed this type of justice on a personal level and used the *lex talionis* until larger communities or towns were founded when it changed to a form of restitution or collective type of punishment. The reason for the shift from personal retaliation to restitution, or to collective punishment dispensed by the recognized authority, elected or not, was a practical one. Personal vendettas could not coexist with an orderly community and, in addition, they would interfere with the authority of the ruler and his financial resources.

Restitution, which in essence avoids any psychological or moral judgment, involves simple reparation or payment for the crime committed, theoretically causing restoration to a previous state. A system of restitution requires offenders to make monetary payments or provide services, either to the victim or to the community at large. Relatively few criminal courts have used restitution extensively, but growing concern for victims' rights has led some judges to require offenders to repay victims for their losses. The supporters of this method are interested in the *bare facts* and not in the *motivations* behind the act. Restitution, however, is not a complete form of justice, especially in cases of major crimes such as rape or murder, where it is obvious that there can be no restoration to a previous state; and actually, not even in such crimes as assault or burglary, because it does not take into consideration the tangible or intangible suffering of the victim.

Retribution, instead, addresses punishment on the basis of the *just deserts theory*, which takes into consideration the intentionality of the offender to commit the crime and supports the contention that the punishment must fit the crime and the culpability of the offender. In retribution the rights and duties of both the victim and the offender him/herself are upheld. This is because the victim has the right "to redress," and the offender has the right not to be punished in excess or to be him or herself victimized. On the other hand, society has the duty to exercise judgment and to punish the offender with equanimity.

If there is no harm, a retributivist would claim there should be no punishment. Retributivists argue that offenders deserve to be punished because they have gained an advantage over others by their crimes, and they must be punished in order to restore a balance among all citizens. The theory of retribution thus sees punishment as deserved and necessary, not to satisfy a desire for revenge, but in order to achieve a sense of justice dispensed by society. It differs from vengeance, which is private and personal (Van den Haag, cited in Conklin, 1992).

A paternalistic view of punishment, contrary to the retributivist reaction of responding in kind to any wrong done, or the social utilitarian view which is more interested in the effects that punishing has on people and society, would not permit the destruction of an offender's character in a substantial way because, regardless of his wrong free choice, he is the possessor of a moral self that we should try not to destroy.

The last of the four R's is rehabilitation and it is an important component in the dispensation of punishment. Rehabilitation sums up both the utilitarian and the humanitarian approaches. Indeed, when dispensing punishment one should attempt to promote the greatest good for the greatest number of people, or the least harm for the greatest number of people (Sidgwick, H., 1907).

It is true that even though the criminal is punished to deter others, he is, at the same time, at least ideally, helped in his or her moral and behavioral rehabilitation. "Rehabilitation is the restoration of criminals to a law-abiding way of life through treatment. More specifically, rehabilitation is the result of any planned intervention focused on the offender that reduces criminal activity, whether that reduction is achieved by changes in personality, abilities, attitudes, values, or behavior. Excluded from rehabilitation are the effects of fear and intimidation—or specific deterrence—and the maturational effects that cause older offenders to leave a life of crime" (Sechrest et al., cited in Conklin, 1992, p. 497).

Punishment is utilized by the utilitarians "to deter potential criminals from committing crimes, to protect the potential victims of crimes from becoming actual victims and to prevent criminals from committing the crimes they have in mind" (Sidgwick, 1907, p. 36). The utilitarian theory poses some restraint on the severity of the sentencing, avoiding unnecessary punishment. In this theoretical approach, the benefits of punishment are shared by potential offenders and potential victims as well: incarceration keeps the individual offender from further offending and the victim from being further victimized. While in prison, the offender, helped by others, such as mental health professionals or teachers, or involved in job training, may reassess his antisocial conduct and possibly be aided in his rehabilitation.

The humanitarian approach seeks to reform the offender while attempting to address his or her plight. It views the offense as a cry for help, and crimes are seen as a consequence of a disturbance of the character of the criminal and of his or her inner emotional problems. Humanitarian doctrine argues that the law has codified criminal behavior, both immoral and illegal, against others, and that those moral truths accepted by the law of the majority call for punishment of the person who commits a criminal offense, but who, at the same time, needs to be reformed for his or her own benefit and for that of society.

Incapacitation is the custodial control of convicted offenders so that they cannot commit crimes that affect the general public (van Dine et al., 1979). Incapacitation must be separated from specific and general deterrence and from rehabilitation as ways to reduce the crime rate. It is based on the idea that offenders will commit a certain number of crimes if they remain in society, and that those crimes can be prevented by placing the offenders in prison. Whether they reform during that time is not the issue, what is important is that they do not commit more crimes and that is why they are placed in prison. The incapacitation rationale for punishment was succinctly stated by a clergyman as follows: "I am concerned that people who assault human lives should be safely contained like nuclear waste so their destruction in our midst will stop" (Byrne, cited in Conklin, 1992).

There are several forms of incapacitation: Collective incapacitation and selective incapacitation. Collective incapacitation is the policy of giving the same prison sentence to everyone convicted of a particular offense (Conklin, 1992). A more refined notion than collective incapacitation is predictive restraint or selective incapacitation. Instead of holding all offenders of a particular type in prison, only those who are the most likely to commit more crime if released would be held. This approach tries to separate high-risk offenders from low-risk offenders and hold only those who are the most likely to be dangerous if released.

"The purpose of corrections is to create justice for all parties, victim, offender, and correctional officers," states Jess Maghan (1997, p. 112). However, if incarceration offers only retribution and not rehabilitation of the offender at the same time, there is no justice for the offender. "Likewise, rehabilitation programs that ignore the victim, or parole and probation approaches that do not consider the very real concern of the public, fail to create justice" (Maghan, 1997, p. 112). For the past two centuries, the concept of rehabilitation of prisoners advanced so far as to propose an individualized type of treatment for each offender, and even though the approaches have been moral, psychological or social, the inmate has always been the center of rehabilitative attention from the system. The solution to the problem should center around the definition of high-risk and low-risk offenders, the imprisonment of the latter and an alternative sentencing program for the former. This would create a more fair judicial system, lessen the overcrowding, rehumanizing the lonely correctional institutions.

During the past twenty years, there has been "a return to determinate sentencing, with a substantial increase in the length of sentencing. Any notion of inmate reformation or rehabilitation, either through evangelical or scientific means, has been largely abandoned in favor of an ideology of rights, in which incarceration as retribution is viewed as proper, and in which equal and identical sentencing would replace the discretionary approach previously highly valued" (Maghan, 1997, p. 102).

DETERRENCE

Deterrence is based on assumptions about why criminals violate the law and how the law can affect their behavior. These assumptions are centuries old, but recently empirical data have been collected to test their accuracy. For instance, much research has been done on the deterrent effect of capital punishment. One strategy has been to compare the homicide rates of states that have the death penalty with the homicide rates of states that do not have the death penalty. Some researchers have studied the homicide rates in a state before and after its abolition of capital punishment to determine if that change affected murder rates. Another method has been to look at murder rates in an area just before and just after executions to see if those executions deter homicide.

A frequently cited study by Ehrlich that used econometric methods did find a deterrent effect of the death penalty. However, the methodological shortcomings of this study are such as to invalidate its conclusions (Conklin, 1992). Another review of the research on the death penalty concluded that although few studies have found a deterrent effect, "the current evidence on [the] effect of capital punishment is inadequate for drawing any substantive conclusions" (Blumstein et al., 1978, p. 62). One cross-national study found that the abolition of the death penalty in a country was followed by a decline in the homicide rate more often than by the increase that deterrence theory would predict (Archer et al., 1983). A study of executions from 1940 to 1986 found a slight but statistically significant association between actual monthly executions and monthly homicide rates, but concluded that the impact of executions on homicides was negligible over a one-year period (Peterson & Bailey, 1989). Two studies (Phillips in 1980 and Stack in 1987, cited in Conklin, 1992) have found that well-publicized executions produce short-term reductions in homicides below the expected number. However, other researchers have found no evidence of even a short-term reduction in homicides (McFarland, 1983; Peterson & Bailey 1988; Bailey & Peterson, 1989), and researchers seem to agree that there is no long-term reduction in homicides after even highly publicized executions. The death penalty has little if anything to do with the occurrence of murder. "Most research is consistent with the conclusion that capital punishment does not deter those crimes for which it has been used in the United States–forcible rape (until 1977) and homicide.... In addition, capital punishment in the United States lacks certainty, with most murderers not sentenced to death and most who are sentenced to death never executed" (Conklin, 1992, p. 457). As Zilboorg (1954) stated, "The man who is about to kill someone does not always, if ever, think of the consequences, still less of such a consequence as capital punishment" (p. 29). But he added, "There is a great deal of psychological tension and emotional power behind the traditional belief in deterrence..." (p. 33). In the past several years, there seems to have been "less and less impulsive type of homicides, the type of homicides that occur in a family situation. We have found that in the past several years homicides are occurring in a more random nature, often lacking any rhyme or reason as to motivation" (personal communication, Mark S. Williams, Assistant District Attorney, Director, Homicide Division, Milwaukee County District Attorney's Office). Many of these persons are aware that if caught and convicted they may be spending the rest of their lives in an incarceration setting. Often, they simply do not care.

CONCLUSION

The present judicial panorama is a mixture of decisions composed of various theories of punishment–retributive, utilitarian and humanitarian. The legal representative–the judge–has discretionary power within a fairly flexible codification of laws. At the same time, psychiatric/psychological input regarding the psychology and psychopathology of the criminal and his offense has become an integral part of the legal process. However, even though punishment is more humane, and probation, early parole, the halfway house, electronic monitoring–the bracelet–continue to be dispensed daily by the judicial system, recidivism is high. Perhaps a Band-Aid® approach is being used in dealing with rebelliousness and violent behavior. We would be in favor of other alternative methods such as the depenalization and decriminalization of minor offenses, which could be dealt with administratively. This approach, not as humiliating as incarceration, would keep the offender in his community, in the midst of those people with whom he will probably continue to live after his release. They may be of emotional, moral and social support to him, and hopefully he will assume a more mature behavior and become respectful of laws and a productive member of society. The possibility of community life under supervision could enable the offender to work and be productive. Through these alternative methods the *jus corrigendi* will take its natural course.

The above overview of punishment demonstrates that law-abiding people have become more humane, less vindictive, and more able to contain their animal instincts when determining punishment. However, even in the twentieth century there have been eruptions of violent collective behavior such as occurred in the lagers in Nazi Germany, during the Stalin regime, in Cambodia, in the case of the desparecidos in South America, or more recently in various countries in Africa and in the former Yugoslavia, all of them remindful of archetypal destructive impulses and memories.

Chapter 8

A VIEW FROM THE BENCH

The dilemma of a judge on the criminal bench in one of America's cities frequently involves a daily and personal struggle of finding a way to resolve cases in a manner which represents a fair and just recognition of the human condition, a proper application of the law, and satisfies the `body politic's' interest in "overseeing" the work of the judiciary.
Judge Maxine Aldridge White

INTRODUCTION

The American criminal justice system is emphatically struggling to address the problems of juvenile offenders and increased violence through a process which is mostly reactive–the expansion of correctional services and facilities. "Nobody seems to doubt that the United States is, comparatively speaking, a violent society.... Violence, it is said, is as American as cherry pie" (Friedman, 1993, p. 173). The murder rate in the United States continues to exceed those of other developed countries. According to Lawrence Friedman, most people have concluded that America's history of violence is simply a part of our tradition and heritage which must be accepted, similar to an ingrained habit.

"In subtle and overt ways, violence has sinister, resourceful and draining effects upon our justice system," wrote Diane Molvig (1997, pp. 10, 12). The Wisconsin State Bar Commission on Violence and the Justice System examined the myriad ways violence impacts the judicial system (Wis. Law. July 1997). Violence and the system's current response to the mild anarchy stemming from such bedlam detracts from the ability of the nation to direct more of its resources in the fight to remain a world power. Although courts have successfully operated to take more and more of these criminals off the streets, no one feels safer and few are satisfied with the criminal justice system. As the State Bar Commission on Violence and the Justice System concludes, violence, both inside and outside of the justice system, impacts not only on public safety but creates a real burden on the case load of the court system and a severe strain on those entrusted with managing the load.

The actual number of violent offenders who commit murder is relatively low. Nonetheless, the synergism that arises from even one violent crime is the greater impact the system needs to address. Those who live in a community gripped by violence are forced to endure the aftermath of a heinous crime being committed and, consequently, are forced to draw on new means of protecting themselves from the threat of violence. Even more frightening is the supposition that these offenders, more often than not, have committed numerous crimes prior to ever being apprehended and charged with a crime in a court of law.

Random, sporadic and private violence continues to gnaw away at the social fabric of many communities. Every day in America three children die from abuse and neglect, and each day 8,523 children are reported abused or neglected. Further, every day in America six children commit suicide, thirteen children are homicide victims and sixteen children are killed by gunfire (Children's Defense Fund, 1997).

According to the statistics reported by the Wisconsin State Bar Commission on Violence and the Justice System, from 1975 to 1995, the incidence of violent crime in Wisconsin more than doubled. In the same report, it is projected that the Wisconsin Department of Corrections' budget will exceed that for higher education in Wisconsin. Despite the above staggering numbers, the vast majority of offenders who come before the criminal justice system are not charged with or convicted of violent crimes, rather the majority of the business of the criminal courts involve very needy people who commit low level non-violent crimes.

In 1995, the criminal courts in Milwaukee County adjudicated over 26,000 criminal and traffic cases. A vast majority of these cases involved low-level offenders whose crimes were driven by addictions to alcohol, drugs and poverty. The most common felony offenses were drug sales, robbery, and property offenses. In 1995, there were 105 homicide cases and 128 sexual assault cases in Milwaukee County (Rosnow, 1997). According to the State Bar Commission on Violence and the Justice System, the number of juvenile arrests for violent crime in Wisconsin increased by nearly eighty percent, from a total of 1,493 to 2,674, between 1985 and 1994. It also reported that in Milwaukee County, 99 percent of all teenage homicides in 1994 resulted from handgun use.

Although violent crimes such as homicide, sexual assault and armed robbery cases were relatively few in number, the violence and pain associated with the homicides and sexual assaults for the victims, their loved ones and the community was immeasurable. Additionally, the costs associated with doing business the way that the criminal justice system currently responds are astronomical. The State Bar Commission on Violence and the Justice System reported that in Wisconsin it costs $52,000 per year to incarcerate one juvenile offender and approximately $20,000 per year for each adult in prison.

Presiding over more than a third of the most violent cases in the county and observing the pain and suffering by innocent victims forces one to look at the system from both sides. Viewing the system from both sides and attempting to provide resolve to the system participants, including the judge, employs one to try and do everything possible to ensure that such violence is reduced. Reflection and growth were results which developed apart from the initial shock and repulsion of the offenders who committed such heinous acts. Through this reflection and growth an understanding was born that there is a massive need to develop strategies which may assist in reducing violence by and against our youth.

Offenders who were found guilty of homicide were sentenced to a substantial prison term. Many received life sentences with littlt or no chance of parole. The main problem with addressing violence in this manner is that an offender has undoubtedly committed, and been convicted of, a serious crime before they are forced to serve time in prison. Reactive measures are needed. However, they do not compensate for the pain and trauma endured by crime victims. Preventative measures which would deter violence and salvage at-risk children would render a more effective result.

The characteristics of offenders and the nature of the crimes they commit expose the soul of a society. The view from the trial bench in an urban city in America provides a snapshot of young offenders, filled with a sense of hopelessness, who violently harm or kill others and do so with little remorse. Like many other case studies, these offenders "appear to be lost, frightened, disillusioned, and alone, and that in the long run, they tend to recoil into the *stage of apathy* and surrender. They move as automatons in a chaotic society where the dyscontrolled, amoral, and antisocial aggressors, themselves victims of a disrupted social milieu, have taken over the streets" (Palermo et al., 1993, p. 257). Many of them have past histories which document the fact that they have either been targets of violence and abuse or have witnessed violence in their own homes and surrounding community. These observers of violence are the ones most likely to perpetrate violence against others during their youth and as adults.

Violent offenders are entering the system at a much earlier age, being convicted of more heinous crimes, and are incarcerated for longer periods of time in prisons which were initially designed to house seasoned criminals. Overall, these young offenders express disregard for, and are hardened towards, what most people consider to be well-established societal norms. This unwillingness to become "functional" citizens has placed these juvenile delinquents on the brink of listlessness and oppressed our court system to the splintering point. Even in a few cases where a supportive parent provided a home and other opportunities such as educational and financial support, it was not enough to counter their move toward violence and the attractiveness of the streets. (See, for example, McCall, 1994. McCall writes about his life as a young black male who grew up in a middle-class two-parent family and still felt that he was devalued by the broader society and had no other option but a life of violence in the streets.)

Early in their lives, many of these violent offenders have themselves been victims in many different situations, including, family violence, sexual abuse, poverty, illiteracy, drug and alcohol addiction, mental health difficulties, and neglect or outright abandonment. Quite often, these offenders display little, if any, evidence that they recognize the consequences of their actions. As opposed to taking responsibility for their own actions, offenders often express their futility by shifting the blame onto others or the "system" as a whole.

The approach by the system to the problem of violence is more one of punishment and retribution as opposed to identification and diversion. The adjudicatory branch of the criminal justice system has had placed upon it the lofty chores of (1) convincing the offender to change by encouraging the offender to embrace self-governing morals and a sense of responsibility; (2) imposing stiff penalties to deter others from committing similar acts; and (3) depriving the offender of the opportunity to commit another unlawful act by imposing lengthy prison terms. Unfortunately, these goals are not deterring violence, at the rate necessary to convince the public that America's streets are safe.

AN OVERVIEW

Is the current approach to crime and punishment correct or are we failing? Are preventive measures being adequately established in our social, economic, educational, religious, and familial institutions to reduce the risk of young people becoming violent offenders? Can we implement more effective measures to stem the tide of violence and identify violent offenders as early as possible and attempt to curb this behavior before crimes are actually committed? Can we afford the loss of life and serious physical and psychological injuries suffered by so many innocent victims in our community who have been marred by this senseless violence?

The criminal justice system has been woefully ineffective in identifying potential violent offenders at any age, let alone early stages of development. Since a significant number of violent crimes are committed by young people, should we address the problems affecting our youth more aggressively and at a much earlier age by expending the necessary resources to connect "at-risk" children with a nurturing environment? The ever-increasing number of children being tried as adults for committing heinous crimes dictates nothing less! If our children are left to grow up unprotected and deprived of even basic living necessities, will we enter the twenty-first century with child predators who operate as if they have no stake in society, no appreciation for the harm they cause to victims, no regard for themselves, and no regard for the communal rules which govern society?

Another issue which must be addressed is whether the criminal justice system is the appropriate proponent of society to be bridled with the daunting task of preventing young people from hurting and killing themselves or others. In a system which mostly relies on incarceration as opposed to recuperation, maturation and rehabilitation these juvenile offenders are likely to be released back onto the cold streets that guided them to the prison doorsteps in the first place. These are all questions which few people know the answer to and even fewer are willing to ask.

Experts agree that prevention is the key to raising non-violent children. Intervention at the earliest possible stage for an "at-risk" child improves the chance that the child will mature into a constructive, as opposed to destructive, member of society. (Deborah Pothrow-Stith, 1991). Additionally, intervention during developmental stages tends to increase the prospect that the child will develop the capacity to comprehend the connection between an individual's actions and the resulting consequences.

WHAT IS GOING ON?

America has more of its citizens behind bars than any other country in the world (Pothrow-Stith, 1991). Moreover, there are more Americans incarcerated right now than at any time in the history of this country. In fact, the number of men and women in American prisons has nearly tripled in the past fifteen years. In addition, the growth rate of the American prison population is unparalleled by any other period in history and unmatched by any other country in the world. These are hardly figures our country can be proud of (American's Behind Bars, 1994). Although an alarming number of citizens are being incarcerated everyday, Americans continue to live in fear of crime. The anger and frustration of the masses is reflected in the promulgation of increased criminal penalties, the building of additional prisons, and the imposition of lengthy prison sentences. Some analysts point to recent statistics showing significant decreases in miscellaneous crime rates; nonetheless, American society continues to be besieged with crime and violence at a ratio which is far out of proportion with our status as one of the most affluent and enlightened nations in the world. More importantly, the average citizen continues to harbor the view that crime is at an all-time high.

A further frustration abounds in the fact that American taxpayers are paying an astonishing amount of tax money towards courts, prisons, and related services. In spite of increased spending, prisons continue to overcrowd and the costs of managing the penal system continues to increase. Couple these facts with the knowledge that courts continue to struggle in handling ever-increasing court dockets and a realization abounds that the current criminal justice system is little more than a volatile situation awaiting the strike of a flint. Moreover, there is little evidence of rehabilitation inside or outside of prison walls.

The successful reintegration of criminals into mainstream society is an overwhelming challenge. Preventive measures have proven inadequate and are often offered, if offered at all, far too late in the lives of potential offenders to make a difference in their conduct or attitude towards society. Alternatives to incarceration, offered in efforts to curtail the staggering number of non-violent offenders incarcerated with violent criminals, have been proven comparably deficient. The mere fact that an excessive number of offenders return to prison is proof enough that incarceration alone is not an effective deterrent to crime.

The court system in America has historically occupied a peculiar role in the social welfare of it citizens as being the keepers of communal sanctity (Friedman, 1993). The criminal trial court is looked upon as the last resort for justice by all parties: the victims, the community, and even the offenders. Many believe that justice is best represented by rigid severity in the court's application of punitive measures, such as the lengthy confinement of lawbreakers. In their capacity as guardians of the court, judges have been placed at the center of a debate on public safety.

In modern times, the work of the criminal court has been significantly affected by situations such as an increase in population, a decrease in stable family structure, decaying morality, and a decline in economic conditions for many Americans. Additional factors which have had a profound effect on the criminal court are shifts in politics and modifications in legislative policies or statutory schemes.

EXPERIENCING THE BENCH

A judge who presides over criminal cases sits on the bench, day in and day out, facing criminal defendants who are charged with a variety of offenses from minor or routine to major crimes. Over ninety-five percent of criminal defendants plead guilty to the charged offense or some lesser version of the charge. The prosecutor and defense attorney offer recommendations and comments to the judge on the issue of sentencing. The lawyers are mindful of the three-pronged standard used by the judge in deciding a sentence: the nature of the offense, the character and background of the offender, and the safety and other interests of the community. The defendant has a right to "allocution," to speak to the judge about the case and the disposition of it. The judge assimilates information from these various sources quickly, assesses the credibility of it based to some extent on judicial training, intuition and "gut," and renders sentence after sentence in numerous cases.

In the not so usual case involving violence against another, assault, or murder, the judge may be engaged over a much longer period of time with substantially more information about the aggravated nature of the crime, the character of the defendant, and the impact of any proposed sentence on the community. One of the most significant factors offered by the state beyond the crime itself, is the offender's past criminal activity and the recency of the criminal history. The defendant often presents a historical perspective on his life and a list of promises that he intends to carry out at some future date.

These and other presenters, some offering conflicting information, often approach the court with the expectation of influencing the outcome of the case. It is not uncommon for the state or the defendant to rely upon expert opinions in presenting a proposed sentence to the court. The judge liberally permits lawyers, victims, family members, community advocates, and other interested persons to address the judge at the sentencing. However, the weight of the decision is left squarely upon the judge who is charged to render a just and fair sentence. The judge is expected to deal with a complex myriad of social, economic, and educational deficiencies, with limited resources and few alternatives to jail and prison. A certain amount of leniency may be considered in not so serious cases, but when bodily harm is involved it is unlikely that a criminal will be exonerated even in cases where the defendant offers a past history of neglect and abuse. The judicial decision of what weight to give to what factors is an important one. It is equally important that the parties and the public both share an interest in these cases.

The judge is the one who is entrusted to put it all together using the appropriate point of the law and legal standards and provide a fair result. Even in this era of heavy scrutiny by the media and by the public in general, and given our ability to gain and share information through technology, the judge must still perform that age-old function of deciding cases based on the facts before the court and the law of the case. The dilemma of a judge on the criminal bench in one of America's cities frequently involves a daily and personal struggle of finding a way to resolve cases in a manner which represents a fair and just recognition of the human condition, a proper application of the law, and satisfies the "body politic's" interest in "overseeing" the work of the judiciary.

LETTERS TO THE COURT

Practically every state court judge who presides over a criminal court receives correspondence from the offenders who have already been sentenced or those who await adjudication by the court. Most offenders know that they will be offered the opportunity to make a statement in open court. Handwritten letters are often filed by offenders. These letters take on many different forms, broken prose and poetry, long loosely connected sentences addressing concerns about the anticipated sentence that the court has the ability to impose and reasons why the particular offender deserves consideration and a lesser sentence. The more serious the crime, the more aspects of his or her personal life the offender is willing to disclose to the judge. Similarly, where a crime carries a lengthy penalty, the more prone an offender is to attempt and explain the reasons behind committing such an egregious crime.

LETTER WRITERS, THEN AND NOW

The concept of prisoners writing letters in an effort to effect an outcome is not a new phenomenon. Famous individuals, especially those who were incarcerated in the course of fighting for justice or liberty, have written letters from prison. Great intellectuals such as Dr. Martin Luther King, Jr., Antonio Gramsci, The Apostle Paul, and a few others, all wrote prolific letters with simple but powerful messages. On April 16, 1963, while in the Birmingham jail, Dr. King wrote an open letter in response to a letter written to him publicly by eight white clergymen complaining that Dr. King's non-violent resistance to segregation might lead to civil disturbances. Dr. King wrote that he was in jail because of injustice. He was "compelled to carry the gospel of freedom beyond his particular hometown...and constantly respond to the Macedonian call for aid for the benefit of others" (Washington 1986, pp. 289-302).

Dr. King's letter, like those written by other famous letter writers, was inspired by a loss of freedom, and the cause for which he lived and was willing to defend even unto death. These letter writers appear to have used their confinement as an opportunity to reflect on the social, economic, or religious injustices that were found in their respective communities. These "now" famous letter writers had different styles–some used prose, oration, emotional appeal, and spiritual conversions to get their ideas across. But regardless of the style, each was effective in stirring the consciousness of society.

The letters written by the famous letter writers are distinctly different in style, content, and motivation from the letters that felonious offenders offer to contemporary criminal courts in America. In the letters written by the famous writers, the personal trials and tribulations suffered by the writers were rarely mentioned, the authors choosing instead to concentrate on societal ills and injustices. This is far from the case with most of the incarcerated letter writers of today.

The most striking difference between the famous letters and the offender letters referenced in this text is that the famous letter writers were jailed because of their philosophical beliefs and for challenging societal injustice in an effort to thwart the disparate treatment of others (Dowd, 1996). Letters written by young violent offenders today are, more often than not, written in an attempt to convince the court that the offender is not "guilty" of the crime they have been charged with, but that society in general is the culprit. Accordingly, letters written by these criminals often become little more than pleas for mercy and leniency.

The testimonies discussed in this chapter were either conferred to the court in the form of a letter prior to sentencing or were received by the court in the form of an oral statement made by a convicted offender prior to sentencing. It is important to note that the external violence these criminals unleash, often on their own families, friends, and communities, is often a result of internal rage and anger these offenders harbor towards society at large. Their letters maintain proclamations of bad associations, bad choices, low self-esteem, and alienation. Consequently, these letters must be considered in conjunction with the backgrounds of these offenders in order to gain insight into who they are and what caused them to become communal malefactors.

WHY SHOULD WE LISTEN?

Many persons inside and outside of the criminal justice system would look upon letters from convicted killers, and other violent offenders facing imprisonment, with suspicion. These letters appear suspect, in that they are written to the judge merely as part of the continuing manipulation of the system by offenders who attempt to throw blame onto others while attempting to characterize themselves as victims. And, in looking at these letters with a suspicious or vengeful eye, it would be easy to conclude that such offenders are not remorseful. However, the fact remains that not all violent offenders are heartless and inhuman. The letters written by these lawbreakers offer the court the opportunity to evaluate the genuineness of the offender's remorse as well as their propensity for repeat offending, if such things may be gauged at all.

In addition, it may be possible to glean constructive information from these letters. Violent offenders, even those demonstrably undeserving of sympathy, can offer information about what situations brought them to prison. The plight suffered by many of these offenders, as conveyed through their letters and court statements, carry striking similarities. Many having experienced the malevolence of society on a grand scale, may be *profiles* of what deficits in our society are likely to result in the production of similar offenders. By gaining such knowledge, society might deter a percentage of "prospective criminals" from violent acts by addressing the source of the problem as early as possible. The severe losses suffered by the crime victims' families, the public's increased fear for safety, and the escalating costs of the criminal justice system provide ample justification for the expenditure of financial and human resources. Intervention at the earliest stage possible can counter the emotional, economical, and environmental forces that appear to be turning some of our children into predators.

The description of issues facing the modern-day criminal court is substantially based on a small but representative sample of offenders in an urban environment who were incarcerated for offenses such as homicide, sexual assault, armed robbery and drug trafficking in Milwaukee County, Wisconsin. Cases involving violent crimes such as these continue to clog court dockets in nearly every state. Undoubtedly, the pattern of cases in Milwaukee County which are described here in would be illustrative of many of the characteristics of offenders incarcerated in prisons throughout America.

THE MIND OF A CRIMINAL

Offenders communicate with the court at various points in the process either through their attorney or by direct written correspondence. Most often the correspondence arrives in the form of letters written just prior to sentencing. These now-convicted offenders proffer justification for their behavior to the court in an effort to explain what prompted their violent acts. The "rationale" offered for their violence, which is set forth in the letters and verbal comments of offenders, generally fall into three categories: (1) Someone other than the offender is responsible for the offender's violent acts (including naivete, peer pressure, gang affiliation, and fear or retribution); (2) the offender's acts were involuntarily caused or influenced by extrinsic factors (including alcohol or drug dependency, psychosis and social history, arising either out of severe neglect and abuse as a child or from the alienation and rage resulting from poverty and social neglect, and mental illness); and (3) the failure of the system to address the offender's problems at an earlier stage (including family abuse, neglect, illiteracy, ineffective juvenile justice programs, and unreliable or unavailable comprehensive rehabilitative and punitive programs).

The characteristics of the conduct exhibited by the offender in many cases often manifest actual or threatened violence against another, sexual assault, or psychological abuse. In some cases, the taking of property for financial purposes to buy personal goods or illegal drugs was offered as the offender's motive for engaging in the violent act. In a number of cases, the use of, or threatened use of, a weapon (typically a firearm) was present. In the cases involving family violence, the victim was often a female being assaulted by a male. Many of the victims who fall prey to these senseless acts are women and children who suffer violence and abuse, most often, at the hands of known perpetrators.

THE CRIES OF A COMMUNITY

During the offender's sentencing hearing, the victim's family cries out for the court to recognize and respond to the extreme pain the offender has caused. It is especially tumultuous for the victim's family when the offender is a familial acquaintance or a person who had been a longtime associate of the victim. At sentencing, it is not uncommon for the victims to direct rhetorical questions towards the offender. In one case, a family asked an offender: Why would someone who professes to love another not only shoot and kill that person but also place her unclothed body in a blanket and throw her over a bridge into an open field?

In a similar case, the family asked the offender why he would cover the victim with a cup of gasoline and strike a match and purposefully set her on fire in his mother's house? The victim suffered tremendously and died from third-degree burns on over 50 percent of her body. This particular offender blamed his criminal conduct on his having smoked three bags of crack cocaine. The offender was oblivious to the magnitude of the pain that he caused the victim as demonstrated by his letter in which he states: "The victim and I had a few misunderstandings; But I am not nor have been a violent person. When you are on drugs, you tend to react in a different way. These are the times when the victim and I had misunderstandings. Our relationship for the most part was based on drugs."

Similarly, one family asked an offender why he would open fire on a playground filled with children simply because he was upset with the basketball players chiding each other over a game of "pick-up," a game in which the offender was not even a participant? Or, as victims often ask in so many cases, why did the offender perpetrate such violence and cause such injury when the victim was unarmed and did absolutely nothing to justify the offender's actions. The rage of the victim's family and the community was captured in a representative way for so many victims, in a case where a child is murdered senselessly. The victim's mother lamented that if possible she would impose the death penalty: "A very *slow* and *painful* death. No man should commit such a heinous act. Only a *BEAST* would react to commands of attack! Only a *BEAST* would commit such a violent act without thinking of the safety of others! Only a *BEAST* would flee such a disastrous scene after committing such a crime! Therefore such a *SAVAGE BEAST* needs to be put to *DEATH* so that he will not have the ability to commit any more tragic acts of violence" (emphasis in original).

Emotions of grief, anger, and frustration are expressed to the court by the victims of these heinous misdeeds. The feelings of outrage and anguish experienced by these victims are eventually passed on to the community at large. In a few cases statements were made at sentencing hearings by community interest groups. Compassion for the severity of these violent acts is further illustrated through the financial donations and other condolences offered to crime victims and their families.

THE BIOLOGY OF AN OFFENDER

The criminal trial court processes a great number of cases. Most of these offenders are poor, illiterate, learning disabled, or otherwise mentally impaired, drug or alcohol addicted "citizens" from dysfunctional families who repeatedly violate the law. The criminal trial court also handles a growing number of cases against violent juvenile offenders and cases in which women are perpetrators. These offenders and their supporters claim that they are driven to crime and violence out of desperation and countless unmet needs. Nevertheless, they usually do not dispute findings that their criminal conduct causes substantial sorrow and torment to the victims of their crimes and the families and friends of these victims.

A combination of destructive traits are routinely found in the case histories of many offenders. Common offender characteristics usually reflect a young minority male, primarily African-American or Hispanic. Racial and ethnic minorities make up an enormous percentage of the prison population. The ratio of whites to non-whites held in penile institutions greatly exceeds the ratio of whites to non-whites in the general population in America. Most offenders had exceedingly low levels of academic achievement, frequently reflecting grade school or high school dropout.

Of the adult aged offenders, most had, at best, a spotty employment history. Psychological impairments, mental health problems, and poor school evaluations gave insights into reasons why these offenders performed poorly on competency evaluations. A number of these lawbreakers showed signs of marginal retardation or total illiteracy. Those who had been given mental diagnosis most often reflected schizophrenia, paranoid type, and most all were described as antisocial personality type, undifferentiated. Depression was reported by many offenders, and several had records reflecting thoughts of or attempts at suicide.

One of the most common factors found in the history of these offenders was the presence of a dysfunctional family. Most had been raised by a single parent, who themselves had often experienced similar impediments of abuse, drug and alcohol addiction, and criminal records. It was not uncommon for the offender's file to reflect a life of social deprivation including poverty, physical or sexual abuse, a history of psychological problems and mental health treatment, drug abuse by caretakers, and personal drug dependency commencing at an early age. Offenders professing gang affiliation viewed membership as a necessity for survival, and in a few cases, the offender's criminal conduct was an act of retaliation grounded in gang affiliation.

The male offenders had often fathered several children whom they failed to support, either financially or emotionally. Female offenders were frequently young, poor, unwed, single parents to children whose fathers were unknown or refused to participate in raising the children. It was not uncommon to find a female offender who had reared numerous children by several different men. The children of offenders often wound up unprotected, undernourished, unhealthy, and uneducated. Several experts have revealed that if adequate measures are not undertaken, the children of these offenders may end up with problems similar to those currently being exhibited by their parents. In other words, many of these children will represent our next generation of criminal offenders if they are not adequately protected and provided for very soon.

Many offenders believe that they have been victims of the system and, as a result, became victimizers themselves. They express concerns that their families have been broken by societal systems such as social services and the criminal justice system. The majority of these offenders believed that their violent act was reasonable under the circumstances and that their show of violence was in response to a hostile, violent, armed threat from another. Frequently, offenders offered some other person or the influences of substances or a watered-down version of self-defense to perceived danger.

The criminal court is forced to deal with these issues in an arena where the pains of the victims and their families come face-to-face with the societal wariness of the perpetrators. In each case, even after the court considers mitigating circumstances such as the horrible treatment offenders received at the hands of family members and societal institutions, the heinous nature of the offender's criminal conduct and the court's concern for the safety of the community almost always mandate a lengthy prison sentence.

At sentencing, the court hears information concerning the role of the offender in the crime, the level, if any, of remorse shown by the offender, prior criminal infractions, and the offender's social, education, employment, mental and physical health history. To its credit, the criminal justice system mandates that a judge listen to and consider this information for a reason.

The information concerning the background of the offender is presented in open court and documented in the sentencing transcript. These transcripts chronicle the severity of the problems entrenched in the offender's life, which, more than likely, developed that person into the societal miscreant courts have been constrained to rehabilitate and develop into a "mainstream American." Even if this prisoner history to influence the future for the offender whose violent act justifies his or her removal from the community, should these prisoner profiles serve as tools for the development of proactive means to reduce the likelihood that some other victim's family will suffer the precious loss of a child or loved one at the hand of an offender who meets society's definition of a thoughtless coward and BEAST?

The horrendous price paid by innocent victims justifies an analysis of the social, educational, psychological, and economic traits exhibited by these offenders. Such an inquiry should be undertaken in a manner sufficient to identify prospective malefactors at as early an age as possible. With any luck, these studies will aid authorities, counselors, parents, and any other person maintaining close contact with "at-risk" children.

The offender generally merges pleas for leniency in sentencing with personal stories of poverty, neglect, abuse and loneliness. Personal history is summarized for the court from files which were often created by the justice system itself at earlier adjudications, such as substantiations of criminal conduct in children's court or as a part of the record in cases brought in prior proceedings to intervene on behalf of the offender who was then the victim of neglect or abuse. Psychological profiles, health history, school records, employment history, and family background materials are also included in the sentencing summary. Such records often document the difficulties and abuse encountered by offenders at earlier and various stages in their lives.

Some of the abuses suffered by these offenders were made known to the "system" on prior occasions where attempts at intervention are customarily documented in case files. In some cases, despite intervention, problems of abuse and neglect continued throughout the early childhood of these offenders. To some extent, the pattern of conduct supports the correlation between the abusive life-style that some offenders were forced to live and the violent conduct they display toward others in the commission of their crimes. Shockingly, it was extremely common for offenders to displace internal violence upon friends and family members. What makes such exhibitions of anger on the part of the offender so frightening is the fact that the majority of the victims who fall prey to the rage of these perpetrators were totally innocent of any wrongdoing towards these lawbreakers.

THE MAKING OF A MISCREANT

In some cases, signs of mental illness are part of the background of the offender. However, the majority of the offenders found to suffer from mental disorders do not offer poor mental health as a justification for their criminal acts, nor do they offer mental illness as grounds for exoneration. Instead, the offenders use diagnoses of psychiatric problems, including antisocial personality disorders, mild mental retardation, and psychosis induced by alcohol or drug addiction, in an effort to explain the motivations in committing such violent acts and as a basis for leniency.

Even in the scant number of cases where the offender had received some support from a parent, teacher, or friend, apparently that support, as we previously stated, was insufficient to counter the appeal of street life and the migration towards violence. Offenders recurrently expressed feelings that the gangs or individuals they associated with, whose goals were similarly driven by crime and violence, valued the existence of the offender in a manner which gave their life meaning and purpose. The lawbreakers maintain that sustaining self-respect among "their crew" was much easier and less intimidating than conforming to societal values which forced the lawbreakers to adopt lifestyles which they felt reflected a devaluation of their lives and intensified the futility of their existence.

For many of these criminals, their living conditions verified, even sanctioned, contentions that the only avenue of advancement was the one that would be achieved through a path laden with violence. An absent or unidentified father, struggling mother, impoverished lifestyle in a violent urban locale, and extensive illiteracy faced these offenders on a day-to-day basis. The uncanny regularity with which the majority of these criminals routinely purport to have endured these situations undoubtedly served as a catalyst in spawning these violent offenders.

Prior to the commission of violent acts such as rape and murder, there was usually little or no evidence of the offenders' commitment to personal accountability or rehabilitation, as many of these criminals are prior offenders, hardened through encounters with the criminal justice system. Instead of learning from their mistakes, many repeat offenders give up on becoming productive community members. In fact, habitual offenders tend to view life as a two-way street, one road leading to incarceration, the other to death. The issue which the system must address is: how can we compel someone to be concerned about the lives of others when they do not care about their own life?

Those offenders who lived within a community where violence was common acquired violent tendencies, even to the most casual disputes. Offenders generally display symptoms of their social situations through conduct which demonstrates that "violence begets violence." An abusive childhood, the lack of parental guidance, discipline, and caring appear to be at the root of the many of these problems. Offenders, who have themselves been violently victimized, regularly victimize others and exhibit a lack of appreciation for personal responsibility, self-sufficiency, and self-control. Also prevalent in the lives of these victimizers are incidents of alcohol and other substance abuse, poor religious values, and a scarcity of morality. The solutions employed to remedy these situations must necessarily include creative innovations pertaining to familial, educational, and social issues.

In one case, for example, an offender was convicted of an armed robbery in which he, along with another adult and a juvenile, entered the victim's homes, seizing valuables at random. The gunman's mother abandoned him at birth by leaving him at the hospital where he was born. He had been sexually abused from the age of one month up until age six by both males and females who were neighbors and friends of his grandmother, his guardian upon abandonment. These sexually abusive adults took sexually explicit photographs of the offender and other children while forcing the performance of oral sex acts. Subsequently, this offender's natural father, who was an alcoholic and physically abusive, assumed custody of him. The offender's father placed him in seclusion and also sexually abused him.

By the time this offender became a teenager he had attempted suicide, both by cutting his wrists and by attempting to hang himself. He was separated from his father at the age of thirteen and returned to the home of the same grandmother where he had previously been sexually abused. While with his grandmother, the offender was placed in a psychiatric hospital for three and one-half months. Upon release from the hospital, he found his natural mother and took up residence with her.

After a short while, the offender discovered that his mother was a cocaine addict and drug dealer. He again attempted unsuccessfully to commit suicide, this time by walking into oncoming traffic. The offender's mother coerced him to run a house where she sold drugs and offered prostitution services. The mother was subsequently convicted of drug dealing and sent to prison. At the time that the offender committed the armed robbery, he was operating in concert with a half-sibling who had "taught" him how to commit an armed robbery.

In summary, the court had before it a young African-American male who grew up in a chaotic family environment where he was abandoned, subjected to severe sexual abuse, and taught to survive by selling drugs, overseeing prostitutes, and committing armed robberies. A young man who had attempted suicide on numerous occasions, had endured several psychiatric hospitalizations, yet continued to exhibit signs of severe depression. He had suffered severe head trauma from being beaten with a stick and, as a result, had extreme difficulty in controlling anger and other impulses. Although this juvenile gunman had made it to high school, he barely had the reading ability of a third-grader. Even more unsettling is the fact that this offender abused other children until he reached age sixteen, thus creating a never-ending circle of abuse, resentment, and despair.

At sentencing, it was reported that the offender commented that: "He is happy now that he is incarcerated because he feels better now that he is medicated." Because of the nature of this offender's crimes, a lengthy term of imprisonment was imposed. The sentence could not be minimized by his personal misfortunes because the crime that he committed was so ruthless. However, the ordeal this young man endured must not be ignored. His pain and the backlash caused by the pentup anger he released on his victims can serve as signposts to expose the many breakdowns in the system, so that others may be saved from his plight.

We as a society can no longer afford to ignore such signposts. The costs in money and human misery are simply too great. Moreover, if we continue to ignore blatant signs of developing violence, soon our society will be overrun with disgruntled adolescents who harbor little regard for their futures and even less regard for life in general. This is because violent offenders such as the young man described above often communicate a sense of hopelessness or feelings of detachment from "societal norms." "Hostility and overt aggressive behavior are most evident in persons who have limited or no sense of self-worth and who can only prove their importance as people through violence or power, or through the acquisition of material goods." (Palermo et al., 1993, p. 256). This sense of hopelessness, despair, and resignation is illustrated in a direct quote from an offender's letter which states:

> Every night my soul puts up a fight. I toss and turn, my bed is made of thorns.... Time passes (ten o'clock, twelve o'clock, three o'clock). I see nothing but darkness, and yet my eyes are open.
> Good and evil run through my mind, my heart is damage[d]. Who will stick by me threw these times? I see many people, but no one notices me and no one can see the overflowing rivers that runs threw the forest down my chin.
> I am lock[ed] out from the outside world, an alien to the inside world.
> Yesterday is today and today will be like tomorrow. I am not the only one, bet yet I'm still alone....
> I am truly sorry for what I have done. I must face the beat of the loud drum. I will chase away fear, stand tall, and wipe away tears. "Justice!" Voices will sing and that will be the end to
> Everything.

CONCLUSION

Certain predictors have been developed by child psychiatrists, and other professionals, which may be helpful in assisting the authoritative agencies in identifying "at-risk" juveniles before they become violent offenders. Intervention efforts in various facets of the justice system must be vigorously pursued, including prompt removal of children from abusive situations, educating parents and the community concerning the need for cooperation and support in efforts to save these at-risk children, and comprehensive treatment programs designed to address juvenile alcohol and drug addiction, teen pregnancy, and lifestyle choices.

The current systemic response of providing a few weeks of social service visits to some of these borderline juvenile delinquents will not breed responsible adults. The bottom line is that offenders who ended up before the criminal justice system as juveniles usually return to the system as adults, still exhibiting many of the same characteristics that caused the offender to enter the system as a juvenile.

These offenders have been flung into a court system which is unprepared to do anything more than warehouse them, carrying the insurmountable load which is the tragic history of their gloom-filled lives on their backs. Although the system acknowledges the hard knocks that these defendants have experienced, they are held to no lesser level of responsibility for their violent conduct. Twentieth-century American justice is administered swiftly and with a great emphasis placed on punishment and retribution. This follows the historical trend of making the criminal justice system more responsive to the public's fear during periods of increased crime and violence.

The problems of crimes and violence are not confined to any particular group, they affect us all. The criminal justice system can share some valuable lessons even from the lives of offenders whose crimes are so egregious that nothing could mitigate or change their criminal sentence. These problems will require a great deal of society's participation and resources to formulate and implement solutions. Until we are willing to devote the proper amount of time, effort, and resources to the identification and treatment of abusive behavior by and against children, America will continue to experience the tragic consequences of this violence.

Chapter 9

CONCLUSION

Even when laws have been written down, they ought not always to remain unaltered.

Aristotle

There is but one law for all, namely, that law which governs all law, the law of our Creator, the law of humanity, justice, equity—the law of nature, and of nations.

Edmund Burke

In reporting the prisoners' letters, we had thought primarily to see their reactions to being confined. However, we came across myriad feelings that the writers expressed to the recipients of their letters. These feelings and their thoughts fell into diverse categories, even though most of the inmates asked for understanding for their plight, for clemency if not yet sentenced, or for a reassessment of the sentences received. The letters appear to be not only a means of communication with the representatives of the legal-judicial system and others but almost a mediation. Many stated, indeed, not only how their offenses occurred and in what they consisted but frequently stated, "I want to tell you who I really am, before you decide about my life." Their written words support their frequently expressed oral statements in regard to their emotions and to their belief that because of the way due process works, they have not always had the opportunity to speak out about themselves in the way in which they would have liked, admitting not only to their faults but also making the system aware of their positive qualities. In other words, their letters demonstrate not only a cry for help but a basic desire for justice.

In their letters, most of the prisoners talk about having grown up in dysfunctional families, frequently abandoned by their fathers, and about their strong attachment to their mothers. A few praise their mothers for the good upbringing they gave them and for their good advice. Most of these offenders dropped out of school by grade ten or eleven, usually because of their dysfunctional families, their illicit drug and alcohol use, their misconduct in school or their gang affiliation. They claim that they needed a father who was not only a provider but an emotional and moral supporter during their growing years. It is generally believed that children who live in an harmonious family, whose fathers are supporting and positive role models and psychologically involved with them, have a more balanced childhood and adolescence and, as a rule, grow up better educated and compassionate towards others, and able to exercise better control of their instinctual drives. Perhaps these prisoners' easy irritability and impulsivity is a reaction against authority which reflects their feelings of rejection by their fathers, and at times by their mothers, during certain periods of their lives. Indeed, "while girls can continue to be part of the kitchen, in the maternal world [the mothers]...push their young sons away to learn their 'maleness'" (Moradi, 1997, p. 40). However, all too often there is no father or any other male to help them and to teach them the right ways of living. It is then that feelings of abandonment, rejection and humiliation occur, and the young person stops growing inside, withdraws from positive social contacts, and assumes an attitude of bravado, keeping under control a self that tends to disintegrate, and that actually often does, when under the effect of stress, group demands, drugs or alcohol, manifesting itself in the chaotic behavior that leads them to prison.

A claim is made by some that many prisoners would not be such if they could have had a good-paying job. That is certainly an important cofactor in the genesis of criminal behavior, but a person who gets such a job must be productive, must have a continuous presence on the job, and has to demonstrate initiative and reliability. Unfortunately, many prisoners do not have those qualities and others that an employer is willing to pay for, such as professional or technical skills, reliability, honesty, diligence and emotional stability. Illicit drug and alcohol use greatly interfere with their acceptable performance on the job. Therefore, they lose their employment and pass from one occupation to another—a peregrination that does nothing other than increase their humiliation and sense of failure.

Many of these prisoners talk about their children and say that they would like to be with them as they are growing up and claim, "I don't want to be like my father—not present for me when I needed him." But, because of their often poor education, lack of skills, social incompetence and lack of discipline, their good wishes are not carried out, and they, like their fathers before them, will become statistics, part of the large cauldron of the culture of poverty. Things may even get worse in this age of social transformation because only a few of these offenders will probably eventually qualify as a *knowledge worker*, a newly emergent dominant group, already envisioned by Peter Drucker in 1959, when he coined the word (Drucker, 1994, p. 67).

Even though, as W. A. Bonger (cited in Bovenkerk, 1993) stated, "there is no special predisposition to crime," we agree with Frank Bovenkerk when he states: "It all depends, of course, on what people do with the inclinations they are born with, which is where social circumstances come in" (p. 271). Criminality, indeed, should be looked upon as behaviors, antisocial in quality, that take place in a particular social setting, at a particular time, within an economic and social construct, demonstrated by people who are the product of their family and their community. Theories about criminal behavior fluctuate, usually between the theory of inborn traits as a cause of poor adjustment to society and the failure of the family and the social environment in which the individual resides. To be objective, one should take into consideration both the above approaches. However, more emphasis should be given to those environmental factors usually believed to be conducive to emotional and behavioral stability. What are the reasons for which society does not create the right environment to enable people to strive for those inalienable rights to life, liberty and the pursuit of happiness, and offset the negative attitudes some people develop and may show while they are growing up in the midst of adversities?

One wonders whether, as stated by one of the prisoners, the African-American male is an endangered species. The majority of recidivistic inmates seem to be comprised of minority groups, and the number of African-American offenders and recidivists is proportionately higher compared to their percentage of the total population of the United States. We are certainly not the only ones to raise this issue. Statistics show that this has been so for many years past. These persons are incarcerated, as the letters of many black prisoners show, for various crimes—against persons and property—at the same time that they are exposed on a daily basis to a flood of illicit drugs and alcohol. It seems from what they write that many of them looked for oblivion from their frustrating, castrating type of life in the ephemeral nirvana of mind-altering substances. As Marc Mauer (cited in Christie, 1993) stated, "From 1984 to 1988, the Black community's percentage of all drug arrests nationally increased from 30 percent to 38 percent. In Michigan drug arrests overall have doubled since 1985, while drug arrests of Blacks have tripled" (p. 121).

Mauer pointed out that "African-American males, who are disproportionately low-income, face a variety of problems, including: The social and economic decline of our inner cities and diminished opportunities for young people; the continuing failure of our schools, health care system, and other institutional supports, to prepare young Black males to occupy legitimate roles in society; continuing poverty and a distribution of wealth which has resulted in even greater disparity between the rich and the poor over the past twenty years" (p. 120). The above social panorama applies as well to other races; many people, not only African-Americans, resort to crime, frequently obnubilated by the use of drugs.

A very important observation that must be made is that of the overcrowding in the jails/prisons, to which some of the letters we reviewed alluded. This is not only due to the lack of a moral and responsible character that is often found in the offenders but also to the deficiency of the mental health facilities, the tightening of commitment procedures, and the criminalization of mentally ill or emotionally disturbed individuals. Their removal from the streets by incarceration, even though through due process, gives an appearance of justice to an inhuman approach. Who are those who, mentally ill, end up in jails/prisons for a fairly long period of time, part of a transinstitutionalization process (Palermo, in press), if not the indigent and the social misfits, most of them belonging to minorities? Michele Foucault, in his book, *Madness and Civilization* (1988), wrote of the confinement of the mentally ill or social misfits in France during the past centuries. The title of his book invites us to a very pertinent reflection. Is there a madness in the way in which society continues to deal with its deviant members? Is this imprisonment of those who are "different"—and here we do not mean murderers or people charged with serious felonies—right and just, or ethical? Is it conducive to positive social gains in the long run to incarcerate the deviants and the misdemeanants or some of the minor felons? Is it economically sound? Is it moral? The answer may come from the prisoners themselves. Their voices, and their written words, at times in a self-serving way, ask for leniency in their punishment, not for freedom. They claim that they are willing to assume their responsibilities, almost as if awakening from a long twilight period they see reality and their wrongdoing, and become aware of their distorted way of living and their past misconduct. Should society give them a chance? Not only a chance to get out of jail/prison faster, or to avoid being placed there in the first place, but give them those opportunities that may change their behavior? Or will they continue to be extruded as a foreign body while encapsulated in a social system that moves them from indigence—the inability to get a self-supporting job—to a place of confinement where they are placed because their resentment about their feelings of social castration exploded in unacceptable behavior? Many of these people seem to have been set in a vicious cycle from which they are unable to escape, and ghetto life certainly does not help but rather creates "the conditions that will confine their [emphasis in original] children to a life sentence among the dispossessed" (Gaylin, 1991, p. 263). Community residents should be helped to create an environment in which people are able to get along together and not engage in criminal activities. "Inner-city crime reduction requires more than strong families, good schools, and ample jobs. It also requires self-determination, community control, and empowerment" (Sulton, 1994, p. 16). How long will it take for society to fully acknowledge its co-responsibility? If their problems are not addressed, and soon, they will join that large number of people who will probably never become a part of the *knowledgeable worker* group of Drucker that is more and more requested in a rapidly-changing world. Does society allow them to survive in misery and punish them when they rebel against their condition, victims of their reaction to contradictory messages of economic markets and the incessant teasing by the advertisements of a hedonistic culture? Do they really deserve this type of treatment? Inmates, themselves, wish to be treated with respect and as stated by Walter Dickey (1994), "it is enormously destructive in human terms to treat the mass of offenders as if they are all highly dangerous and sophisticated" (p. 15).

We wonder whether this approach is correct. These people have been given Constitutional guarantees; however, they are not able to pursue them because of the invisible chains reminiscent of times past. These are chains of an economic type, the heaviness of which is increased by the demoralizing effect of a lifelong, socially supported income, called entitlement. One can certainly ask, as many do, entitlement for what? Could it be that these entitlements keep them out of the mainstream of society, doing more damage to them?

The feelings among the African-American inmates are that they are treated differently, even by Lady Justice, who should be blindfolded. This, too, has increased their dissatisfaction with the judicial system as shown in some of the letters we have perused. Bruce Wright (1987), former New York Supreme Court Justice, aptly stated, "If the letters I receive [from the prisoners] define a mood, it is that the imprisoned writers believe they never had a fair trial and that none was even possible" (p. 208). This has contributed to the philosophy of Afro-centrism and tends to a de facto race separation in the United States.

We, too, feel that from a sociological point of view the way justice is distributed is often tantamount to injustice for all–victims, victimizers, the triers of justice, and primarily society at large. "The hard fact is that none of us know what to do about crime, other than hope that our persons and homes will be secure. But in our desperation to do something, we send offenders to jail" (Wright, p. 203).

It is almost a revolving door. Is the system unconsciously promoting recidivism? Is it society's resentment and anger that impedes and clouds our objectivity and decisional capacity in how to deal with at least the lesser criminal offenders? The voice of prisoners still echo in the correctional institutions. Bad Habits?–"It is like an addiction. I can't stop misbehaving. I don't know why," said an inmate. Wachtler (1997) stated, "Prisons for the incarceration of violent criminals are necessary. Predators who destroy our cities and communities, who cause our citizenry to live behind triple-locked doors should be taken off the street. But I am convinced that it is a wasteful, counterproductive distraction to use prisons for the non-violent offender who is capable of redemption or rehabilitation" (p. 23). He added, "A fifteen-year-old delinquent may well emerge from his incarceration with hardened adult criminals having had his juvenile criminal skills increased and intensified" (p. 54). While it is true that the often long-term incarceration of some young people leaves one dubious about its fairness and usefulness, it must be recognized that their crimes are often heinous. Nevertheless, it is a fact that offenders' misbehavior differs and that one should apply a differential type of punishment for non-violent and violent crimes and that "the goal of imprisonment should be to promote public safety instead of to punish sinners" (Wachtler, 1997, p. 22).

In order to understand the prisoners and look at them in a humane fashion, it is necessary to learn about their background, their life in the ghetto, and the factors, historical or other, which led to their criminal activity. Crime is the outcome of many factors. We believe that it is worth repeating that one of the major factors is that many black American children are not exposed to an adequate parental role model, do not have the opportunity to live in a harmonious family, where they can learn duties and responsibilities from their parents. The majority of black children in America today are growing up without the example of a healthy marriage between their parents. "They do not have the opportunity to live with and learn from two parents who are balancing the ups and downs of love and anger, who are handling responsibility, earning a living, struggling with the commitment to stay together. This is a profound disadvantage for children of both sexes, especially those—half of all black children—who are growing up poor" (Pothrow-Stith, 1991, p. 78).

The criminal justice system is sinking under the weight of massive case loads of low-level criminals who are desperately in need of social intervention. Despite this, public awareness of the criminal justice system is based on an unrepresentative number of cases in which the offenders have committed some heinous act of violence or abuse against innocent citizens or child victims. Ironically, these violent offenders provide lessons that are discussed but seldom heeded. Why do criminal justice professionals and social engineers ignore the lessons, the message, the penalty, and the pain gleaned from these and many other youthful offenders? If we do not provide for, protect and nurture all of America's children, we create, as previously stated, an injustice for all—for the victims of these young predators, for the community that bears the cost, and for the nation as a whole as the quality of life deteriorates for so many of its citizens. Is this an injustice for all of us, or does crime really provide economic and political incentives that the American public is not willing to forego, regardless of the nature of the industry from which these benefits are derived?

The punishment component of practically every criminal case is almost always defined by the state as incarceration. Rarely is supervision with accountable and responsible work or other restorative program viewed as punishment. The imposition of prison or jail time is an easier and much preferred solution regardless of the crime. Alternatives to incarceration which require offender performance in lieu of incarceration would be more punitive than jail for the numerous offenders who have not been subjected to the routines of earning a living and remaining substance-free.

According to the Children's Defense Fund's 1997 report on the State of America's Children, every day in America 2,556 children are born into poverty and 14.7 million of America's children live in poverty. The human cost and misery associated with being poor *and* growing up in and around violence and abuse are substantial. The adverse impact of crime on the community in general is enormous, but the impact of crime on minorities and other marginalized communities is much more severe in some respects. Imprisonment of the thousands of low-level offenders creates multiple problems–detrimental to the system, the victims, the communities, and the families of offenders. High incarceration rates in African-American communities, for example, bring a host of other negative consequences to already failing and dysfunctional families. Among the 26,000 criminal cases adjudicated in Milwaukee County Circuit Court in 1995, over 17,000 or 65.8 percent were filed against non-white persons. About twenty-one of every 100 non-white males age eighteen or older in Milwaukee County were the subject of a case adjudicated in 1995. By contrast, only 2.8 cases for every 100 white males age eighteen or older were. (Rosnow, 1995).

The failed social programs of days gone by are ready references for those who dare propose spending tax dollars on social programs in lieu of incarceration as a measure of public safety. Personal responsibility and accountability are recognized as legitimate goals, but the system does little more than demand that these miscreants obtain such control. Regardless of the circumstances of their background, offenders are viewed as blameworthy, irresponsible and deserving of their plight. They certainly gain no sympathy from the justice system, especially in those cases where their criminal acts are violent. Even in cases involving less serious or petty crimes, offenders find few who will view a background of abuse, poverty and other dire circumstances as factors which militate toward community-based intervention.

Although everyone agrees that these offenders once released should be responsible, accountable and productive citizens, no one is willing to set forth a blueprint to help accomplish such rehabilitation. After imprisonment, offenders can expect to receive even more rejection from potential employers, even for low-paying or temporary jobs with no medical or other benefits because of their many problems in combination with a criminal record. These ex-prisoners are viewed as negative role models regardless of whether their crimes were serious or relatively minor. The suspicion that they will repeat criminal activity is borne out after even brief periods of release. The offenders' inability to earn a living is further reduced by an already dismal record of no skill, little education and a lack of support. Recidivist behavior should not be a surprising result.

The annual cost of corrections is estimated at $35 billion nationwide and is in the first instance problematic for state and local governments. Spending for incarceration far exceeds spending for education in most states (Mauer, 1996). With such a tab one should question why the nation is not combating the crime problem through more investments in education alternatives to prison and other preventive measures. The economic shift from a manufacturing and industrial nation to one where information, technology, and services dominate the skilled labor market has had a profound and disproportionate impact on many groups.

African-American males and other historically marginalized groups have been more harshly affected by this economic trend. The economics of the criminal justice system, the growing number of persons employed by police departments, courts, prisons, and other related professional jobs have certainly been a positive aspect for those who benefit from such employment. The industry surrounding the building, financing and management of jails and prisons has grown tremendously (Christie, 1993). Few if any positive opportunities exist for criminal offenders in this economic quagmire. Instead, criminal employment with drug dealers and fences of stolen goods are the type of alternatives that generally ensure that offenders are returned to the criminal justice system.

With the rapid growth of prisons and prison building initiatives, policymakers are avoiding any discussions which include alternatives to prison. The "three-strikes" laws, the increase in funding for prison and jail construction projects, and the truth-in-sentencing proposals continue to promise a steady flow of prisoners to fill these new cells. The use of prison labor by governmental units, and the extension of "free" prison labor offers into the work force, provide another economic incentive to a costly crime control system.

The magnitude of the crime problem was captured by Dr. Louis Sullivan, former Secretary of the Department of Health and Human Services, when he lamented that in 100 hours on our streets we lose more young men than those killed in 100 hours of ground war in the Persian Gulf (Witkin, 1991, p. 26). Still, American communities and the criminal justice system remain complacent about the large number of children who grow up neglected, abused, abandoned and poor. These children often end up in prison or dead at a very young age. President Bill Clinton acknowledged that across the country children are killing children for shoes, for jackets, for turf (Witkin, 1991). The president promotes a three-pronged strategy for prevention, intervention and enforcement to combat violence using a comprehensive approach (The President's Crime Prevention Council, Quarterly, April 1997).

Drugs, death, guns and gangs are all commonplace in the lives of these offenders. These offenders readily admit full awareness of the dangers associated with drugs and that if the dealer is not compensated in cash, the in-kind payment could very well be paid in blood. The pain and suffering caused by these offenders should be motive enough to develop responses which reduce the likelihood that more youths will die on the streets, suffer abuse at the hands of adults, or become violent predators preying on more and more innocent citizens. Our failure to deal with potential offenders at an earlier stage results in broken lives for crime victims and their loved ones, lengthy incarceration or life sentences for the offenders, and anguish for the families of offenders—all paid for with an ever-increasing amount of tax dollars.

Why do we refuse to intervene in the lives of young people who are being harvested as "villains" in chilling and unfit environments? Why are comprehensive intervention and community-based treatment programs so unpopular and frowned upon in favor of incarceration by policymakers and the public? These young people who are destined for a life of crime would have some other chances in life if more comprehensive intervention were undertaken at the earliest possible stage in their development. "The crime and disorder which flow from hopeless poverty, unloved children, and drug abuse can't be solved merely by bottomless prisons, mandatory minimum sentences, or more police" (Freeh, 1993, pp. A1, A16).

Therapeutic jurisprudence is one way of managing an already overcrowded criminal justice system and curtailing the increasing public costs of incarceration. Both juvenile and adult criminal justice programs can identify and counteract negative dysfunctional family influences and other social influences, address substance abuse problems, and provide motivations for good behavior. Many of the lessons and experiences learned from studying the lives of these offenders can be incorporated into the coordination of services between the court and other systems, such as school, community agencies, churches, and family to provide a more solid base upon which these poor, disenfranchised youths can gain a start at life.

These violent offenders are not experts at anything, except violence itself. Although the legacy of violence is marked annually in Milwaukee County by fewer than 200 cases, those are the images which saturate the media and remind us of the fragility of life. It behooves us to discover why so many young offenders seem to be desensitized to violence as never before and why they have developed a resolve for death more so than for life.

For many offenders, expressions of hopelessness in their recitations and letters to the court point out the terrible wrath that poverty and alienation have taken in the lives of these miscreants. The costs associated with the warehousing of these offenders are phenomenal, as we have often stated. And an immeasurable amount of future costs can be anticipated if the old adage continues to have truth that "violence begets violence." The case files of many violent offenders substantiate that violence was indeed played out over and over in the lives of the offenders before the court. Abusive family histories, family breakdowns, and illiteracy further fuel the death fire that burns ever so bright in the lives of these young violent offenders. The paths which lead to these young offenders becoming violent and abusive adults are covered with myriad examples of death, imprisonment, drug addiction, sexual abuse, abandonment, and social and economic poverty.

The violence is aggravated among youthful and adult offenders alike by the ready presence and quick use of firearms. The lack of self-esteem and purpose experienced by so many of these offenders make it more likely than not that they will express power over disputes through the display and use of guns. Many violent offenders expressed fear that they had to kill or be killed, and many had already experienced being shot or beaten for money, drugs or for disrespecting someone who commanded respect, but only with a gun.

The case captions in criminal courts change daily, but their stories are so strikingly similar: They are primarily young minority males, mostly African-Americans, whose lives read like a book of tragedies. They shoot and kill even their best friends; or they stab or shoot their girlfriends with no idea of what the dispute was about; or they shoot and kill innocent victims in drive-by shootings; or they rob and steal from rival gang members and beat and shoot the losers; or they carry out their rage by spraying bullets onto playgrounds, wounding and killing innocent children. It is useless in court to try to pry a rational response to the question of why, because none is forthcoming. The system is overburdened with persons in need of community-based programs, such as drug treatment and educational and vocational training for adults and youth alike.

Most of the prisoners' letters examined as part of the subject of this book were written by a small number of offenders who had been convicted of violent crimes. However, the overwhelming majority of the business of the criminal courts involves a struggle by judges, prosecutors, defense attorneys, the police and other system participants to manage a high volume of less violent, recidivist offenders who pass through the system like a sieve, repeatedly violating the law by stealing, using or selling small amounts of drugs, battering family members, or violating some form of the criminal traffic laws.

The criminal courts employ some form of case management, but the vast majority of cases pass through a routinized process from arrest to sentence with little fanfare. The courts rarely employ, with meaning, any judicially supervised community-based supervision. The system relies on probation and parole to capture the offenders' attention and to repair years of abuse, neglect, illiteracy, and antisocial behavior through programming and intervention. There is little dispute that the current system of probation and parole requires and provides very little supervision, and many recidivate while on supervision. Offenders continue to exist in the drug- and crime-infested neighborhoods and realize that, given the size of the probation or parole agent's case load, they can avoid supervision with little if any risk of sanctions.

Failure to treat low-level offenders charged with similar crimes, such as theft, battery and drug possession, by systemically requiring individualized and comprehensive responses has created a system which is mocked by all as a "cattle call" and which hails huge rates of recidivism. The criminal justice system has failed to combine criminal justice resources with other disciplines to combat social, economic, and health crisis. Such a partnership would encourage the delivery of criminal justice system resources in a manner which would increase public safety, locking up those who pose a threat to the community while providing alternatives for intervention to those who are financial drags on the community but who pose no safety risk.

As we approach the twenty-first century, "in many ways, fear *for* our children's safety [has been] twisted into fear *of* our children" (Children Defense Fund, 1997, p. 61). Youth violence is now down for the first time in a decade following a big increase in violence which was driven substantially by gun-related violence. However, the Children's Defense Fund's 1997 report indicate that based on the 1996 figures child abuse and neglect are increasing. For example, in 1995, 996,000 children–more than 2,700 per day–were abused and neglected according to the National Committee to prevent Child Abuse. In fact, between 1985 and 1995 there was a 61 percent increase in the number of children reported abused and neglected.

The prisoner case histories can motivate our communities to attack serious flaws in the growth, development and treatment of children, and to discard the hype and seek solutions which are just and fair. To do otherwise is to merely accept the costs in human lives and resources in a nation where preventive measures can be employed to respond early and definitively to serious factors which can turn a child into a "danger to the community."

In the ultimate analysis, the problems of the offenders are multi-factorial and obviously have roots not only in the offenders themselves but also in society itself. A cooperative, concerted effort is warranted at the community level in order to address hands-on the ills of society, its discrimination, and its inequality of care for its citizens. A sensible and sensate life should be returned to the community (Bellah et al., 1991), and only unselfish and humane citizenship can do it–not just those social services involved in the management of entitlements while limited by legalities and the bureaucratic process (Howard, 1994). It calls for uniting the common interests of both victim and victimizers if a truly moral and good society is to be achieved. "Will common sense...bring a return to that good society that is so vociferously, but often hypocritically, sought? Will justice be again *a just state of affairs* and not merely a word that seems to have lost its meaning? Only time will tell if those inalienable rights [people] are endowed with will again become the basis for [their] endeavors, so that life will again find its essence, liberty will be freedom with dignity and responsibility, and happiness will be the achievement of an ultimate common good" (Palermo, 1996b).

Appendix 1

STATISTICS

1995

Law enforcement agencies made over 2.7 million arrests of juveniles (persons under age 18) in 1994. Of crimes cleared by law enforcement agencies, juveniles accounted for 14 percent of the total number of violent crimes and 19 percent of the violent crime arrests. Of these, one in seven violent crime arrests was that of a female, female juvenile violent crime arrests having more than doubled between 1985 and 1994. During the same time period, the percentage increases in arrests were greater for juveniles than for adults. Juvenile drug arrests increased 42 percent from 1993 to 1994. "If trends continue as they have over the past 10 years, juvenile arrests for violent crime will more than double by the year 2010" (Snyder et al., 1997, p. 15).

In 1995, Walinksy wrote that "[e]ight percent of those polled (implying 560,000 New Yorkers) said their houses or apartments had been broken into, twenty-two percent (1,540,000) said their cars had been broken into. In all, forty-two percent (nearly 3,000,000 New Yorkers) said they had been the victim of crime in 1993. And...about 2,000 were murdered" (p. 44). In 1995 the estimated number of incarcerated people in the United States was 1,585,400; in other words, 600 persons per 100,000 United States' residents were held in custody during that time period. Of the above number, two-thirds, or 1,078,357, were in the custody of the fifty states, the District of Columbia and the federal government, while the remaining one-third (507,044) were held in local jails. Further, as of June 30, 1995, "the nation's local jails held or supervised an estimated 541,913 persons; of that number, 34,869 were in community supervision programs such as electronic monitoring, house detention, and day reporting" (Gillard & Beck, p. 1). It is understood that people in the supervised programs mentioned above usually spend some time in jail or other correctional institutions prior to their release to such programs. What is more disturbing is the report that "an estimated 7,888 juveniles (under age eighteen), were held in local jails," and, even worse, "over three-quarters were tried or awaiting trial as adults" as of June 30, 1995 (Gillard & Beck, 1996, p. 1). These statistics are quite discouraging when one considers that during the twelve months of 1995 the prison population grew by 72,059 prisoners–an increase of almost seven (6.8) percent since year-end 1994.

As of December 31, 1995, state prison systems were operating between 14 percent and 25 percent over their reported capacity; the federal system, 26 percent over its capacity (Gillard & Beck, 1996). The proper ratio of prisoner per square feet of cell space and the flexible and humane management of jails/prisons is of great importance in order to achieve better adaptability of the prisoners to a carceral system. Adaptability may allow rehabilitation and possibly decrease recidivism. Because of the shortage of jail/prison beds and overcrowding, over the twelve-month period from June 30, 1994, to June 30, 1995, "local jails added space for 41,439 inmates, an annual increase of 8%" (Gillard & Beck, 1996, p. 1). A recent trend in the attempt to overcome the overcrowding in correctional institutions has been to either build new, larger jails/prisons, or to board prisoners out to other state correctional institutions which have vacancies due to their having built larger prisons in the recent past. This new construction of correctional institutions does not seem to be sufficient, and at state and federal levels new, larger jail/prison construction is being pushed, based on their projection which seems to expect higher numbers of violent crimes in the proximate future. It can be argued that such a pessimistic attitude undermines and demotivates any reasonable effort that could or should be made towards the rehabilitation and treatment of the social/psychological factors at the basis of the criminal behavior in the many offenders. This should not be misinterpreted; we believe that seriously, violent, antisocial people must be incarcerated after due process and if the law of the land so decides, both for the protection of society and in an attempt to rehabilitate the offender.

The number of women in state and federal prisons in 1994 was 56,895; in 1995 it reached 63,998; those not in custody increased 6.5 percent, from 64,340 to 68,654 during the same period (Gillard &

Beck, 1996). From a sociological point of view, the fact that prison growth rates were nearly equal for both the male and female population is of interest.

A review of a statistical analysis of the Bureau of Justice Statistics reveals that the racial demographic characteristic of inmates in 1995 was unchanged when compared to 1990. "At midyear 1995 a majority of local jail inmates were black or Hispanic" (Gillard & Beck, 1996, p. 10). The survey revealed, in fact, that 43.5 percent were black non-Hispanics, 40.1 percent were white non-Hispanics, 14.7 percent were Hispanics, and other races were 1.7 percent.

Firearms are a frequent weapon in major offenses and their use tells a great deal about the personality of the offender. A 1995 U.S. Justice Department statistical report shows that the "weapons arrestees are predominantly male, age eighteen or over, and white. However, weapons arrest rates per 100,000 population were highest for teens and for blacks...and weapons offenders are making up an increasing proportion of admission to State and Federal prisons" (Greenfeld & Zawitz, 1995, p. 1). Weapons arrest rates are reported to have been five times greater for blacks than for whites–362 arrests per 100,00 population for blacks compared to 70 arrests per 100,000 population for whites; in addition there were 40 arrests per 100,000 for others. In addition, "The growth in juvenile homicide victimizations from the mid 1980s though 1994 was completely firearm-related" (Snyder et al., 1996, p. 2). The trend of possession and arrest for weapons offenses among juveniles is rapidly climbing; males at age eighteen had the highest per capita arrest rate for weapons offenses. (The frequent justification given by them for possession of a handgun was possible self-defense in a dangerous neighborhood.) Those persons arrested for weapon use (handgun) against another person usually had had previous charges of fines (1.%), pay restitution (7%), community service (5%), or sentencing to treatment (4%) for a previous, less serious conviction. These statistics indicate that at times offenses escalate from misdemeanors to felonies and that better, more thorough evaluations of offenders is necessary to prevent the dire consequences of the use of weapons against others. "In 1991 an estimated 12,700 weapons offenders were in State prisons, and 3,100 were in Federal prisons" (Greenfeld & Zawitz, 1995, p. 6).

The use of weapons by offenders and the frequency of murder in the domesticity of people's homes is frequent. Unfortunately, domestic violence is not limited to battery, substantial battery or rape but at times reaches the point of murder. A 1995 report from the U. S. Department of Justice shows that in 1988 the justice systems in the seventy-five largest counties in the United States had 540 spousal murder cases. There were 318 husbands who murdered their wives compared to twenty-two wives who murdered their husbands (Langan & Dawson, 1995).

1996

Bureau of Justice Statistics show that at midyear 1996 an estimated 1,630,940 persons were incarcerated in the Nation's prisons and jails. Six hundred fifteen persons per 100,000 U.S. residents were held in federal and state prisons and local jails. Two-thirds of those prisoners (1,112,448) were in the custody of the 50 states, the District of Columbia, and the federal government. The other third (518,492) were held in local jails. On June 30, 1996, 1,164,356 prisoners were in custody or being held under the legal authority of a prison system outside its facilities under federal or state jurisdiction. This was an increase of 5.3 percent from midyear 1995. The states and the District of Columbia had an increase of 54,549 prisoners and the federal system of 4,256. An estimated 591,469 offenders were held or supervised by local jail authorities. Twelve percent of these offenders (72,977) were supervised outside jail facilities in various alternative programs including community service, work release, weekend reporting, and electronic monitoring. "At midyear 1996 there were an estimated 420 prison inmates per 100,000 U.S. residents—up from 292 at year-end 1990" (Gillard & Beck, 1997, p. 1). Since 1990 the number of jail inmates per 100,000 U.S. residents rose from 163 to 196, and by June 28, 1996, there were an estimated 518,492 inmates held in the nation's local jails, up from 506,044 at midyear 1995. This was a 4.4 percent increase in the total incarcerated population from the prior twelve months. From midyear 1995 to midyear 1996 there was a 5.5 percent increase in the number of inmates in state and federal prisons and a 2.3 percent increase in those held in local jails. During the same period, the number of inmates under state or federal jurisdiction are reported to have risen 5.3 percent (Gillard & Beck, 1997). The incarceration rate of state and federal prisoners sentenced to more than a year reached 420 per 100,000 U.S. residents on June 30, 1996.

California showed 39 percent (10,954) of the growth in the prison populations during the twelve month-period ending June 30, 1996, the federal system (4,256), Pennsylvania (4,095), and North Carolina (3,853). During that period, the total prison population increased at least 10 percent in 13 states, with Nebraska reporting the largest increase (16.0%), followed by Montana (15.2%), North Carolina (14.4%), Oregon (14.1%), Wisconsin (13.9%), and Pennsylvania (13.7%). Only two states, New Hampshire (0.7%) and Connecticut (0.2%), reported a decline. Interestingly, the District of Columbia experienced a large decline in its prison population (6.9%). Texas had the highest rate of incarceration with 659 sentenced prisoners per 100,000 state residents. It was followed by Louisiana (611 per 100,000), Oklahoma (580), and South Carolina (540). Three States— North Dakota (90), Minnesota (108), and Maine (112)—had rates that were less than a third of the national rate. The District of Columbia held 1,444 sentenced prisoners per 100,000 residents at midyear 1996 (Gillard & Beck, 1997). An estimated 591,469 offenders were held in or supervised by the nation's local jails on June 28, 1996. Jail authorities supervised 12 percent of these offenders (72,977) in alternative programs outside the jail facilities. An estimated 518,492 offenders were housed in local jails (Gillard & Beck, 1997).

There was an increase in the number of women under the jurisdiction of state and federal prison authorities from 69,161 to 73,607, an increase of 6.4 percent during the 12 months ending June 30, 1996. Nevertheless, "the lifetime chances of a person going to prison are higher for men (9.0%) than for women (1.1%) and higher for blacks (16.2%) and Hispanics (9.4%) than for whites (2.5%)" (Bonczar & Beck, 1997, p. 1). If these rates of incarceration remain unchanged, an estimated one of every twenty persons (5.1%) will serve some time in a prison during their lifetime, with men (9.0%) being over eight times more likely than women (1.1%) to be incarcerated in prison at least once. "Among men, blacks (28.5%) are about twice as likely as Hispanics (16.0%) and 6 times more likely than whites (4.4%) to be admitted to prison during their life" (Bonczar & Beck, 1997, p. 1).

The type of offense leading to the first admission to prison varied with the age of the offender. About 22 percent of the first-time prisoners 45 years of age or older had committed a sexual assault, compared to fewer than 5 percent of those under age 25. Almost 20 percent of first-time prisoners under the age of 20 had committed robbery and 13 percent burglary, compared to those age 45 or older of whom only 1 percent had committed robbery and fewer than 1 percent burglary. The percentage of persons admitted for a public-order offense (such as driving under the influence, commercialized vice, weapons offenses, and federal regulatory offenses) increased with age. Two-thirds of all persons who entered prison for the first time were found to have had a prior sentence to probation and one-third had been sentenced to a local jail or served time in a juvenile facility; those persons entering state prisons were more likely than those entering federal prison to have had prior sentences to jail or probation. "On average, persons entering state prison for the first time had received a total maximum sentence of eighty-six months while those entering federal prison received a sentence of seventy-three months...nearly two-thirds will have been on probation and a third will have served a sentence to a local jail or juvenile facility before entering prison" (Bonczar & Beck, 1997, p. 5).

The above statistics support the fact that even though most adult major criminal offenses are reported as diminishing in 1997, especially homicides, juvenile offenses are on the increase. Further, more offenders are spending more time in the carceral system. This is the basic factor in increasing overcrowding and of the building of more correctional institutions with a higher capacity. The above is the outcome of a tougher approach to crime.

Appendix 2

EXAMPLES OF INMATE RULES AND JARGON

The Inmate Code

1. Don't interfere with the interests of other inmates. Never rat on a con.
2. Don't quarrel with other inmates. Play it cool.
3. Don't exploit other inmates.
4. Maintain yourself. Don't whine or cop out.
5. Don't trust the guards or the things they stand for. Officials are wrong and inmates are right.

Inmate Slang

Fish: new inmate
Get-back: revenge
Hack or screw: correctional officer
Play for the gate: trying to look good for the parole board
Script: money
Shank: knife or other weapon with a blade
Snitch: a rat
Waste: kill someone
Hole: solitary confinement

Argot rules

1. *Rat:* An inmate who squeals or "rats" on other inmates and hence is viewed negatively by other inmates.
2. *Center man:* An inmate who aligns himself/herself with the guards

Prepared by Prof. Mary Anne Farkas
Professor of Criminology, Marquette University

and supports them in their interactions with inmates. Not trusted, and disliked by other inmates.

3. *Gorilla:* Inmates who use force or threat of force to intimidate other inmates into giving up goods or favors.

4. *Merchant/Peddler:* Exploiters of other inmates by selling them things which they pilfered or stole.

5. *Punks:* Inmates who have been coerced into homosexual relations with other inmates or chose such a role to acquire goods and services or to obtain protection from predatory inmates.

6. *Ball Busters:* Inmates who are in constant defiance of correctional staff. They are viewed negatively by other inmates because they cause problems through their defiance. They upset the "apple cart."

REFERENCES

Abrahamsen, D. (1952). *Who Are the Guilty?* New York: Rinehart & Co.

Alexander, F. (1948). *Fundamentals of Psychoanalysis.* New York: W. W. Norton.

American's Behind Bars: The International Use of Incarceration, 1992-1993. (1994). Washington., DC: The Sentencing Project Report, September.

APA–American Psychiatric Association. (1994). *Diagnostic and Statistical Manual of Mental Disorders,* Fourth Edition. Washington, DC: American Psychiatric Association.

Archer, D., Gartner, R., & Beittel, M. (1983). Homicide and the Death Penalty: A Cross-National Test of a Deterrence Hypothesis. *Journal of Criminal Law and Criminology,* 74:991–1013.

Arieti, S. (1967). *The Intrapsychic Self.* New York: Basic Books.

Bailey, W.C., & Peterson, R.D. (1989). Murder and Capital Punishment: A Monthly Time-Series Analysis of Execution Publicity. *American Sociological Review,* 54:722–743.

Ball, R.A. (1997). Prison Conditions at the Extreme. *Journal of Contemporary Criminal Justice,* 13(1):55-72.

Bartollas, C., & Conrad, J.P. (1992). *Introduction to Corrections.* New York: Harper Collins,

Baum, D. (1996). *Smoke and Mirrors. The War on Drugs and The Politics of Failure.* Boston: Little, Brown.

Beccaria, The Marquis of Milan. With a Commentary by M. De Voltaire. (1872). *An Essay on Crimes and Punishments.* Albany: W.C. Little.

Beccaria, C.: *An Essay on Crimes and Punishments.* Adolph Caso (Ed.). Boston: International Pocket Library, ([1775] 1993).

Bellah, R. N., Madsen, R., Sullivan, W. M., Swidler, A., & Tipton, S. M. (1991). *The Good Society.* New York: Knopf.

Bennett, W. J., DiIulio, J. J., Jr., & Walters, J. P. (1996). *Body Count.* New York: Simon & Schuster.

Benson, Bruce L., & David W. Rasmussen. (1996). *Illicit Drugs and Crime.* Oakland, CA: Independent Institute.

Berkowitz, M., Mueller, C., Schnell, S., & Padberg, M. (1986). Moral Reasoning and Judgment of Aggression. *Journal of Personality and Social Psychology,* 31:885-891.

BJA (Bureau of Justice Assistance). (1997). *Urban Street Gang Enforcement.* Bureau of Justice Assistance Homograph. NCJ161845, January. Washington, DC: U.S. Department of Justice.

Blackstone, W., Sir. (1851). *Commentaries on the Laws of England: In 4 Books.* New York: W.E. Dean.

Blankenhorn, D. (1995). *Fatherless America.* New York: Basic Books/Harper Collins.

229

Blumstein, A., Cohen, J., & Nagin, D. (1978). *Deterrence and Incapacitation: Estimating the Effects of Criminal Sanctions on Crime Rates.* Washington, DC: National Academy of Sciences.

Bonczar, Thomas P., & Beck, Allen J. (1997). Lifetime Likelihood of Going to State or Federal Prison. *Bureau of Justice Statistics Special Report,* March 1997, NCJ160092. U.S. Department of Justice, Washington, DC.

Bovenkerk, J. (1993). Crime and the Multi-Ethnic Society: A View from Europe. *Crime, Law and Social Change,* 19(3):271-280.

Brahce, C. I., & Bachand, D. J. (1989). A Comparison of Retiree Criminal Characteristics with Habitual and Nonhabitual Older Offenders from an Urban Population. In: S. Chaneles & C. Cathleen (Eds.), *Older Offenders: Current Trends* (pp. 45-60). New York: Haworth Press.

Brill, H., & Malzberg, B. (1962). Statistical Report Based on the Arrest Records of 5,354 Male Ex-Patients Released from New York Hospitals During the Period 1946-1948. *Mental Hospital Service Supplement,* 153. Washington, DC: American Psychiatric Association.

Bromberg, W. (1965). *Crime and the Mind.* New York: Macmillan.

Burkett, R. C., & Myers, M. D. (1995). Axis I and Personality Comorbidity in Adolescents with Conduct Disorder. *Bull Am Acad Psychiatry Law,* 23(1):73-82.

Butterfield, F. (1995). *All God's Children: The Bosket Family and the American Tradition of Violence.* New York: Knopf.

Camp, B. M., & Camp, C. J. (1985). *Prison Gangs: Their Extent Nature and Impact on Prisons.* Washington, DC: U.S. Government Printing Office.

Campagna, A., & Harter, S. (1975). Moral Judgment in Sociopathic and Normal Children. *Journal of Personality and Social Psychology,* 31:199-205.

Chaiken, J. M., & Chaiken, M. R. (1982). *Varieties of Criminal Behavior.* Santa Monica, CA: Rand.

Chess, S., & Thomas, A. (1991). Continuities and Discontinuities in Temperament. In: L. Robins & M. Rutter, (Eds.). *Straight and Devious Pathways from Childhood to Adulthood* (pp. 205-220). New York: Cambridge University Press.

State of American's Children, The. Yearbook 1997. (1997). Washington, DC: Childrens' Defense Fund.

Christie, N. (1993). *Crime Control as Industry.* London: Routledge.

Clark, Ramsey. (1972). Prison: Factories of Crime. In: B. M. Atkins & H. R. Glick (Eds.), *Prisons, Protest, and Politics* (pp. 15-24). Englewood Cliffs, NJ: Prentice-Hall.

Cleckley, H. (1955). *The Mask of Sanity.* St. Louis, Mosby.

Cocozza, J., Melick, M., & Steadman, H. (1978). Trends in Violent Crime Among Ex-Mental Patients. *Criminology,* 16:317-334.

Cohen, S., & Taylor, L. (1972). *Psychological Survival.* Harmondsworth: Penguin.

Conklin, J. E. (1992). *Criminology,* 4th ed. New York: Macmillan.

Craig, R. D., & Truitt, K. (1996). Moral Problem Solving Among Inmates in a Maximum Security Correctional Institution. *International Journal of Offender Therapy and Comparative Criminology,* 40(3):243-252.

Dante, A. ([1307] 1982). *The Divine Comedy of Dante Alighieri. Inferno.* A. Mandelbaum (Trans.). New York: Bantam.

Deaglio, E. (1995). In: Adriano Sofri (Ed.), *Rapporto degli Ispettori Europei sullo Stato delle Carceri in Italia (A Report of the European Inspectors on the Condition of Prisons in Italy)*. Palermo, Italy: Sellerino.

Deardorff, P., & Finch, A. (1975). Empathy and Socialization in Repeat Offenders, First Offenders and Normals. *Journal of Counseling Psychology*, 22:453-455.

Dickey, W. (1994). Who Are the Offenders? *In Context.* 38:15.

DiIulio, J. J. (1994). *Saving the Children: Criminal Justice and Social Policy.* Presented at the Conference on Social Policies for Children, Center of Domestic and Comparative Policy Studies, Woodrow Wilson School, Princeton University (May 25-26).

DiIulio, J. J. (1990). *Courts, Corrections, and the Constitution.* New York: Oxford University Press.

Dinitz, S., Ferracuti, F., & Piperno, A. (1976). *Deterioramento Mentale da Detenzione (Mental Deterioration as a Result of Detention).* Rome, Italy: Ministry of Grace and Justice.

DiTullio, B. (1960). *Principî di Criminologia Clinica e Psichiatria Forense (Principles of Clinical Criminology and Forensic Psychiatry).* Rome, Italy: Istituto di Medicina Sociale.

Dizionario Enciclopedico Italiano-Treccani. s.v. Justinian Code. Rome: Istituto Poligrafico dello Stato, 1970, vol. V, p. 452-453.

Dowd, S. (Ed.). (1996). *This Prison Where I live. The Pen Anthology of Imprisoned Writers.* London: Cassell.

Drucker, P. F. (1994). The Age of Social Transformation. *Atlantic Monthly.* November, pp. 53-80.

Dumm, T. L.: *Democracy and Punishment.* Madison: University of Wisconsin Press, 1987.

Durkheim, E. (1972). Crime as Normal Behavior. Rules of Sociological Method. In: D. Dressler (Ed.), *Readings in Criminology and Penology* (pp. 4-9). Glencoe, IL: The Free Press.

East, Sir N. (1951). *Society and the Criminal.* Springfield: Charles C. Thomas, Publisher.

Ellis, D., Grasmick, H. G., & Gilman, B. (1989). Violence in Prisons: A Sociological Analysis. *Am J Sociology*, 80:16-43.

Ellis, H. ([1890]1973). *The Criminal.* Reprinted from the 5th edition. Montclair, NJ: Patterson Smith.

Ellis, L. (1990). Universal Behavioral and Demographic Correlates of Criminal Behavior: Toward Common Ground in the Assessment of Criminological Theories. In: Ellis, L., & Hoffman, H. (Eds.), *Crime in Biological, Social, and Moral Contexts* (pp. 36-49). New York: Praeger.

Ellis, L., & Hoffman, H. (Eds.). (1990). *Crime in Biological, Social, and Moral Contexts.* New York: Praeger.

Eysenck, H. J. (1977). *Crime and Personality*, rev. ed. London: Routledge & Kegan Paul.

Faine, J. R. (1973). A Self-Consistency Approach to Prisonization. *Sociological Quarterly*, 14(4):576-588.

Farrington, D. P., Loeber, R., & Van Kammen, V. B. (1990). Long-Term Criminal Outcomes of Hyperactivity-Impulsivity-Attention Deficit and Conduct Problems in Childhood. In: L. Robins & M. Rutter (Eds.), *Straight and Devious Pathways from Childhood to Adulthood* (pp. 62-81). New York: Cambridge University Press.

Ferracuti, F. (Ed.). (1989). *Carcere e Trattamento (Prisons and Treatment). Trattato di Criminologia, Medicina Criminologica e Psichiatria Forense (Treatise on Criminology, Criminological Medicine and Forensic Psychiatry)*, vol. 11. Milan, Italy: Giuffrè.

Fisher, S., Raskin, A., & Unlenhuth, E. H. (Eds.). (1987). *Cocaine: Clinical and Biobehavioral Aspects.* New York: Oxford University Press.

Fong, R. S. (1991). *The Organizational Structure of Prison Gangs: A Texas Case Study.* Federal Probation, March, pp. 36-43.

Foucault, M. (1979). *Discipline and Punish: The Birth of the Prison.* A. Sheridan (Trans.). New York: Vintage.

Foucault, M. (1988). *Madness and Civilization.* R. Howard (Trans.). New York: Vintage Books, 1988.

Freeh, L. J. (1993). Strategies to End the Carnage. *Washington Post,* October 27, 1993, A1, A16.

Friedman, L. M. (1985). *A History of American Law,* 2nd ed. New York: Simon & Schuster.

Friedman, L. M. (1993). *Crime and Punishment in American History.* New York: Basic Books.

Friedman, L. M., & Percival, R. V. (1982). *Roots of Justice.* Chapel Hill: University of North Carolina Press.

Garland, D. (1990). *Punishment and Modern Society.* New York: Oxford University Press.

Gaylin, W. (1991). *On Being and Becoming Human.* New York: Penguin.

Gemelli, A., & Zunini, G. (1949). *Introduzione alla Psicologia.* Milan, Italy: Vita e Pensiero.

Gerstein, D. R., & Lewin, L. S. (1990). Special Report: Treating Drug Problems. *N Eng J Med,* 323:844-848.

Gibbons, D. (1965). Offender Typologies. Two Decades Later. *Br J Criminology,* 15:141-156.

Gillard, D. K., & Beck, A. J. (1996). Prison and Jail Inmates, 1995. *Bureau of Justice Statistics Bulletin,* NCJ-161132. U.S. Department of Justice, Washington, DC. August.

Gillard, D. K., & Beck, A. J. (1997). Prison and Jail Inmates at Midyear 1996. *Bureau of Justice Statistics Bulletin,* NCJ-162843. U.S. Department of Justice, Washington, DC. January.

Giovannoni, J. M., & Gurel, L. (1967). Socially Disruptive Behavior of Ex-Mental Patients. *Arch Gen Psychiatry,* 17:146-153.

Glueck, S., & Glueck, E. T. (1930). *Five Hundred Criminal Careers.* New York: Knopf.

Greenfeld, L. A., & Zawitz, M. W. (1995). Weapons Offenses and Offenders. Bureau of Justice Statistics Selected Findings, NCJ-155284. U.S. Department of Justice, Washington, DC. November.

Griffith, L. (1993). *The Fall of the Prison. Biblical Perspectives on Prison Abolition.* Grand Rapids, MI: William B. Eerdmans.

Guttmacher, M. S. (1960). *The Mind of the Murderer.* New York: Farrar, Strauss and Cudahy.

Guttmacher, M. S. (1972a). The Normal Murderer. In: D. Dressler (Ed.), *Readings in Criminology and Penology* (pp. 99-105). Glencoe, IL: The Free Press.

Guttmacher, M. S. (1972b). The Psychiatric Approach to Crime and Correction. In: D. Dressler (Ed.), *Readings in Criminology and Penology* (pp. 294-300). Glencoe, IL: The Free Press.

Guy, E., Platt, J. J., Swerling, I., & Bullock S. (1985). Mental Health Status of Prisoners in an Urban Jail. *Criminal Justice and Behavior,* 12:29-53.

Häfner, H., & Böker, W. (1973). Mentally Disordered Violent Offenders. *Social Psychiatry,* 8:220-229.

Haley, J. O. (1994a). A Spiral of Success. *In Context.* 38:32-34.

Haley, J. O. (1994b). Victim-Offender Mediation: International Success. *In Context.* 38:34.

Hare, R. M., & McPherson, L. M. (1984). Violent and Aggressive Behavior by Criminal Psychopaths. *International Journal of Offender Therapy and Comparative Criminology,* 7:35-50.

Hofer, P. (1988). Prisonization and Recidivism. A Psychological Perspective. *International Journal of Offender Therapy and Comparative Criminology,* 32:95-106.

Hoffer, P .C., & Scott, W .B. (Eds.). (1984). *Criminal Proceedings in Colonial Virginia, Richmond County, 1711-1754.* Athens, GA: University of Georgia Press.

Homant, R. J., & Dean, D. G. (1988). The Effect of Prisonization and Self-Esteem on Inmates' Career Maturity. *Journal of Offender Counseling, Services and Rehabilitation,* 12(2):19-40.

Howard, P. K. (1994). *The Death of Common Sense.* New York: Warner.

Huessy, H. R., & Howell, D. C. (1985). Relationships Between Adult and Childhood Behavior Disorders. *Psychiatric Journal of the University of Ottawa,* 48:566-574.

Hutson, H. R., Anglin, D., Kyriacon, D. N., Hart, J., & Spears K. (1996). The Epidemic of Gang-Related Homicides in Los Angeles County. From 1979 Through 1994. *JAMA,* 274(13):1031-1036.

James, J. F., Gregory, D., Jones, R. K., & Chiles, J. A. (1989). The Mentally Ill in Prisons: A Review. *Hosp Community Psychiatry,* 11:674-677.

Johnson, J. (1984). *Removing the Chronically Mentally Ill from Jail.* Washington, DC: National Coalition for Jail Reform.

Kant, I. ([1797] 1985). The Right to Punish. In: J. G. Murphy, *Punishment and Rehabilitation,* 2nd ed. (pp. 20-23). Belmont, CA: Wadsworth.

Kaplan, H. I., Sadock, B. J., & Grebb, J. A. (1994). *Synopsis of Psychiatry.* Baltimore: Williams & Wilkins.

Kaufmann, W. (1974). *Nietzsche,* 4th ed. Princeton: Princeton University Press.

Kaufmann, W. (1975). *Nietzsche. Thus Spoke Zarathustra.* New York: Penguin Books.

Kempin, F. G. (1963). *Legal History: Law and Social Change.* Englewood Cliffs, NJ: Prentice-Hall.

Lamothe, P., & Gravier, B. (1990). La Psichiatria Forense Francese (French Forensic Psychiatry). In: F. Ferracuti (Ed.), *Trattato di Criminologia, Medicina Criminologica e Psichiatria Forense, (Treatise on Criminology, Criminological Medicine and Forensic Psychiatry)*, vol. 13. (pp. 169-184). Milan, Italy: Giuffrè.

Langan, P. A., & Dawson, John M. (1995). Spouse Murder Defendants in Large Urban Counties. Bureau of Justice Statistics Executive Summary, BCJ-156831, U.S. Department of Justice, Washington, DC. September.

Laurent, F. W. (1959). *The Business of a Trial Court, 100 Years of Cases; A Census of the Actions and Special Proceedings in the Circuit Court for Chippewa County, Wisconsin, 1855-1954.* Madison: University of Wisconsin Press.

Lindvquist, P., & Allebeck, P. (1990). Schizophrenia and Crime: A Longitudinal Follow-Up of 644 Schizophrenics in Stockholm. *Br J Psychiatry*, 157:3345-3350.

Lombroso, C. (1911). *Crime: Its Causes and Remedies.* H.P. Horton (Trans.). Boston: Little, Brown.

Lombroso, C. ([1888]1996). *Palimsesti del Carcere* (Palimpsests from Prison). Florence, Italy: Ponte alle Grazie.

Lombroso-Ferrero, G. (1972). *Criminal Man, According to the Classification of Cesare Lombroso.* Montclair, NJ: Patterson Smith.

Luberto, S., Zavatti, P., & Gualandri, G. (1993). Tipologia di Reato e Malattia Mentale. Indagine Campionaria su Pazienti in Trattamento Psichiatrico (Type of Crime and Mental Disease. A Sample Study of Patients in Psychiatric Treatment). *Quaderni di Psichiatria Forense (Journal of Forensic Psychiatry)*, 1:78-103.

Mackenzie, M. M. (1981). *Plato on Punishment.* Los Angeles: University of California Press.

Maghan, J. (1997). The Dilemmas of Corrections and the Legacy of David Fogel. *International Journal of Offender Therapy and Comparative Criminology*, 41(2):101-120.

Mauer, M. (1996). Punishing More Wisely. *Legal Times.* Sept. 2.

McCall, N. (1994). *Makes Me Wanna Holler.* New York: Random House.

McFarland, S. G. (1983). Is Capital Punishment a Short-Term Deterrent to Homicide? A Study of the Effects of Four Recent American Executions. *Journal of Criminal Law and Criminology*, 74:1014-1032

Megargee, E. I., & Bohn, M. J. (1979). *Classifying Criminal Offenders. A New System Based on the MMPI.* Beverly Hills: Sage.

Menninger, Karl. (1968). *The Crime of Punishment.* New York: Viking Press.

Menninger, Karl. (1972) The Crime of Punishment. In: B. M. Atkins & H. R. Glick (Eds.), *Prisons, Protest, and Politics* (pp. 40-54). Englewood Cliffs, NJ: Prentice-Hall.

Merton, R. K. (1972). The Doctrine of "Socially Derived Sin." In: D. Dressler (Ed.), *Readings in Criminology and Penology* (pp. 377-393). Glencoe, IL: The Free Press.

Miller, N. S. (1996). Economics and Politics of Addiction. *Addiction Psychiatry Board Review Course Notes.* Terre Haute, IN: Osler Institute.

Molvig, D. (1997). *Violence and the Judicial system: Stemming the Tide of Violence in Our Courthouses.* Madison: Wisconsin State Bar Commission on Violence and the Justice System. 70 Wis. Law. July.

Monahan, J. (1996). Mental Illness and Violent Crime: A Summary of a Presentation of John Monahan, Ph.D. *National Institute of Justice Research Preview.* Washington, DC: U.S. Department of Justice. October.

Monahan, J., & Steadman, H. (1983). Crime and Mental Disorder: An Epidemiologic Approach. In: N. Morris & M. Tonry (Eds.), *Crime and Justice, An Annual Review of the Literature,* vol. 4 (pp. 145-189). Chicago: University of Chicago Press.

Montesquieu, C. ([1748] 1994). *The Spirit of the Laws.* In: A. M. Cohler, C. M. Basia, & H. S. Stone (Eds. and Trans.). New York: Cambridge University Press.

Moradi, R. S. (1997). The Father-Child Connection: A Struggle of Contemporary Man. In: Special Report: Child and Adolescent Psychiatry. *Psychiatric Times,* 14(1):40.

Morris, H. (1985). Persons and Punishment. In: J. G. Murphy, *Punishment and Rehabilitation,* 2nd ed. (pp. 24-41). Belmont, CA: Wadsworth.

Morris, N. (1973). *The Habitual Criminal.* Westport, CT: Greenwood Press.

Morris, N. (1995). The Contemporary Prison. In: Morris, N., & Rothman, D. J. (Eds.), *The Oxford History of the Prison. The Practice of Punishment in Western Society* (pp. 227-259). New York: Oxford University Press.

Morris, N., & Rothman, D. J. (Eds.). (1995). *The Oxford History of the Prison. The Practice of Punishment in Western Society.* New York: Oxford University Press.

Nesser, J. J., & Takoulas, D. (1997). Bursting at the Seams: Prison Overcrowding: A Brief Overview. http://www.penlex.org.uk/takoulas, June 24.

Noyes, A. P., & Kolb, J. C. (1958). *Modern Clinical Psychiatry.* Philadelphia: W. B. Saunders.

Nylander, I. (1979). A 20-Year Prospective Follow-Up Study of 2,164 Cases at the Child Guidance Clinics in Stockholm. *Acta Paediatr Scand,* supplement 276.

Offord, D. R., Sullivan, K., Allen, N., & Abrams, N. (1979). Delinquency and Hyperactivity. *J Nerv Ment Dis,* 167:734-741.

Palermo, G. B. (1994a). *The Faces of Violence.* Springfield: Charles C. Thomas, Publisher.

Palermo, G. B. (1994b). The Plight of the Deinstitutionalized Chronic Schizophrenic. In: J. F. Monagle & D. C. Thomasma (Eds.), *Health Care Ethics: Critical Issues* (pp. 133-145). Gaithersburg, MD: Aspen.

Palermo, G. B. (1996a). The City Under Siege: Drugs and Crime. *Journal of Interdisciplinary Studies,* 8(1/2):1-18.

Palermo, G. B. (1996b). We Are in Trouble, Society. In: In My Opinion. *Milwaukee Journal-Sentinal,* April 3, 13A.

Palermo, G. B. Transinstitutionalization and an Overburdened Judicial System. *Medicine and Law.* In press.

Palermo, G. B., & Scott, E. M. (1997). *The Paranoid: In and Out of Prison.* Springfield: Charles C Thomas, Publisher.

Palermo, G. B., Smith, M. B., & Liska, F. J. (1991a). Jails Versus Mental Hospitals: A Social Dilemma. *International Journal of Offender Therapy and Comparative Criminology,* 35(2):97-106.

236   *Letters from Prison*

Palermo, G. B., Smith, M. B., & Liska, F. J. (1991b). Jails Versus Mental Hospitals: The Milwaukee Approach to a Social Dilemma. *International Journal of Offender Therapy and Comparative Criminology*. 35(3):205-216.

Palermo, G. B., Gumz, E. J., & Liska, F. J. (1992a). Mental Illness and Criminal Behavior Revisited. *International Journal of Offender Therapy and Comparative Criminology*, 36(1):53-61.

Palermo, G. B., Gumz, E. J., Smith, M. B., & Liska, F. J. (1992b). Escape from Psychiatrization: A Statistical Analysis of Referrals to a Forensic Unit. *International Journal of Offender Therapy and Comparative Criminology*, 36(2):89-102.

Palermo, G. B., Knudten, R., Simpson, D., Turci, V., & Davis, H. (1993). Modes of Defensive Behavior in a Violent Society. *International Journal of Offender Therapy and Comparative Criminology*, 37(3):251-260.

Peat, B., & Winfree, L. T. (1992). Reducing the Intrainstitutional Effects of "Prisonization": A Study of a Therapeutic Community for Drug Using Inmates. *Criminal Justice and Behavior*, 19(2):206-225.

Peters, E. M. (1995). Prison Before the Prison: The Ancient and Medieval Worlds. In: N. Morris & D. J. Rothman (Eds.), *The Oxford History of the Prison. The Practice of Punishment in Western Society* (pp. 3-47). New York: Oxford University Press.

Peterson, R. D., & Bailey, W. C. (1988). Murder and Capital Punishment in the Evolving Context of the Post-Furman Era. *Social Forces*, 66:774-807.

Piperno, A. (1989). La Prisonizzazione: Teoria e Ricerca (Prisonization: Theory and Research). In: F. Ferracuti (Ed.), *Trattato di Criminologia, Medicina Criminologica e Psichiatria Forense (Treatise on Criminology, Criminological Medicine and Forensic Psychiatry)*, vol. 11 (pp. 57-68). Milan, Italy: Giuffrè.

Post, S. G. (1992). Grass-Roots Reflections on Substance Abuse. A Community Dialogue Approach. *Second Opinion*, 18(1):33-47.

Pothrow-Stith, D. (1991). *Deadly Consequences*. With M.Weissman. New York: Harper Perennial.

Rappeport, J. R., & Lassen, G. (1965). Dangerousness–Arrest Rate Comparisons of Discharged Patients and the General Population. *Am J Psychiatry*, 121:776-783.

Richards, S. C., & Jones, R. S. (1997). Perpetual Incarceration Machine. *Journal of Contemporary Criminal Justice*, 13(1):4-22.

Robins, L. N. (1956). *Deviant Children Grown Up: A Sociological and Psychiatric Study of Sociopathic Personality*. Baltimore: Williams & Wilkins.

Rokach, A., & Koledin, S. (1997). Loneliness in Jail: A Study of the Loneliness of Incarcerated Men. *International Journal of Offender Therapy and Comparative Criminology*, 41(2):168-179.

Rosnow, M. (1995). Victims of Crime–Victims of Bias: An Analysis of Criminal and Traffic Cases Adjudicated in Milwaukee County Circuit Court. Madison: *Wisconsin Correctional Service Report*, 1995, p. 13.

Rousseau, J. J. ([1762]1968). *The Social Contract*. M. Cranston (Trans.). London: Penguin Classics.

Rowan, C. T. (1993). *Dream Makers, Dream Breakers. The World of Thurgood Marshall*. Boston: Little Brown.

Sapp, A. D. (1989). Arrests for Major Crimes: Trends and Patterns for Elderly Offenders. In: S. Chaneles & C. Cathleen (Eds.), *Older Offenders: Current Trends* (pp. 19-44). New York: Haworth Press.

Scott, E. M. (1997). When Is A Prisoner Real? *International Journal of Offender Therapy and Comparative Criminology*, 41(2):99-100.

Sellin, T. (1972). Crime as Violation of Conduct Norms. In: D. Dressler (Ed.), *Readings in Criminology and Penology* (pp. 10-19). Glencoe, IL: The Free Press.

Shapiro, D. (1965). *Neurotic Styles.* New York: Basic Books.

Shaw, L. M. (1994). Love & Forgiveness Behind Bars. *In Context.* 38:51-53.

Shaw, Richard D. (1995). *Chaplains to the Imprisoned.* New York: Haworth Press.

Sheldon, W. H. (1942). *The Varieties of Temperament: A Psychology of Constitutional Differences.* With S. S. Stevens. New York: Harper & Brothers.

Sidgwick, H. (1907). Methods of Ethics. London: Macmillan.

Singh, B. K., & Joe, G. W. (1981). Substance Abuse and Arrests: Variations in Pretreatment Arrests of Clients in Drug Treatment Program. *Criminology*, 19(3):315-327.

Smith, N. J., Ivanoff, A., & Jang, S. J. (1994). Changes in Psychological Maladaptation Among Inmates Parasuicides. *Criminal Justice and Behavior*, 21(3):357-365.

Snyder, H. N., Sickmund, M., & Poe-Yamagata, E. (1996). *Juvenile Offenders and Victims: 1996 Update on Violence. Statistics Summary.* Washington, DC: Office of Juvenile Justice and Delinquency Prevention. February.

Sofri, A. (Ed.). (1995). *Rapporto degli Ispettori Europei sullo Stato delle Carceri in Italia (A Report of the European Inspectors on the Condition of Prisons in Italy).* Palermo, Italy: Sellerino.

Stang, David P. (1972). The Inability of Corrections to Correct. In: B. M. Atkins & H. R. Glick (Eds.), *Prisons, Protest, and Politics* (pp. 25-39). Englewood Cliffs, NJ: Prentice-Hall.

Steadman, H. J., Fabrisek, S., Dvorkin, J., & Holohean, E. J. (1987). A Survey of Mental Disability Among State Prison Inmates. *Hosp Community Psychiatry*, 38:1086-1090.

Stojkovic, S., & Lovell, R. (1992). *Corrections: An Introduction.* Cincinnati: Anderson Publishing.

Strick, S. E. (1989). A Demographic Study of 100 Admissions to a Female Forensic Center: Incidences of Multiple Charges and Multiple Diagnoses. *J Psychiatry and Law*, 17:435-448.

Sulton, A. T. (1994). Empowering Communities: Compassion at Work. *In Context.* 38:16-17.

Sutherland, E. H. (1955). *Principles of Criminology*, 5th ed., rev. by D. R. Cressey. New York: Lippincott.

Swetz, A., Saline, M. E., Stough, T., & Brewer, T. (1989). The Prevalence of Mental Illness in a State Correctional Institution for Men. *Journal of Prison and Jail Health*, 8:3-15.

Sykes, G. M. (1958). *The Society of Captives.* Princeton: Princeton University Press.

Szasz, Thomas S. (1963). *Law, Liberty, and Psychiatry.* New York: Macmillan.

Taylor, A. (1961). Social Isolation and Imprisonment. *Psychiatry*, 3:373-376.

Taylor, T., & Watt, D. C. (1977). The Relation of Deviant Symptoms and Behaviour in a Normal Population to Subsequent Delinquency and Maladjustment. *Psychological Medicine*, 7:163-169.

Teplin, L. A. (1990). The Prevalence of Severe Mental Disorder Among Male Urban Jail Detainees: Comparison with Epidemiologic Catchment Area Program. *Am J Public Health*, 80(6):663-667.

Thomas, C. W. (1973). A Study of External Factors Associated with the Impact of Imprisonment. *Journal of Research in Crime and Delinquency*, 10(1):13-21.

Toch, Hans. (1969). *Violent Men*. Chicago: Aldine.

Toch, H., Adams, K., & Grant, J. D. (1989). *Coping: Maladaptation in Prisons*. New Brunswick, NJ: Transaction Books.

Torrey, E. F. (1997). *Out of the Shadows*. New York: Wiley.

Towberman, D. B. (1994). Psychosocial Antecedents of Chronic Delinquency. In: N. J. Pallone (Ed.), *Young Victims, Young Offenders. Current Issues in Policy and Treatment* (pp. 151-164). New York: Haworth Press.

Turner, G. S., & Champion, D. J. (1989). The Elderly Offender and Sentencing Leniency. In: S. Chaneles & C. Cathleen (Eds.), *Older Offenders: Current Trends* (pp. 125-140). New York: Haworth Press.

van Gelder, S. (1994). The Ecology of Justice. *In Context*. 38:1-14.

Van Court, B. (1994). Doing Time: Using Prison as a Time for Healing. *In Context*. 38:50-51.

Wachholz, S., & Mullaly, R. (1995). Policing the Deinstitutionalized Mentally Ill: Toward an Understanding of its Function. *Crime, Law and Social Change*, 19:281-300.

Wachtler, S. (1997). *After the Madness*. New York: Random House.

Walinsky, A. (1995). The Crisis of Public Order. *The Atlantic Monthly*, July, pp. 39-54.

Walsh, W. F. (1923). *Outlines of the History of English and American Law*. New York: New York University Press.

Ward, D., & Kassebaum, G. (1965). *Women's Prison: Sex and Social Structure*. Chicago: Aldine.

Washington, J. (Ed.). (1986). Letter from Birmingham City Jail. In: *A Testament of Hope. The Essential Writings and Speeches of Martin Luther King, Jr.* (pp. 289-302). San Francisco: Harper Collins.

Washington, P. A. (1989). Mature Mentally Ill Offenders in California Jails. In: S. Chaneles & C. Cathleen (Eds.), *Older Offenders: Current Trends* (pp. 161-173). New York: Haworth Press.

Wheeler, S. (1961). Socialization in Correctional Communities. *American Sociological Review*. 697 ss.

Wilson, C. (1984). *A Criminal History of Mankind*. New York: Carroll & Graf.

Wilson, J. Q., & Herrnstein, R. J. (1985). *Crime and Human Nature*. New York: Simon and Schuster.

Winfree, L. T., Mays, G. L., Crowley, J. E., & Peat, B. J. (1994). Drug History and Prisonization: Toward Understanding Variations in Inmate Institutional Adaptations. *International Journal of Offender Therapy and Comparative Criminology*, 38(4):281-296.

Winnicott, D. (1965). *The Maturational Processes and Facilitating Environment: Studies in the Theory of Emotional Development.* New York: International Universities Press.

Wish, E. D. (1987). *Drug Use Forecasting: New York: 1984-1986.* Washington, DC: U.S. Department of Justice, National Institute of Justice.

Wish, E. D., & Johnson, B. D. (1986). The Impact of Substance Abuse on Criminal Careers. In: A. Blumstein, J. Cohen, J. A. Roth, and C. A. Visher (Eds.), *Criminal Careers and Career Criminals,* vol. II (pp. 52-88). Washington, DC: National Academy Press.

Witkin, G. (1991). Kills Who Kill. *U.S. News & World Report,* April 8, pp. 26-32.

Wren, C. S. (1996). Marijuana Use by Youths Rebounding After Decline. *New York Times,* 20 February, A12.

Wren, C. S. (1997). Use of Heroin Is Rising in Cities, Study Says. *New York Times,* June 25, A12.

Wright, B. (1993). *Black Robes–White Justice.* New York: Lyle Stuart Book, Carol Publishing.

Wright, K. N. (1993). Prison Environment and Behavioral Outcomes. *Journal of Offender Rehabilitation,* 20(1-2):93-113.

Zilboorg, Gregory (1954). *The Psychology of the Criminal Act and Punishment.* New York: Harcourt, Brace.

Zingraff, M. T. (1975). Prisonization as an Inhibitor of Effective Resocialization. *Criminology,* 13(3):366-388.

Zitrin, A., Hardesty, A. S., Burdock, E. I., & Drossman, A. K. (1976). Crime and Violence Among Mental Patients. *Am J Psychiatry,* 133(2):42-149.

NAME INDEX

SUBJECT INDEX

A

African-Americans, 55, 64, 82, 199–206, 210–21 (*see also* Letters, prisoners)
Aeschylus (*see* Name Index)
Aggression, 55, 57, 61
Aristotle (*see* Name Index)
Alcohol abuse, 63, 65, 78–81
    overview, 78–81
    personality characteristics, 80–81
    portrait of criminal offender, 199–206
Anglo-Saxon terminology
    companions, 8
    dooms, 8
    hundred court, 9
    national assembly, 9
    reeve, 9, 11
    royalty, 9
    shire court, 9, 11
    thegns, 9
Anglo-Saxons, 7–10, 172 (*see also* History of criminal court)
    English immigration, 9
    evolution of criminal justice system, 8–10
    Germanic emigration, 8–9
    royal rule, 9–10
    tribal system, 8, 9–10
Antisocial personality disorder, 51, 53, 57, 59, 61, 62, 64, 65, 69–77, 158, 165 (*see also* Psychopathic personality)
    behavior traits, 69–77
    characteristics, 72
    drug abusers, 81–87
    incarceration, 1675–68
    portrait, criminal offender, 199–206
    portrait, psychopath, 72–77, 158–59
    theories of behavior evolution, 69–72
Appeals process
    Anglo-Saxon, 9
Apprehension procedures, 5
Attention deficit/hyperactivity disorder, 67

B

Behavior modification, 32, 155–62
Biblical references to law, 7
Biotypology, 59

C

Character and temperament, 57–64 (*see also* Prisoners, personality traits)
    aggression, 55, 57, 61
    antisocial personality disorder, 51, 53, 57, 59, 61, 62, 64, 65, 69–77, 158–59, 165
    biotypology, 59
    character, definitions, 57–58, 60
    criminal offense category, 61
    education and morality, 60, 64
    impulsive, 53, 56, 57, 64, 66–68, 69–77
    neurotransmitter hypothesis, 59
    neurovegetative predisposition, 59–60
    psychopathic behaviors (*see* Psychopathic personality)
    socio-moral values, 61 (*see also* Antisocial personality disorder)
    temperament, categories, 58
    temperament, characteristics, 58–59
    typology of criminal conduct (*see* Typology of criminal conduct)
Character witnesses, 15
Civil law, 10
Code of Hammurabi, 7, 31
Colonial courts, 18–25
    benefit of clergy, 24
    chartered colonies, 21
    common laws, 19
    county courts, 18
    court of appeals, 22
    crown colonies, 21
    English law based, 21
    ideology and religion based, 21
    magistrate's authority, 23